Democracy from Above

Since the momentous events of the late 1980s, democratic transition has been a widely studied phenomenon. Most scholars who have investigated the causes and implications of the global trend to democracy have argued that domestic politics is the leading determinant in the success or failure of transitions to democracy. Jon C. Pevehouse argues that international factors, specifically regional organizations, play an important role in the transition to and endurance of democracy. Domestic elites use membership of regional organizations to advance the cause of democracy since these organizations can manipulate the costs and benefits of democracy to important societal groups such as business elites or the military. Six cases (Hungary, Peru, Greece, Paraguay, Guatemala, and Turkey) are used to examine the causal processes behind the statistical association between regional organizations and democratization. These findings bridge international relations and comparative politics while also providing guidelines for policymakers who wish to use regional organizations to promote democracy.

JON C. PEVEHOUSE is Associate Professor at the University of Wisconsin. He has published in journals such as the *American Political Science Review*, *American Journal of Political Science*, *International Organization*, *Journal of Politics*, and *Journal of Conflict Resolution*.

Democracy from Above

Regional organizations and democratization

Jon C. Pevehouse
University of Wisconsin, Madison

CAMBRIDGE
UNIVERSITY PRESS

PUBLISHED BY THE PRESS SYNDICATE OF THE UNIVERSITY OF CAMBRIDGE
The Pitt Building, Trumpington Street, Cambridge, United Kingdom

CAMBRIDGE UNIVERSITY PRESS
The Edinburgh Building, Cambridge, CB2 2RU, UK
40 West 20th Street, New York, NY 10011–4211, USA
477 Williamstown Road, Port Melbourne, VIC 3207, Australia
Ruiz de Alarcón 13, 28014 Madrid, Spain
Dock House, The Waterfront, Cape Town 8001, South Africa

http://www.cambridge.org

First published 2005

Printed in the United Kingdom at the University Press, Cambridge

Typeface Plantin 10/12 pt.   *System* LaTeX 2$_\varepsilon$ [TB]

A catalogue record for this book is available from the British Library

Library of Congress Cataloguing in Publication data
Pevehouse, Jon C.
Democracy from above:regional organizations and democratization / Jon C.
Pevehouse.
    p.   cm.
Includes bibliographical references and index.
ISBN 0 521 84482 7 – ISBN 0 521 60658 6 (pb.)
1. International agencies – Case studies.   2. Regionalism (International
organization) – Case studies.   3. Democratization – Case studies.   I. Title.
JZ5330.P48   2005
320.9 – dc22   2004051851

ISBN 0 521 84482 7 hardback
ISBN 0 521 60658 6 paperpack

Dedicated to my mother and father,
who taught me the importance of
education, hard work, and modesty;
and who demonstrated the value of all three.

Contents

Figures and tables

Figures

Tables

Acknowledgments

Many graduate students are lucky to find one wonderful advisor with whom they may share ideas and whom they may ask for help during the difficult times of writing. I was lucky enough to have three advisors who have graciously helped me through this process. Ed Mansfield has helped guide this project from the outset. I thank him for all of the time and effort he has spent not only on this project, but in shaping my outlook as a scholar. I hope someday to be as valuable as an advisor to someone as he has been to me.

I am also extremely grateful to Don Sylvan, who was a constant source of feedback on both ideas and written work. He was the best all-purpose advisor and friend a person could hope for. Tim Frye was also an invaluable source of advice. Tim pushed me to think more theoretically about my puzzle while exposing me to new literature and ideas that greatly improved this project.

My graduate school colleagues were also of tremendous assistance throughout many stages of this project, including reading drafts and listening to me drone on at length. David Bearce, Pat McDonald, Hiro Fukushima, Kathy Powers, Scott Orr, Kevin Sweeney, Paul Vasquez, and Louise Steen-Sprang all undertook this job with good humor while providing insightful comments.

At the dissertation stage, I received valuable feedback from seminar participants at the following institutions: Colorado, SUNY-Binghamton, American, Maryland, Harvard, and Wisconsin. As I moved into book stage, I benefited greatly from seminars at Chicago, Notre Dame, UC-San Diego, and Yale.

In addition, Dan Drezner, Dan Reiter, Beth Simmons, Michael Barnett, Joshua Goldstein, Deborah Gerner, Phil Schrodt, Helen Milner, Eric Reinhardt, Jason Wittenberg, Kristian Gleditsch, William Howell, and Leigh Payne have provided helpful comments on drafts of various chapters.

I would like to thank my family, including my mother, father, sisters, nieces, and nephew, who all provided emotional support that helped to sustain my sanity throughout this process. Another key figure in moving this book to its completion was our dog Ernie, who always seemed to like the project, especially as we discussed matters on walks. Finally, my wife, Elizabeth, has endured this project with an extraordinary amount of patience, kindness, and care. Without her love and support, I can honestly say this project would never have been completed.

Portions of the theory chapter have previously appeared in two articles: "Democracy from the Outside-In? International Organizations and Democratization", *International Organization* 56 (Summer 2002): 515–49 and "With a Little Help from My Friends? Regional Organizations and the Consolidation of Democracy", *American Journal of Political Science* 46 (July 2002): 611–26. Although the statistical models in this book are similar to the article versions, the data has been changed significantly since those publications.

Abbreviations

ABEIP	Argentina-Brazil Economic Integration Pact
ACC	Arab Cooperation Council
ANZUS	Australia, New Zealand, and United States Alliance
APEC	Asia-Pacific Economic Cooperation
ASEAN	Association of Southeast Asian Nations
ASPAC	Asian and Pacific Council
BSEC	Black Sea Economic Cooperation
CACM	Central American Common Market
CARICOM	Caribbean Community and Common Market
CBSS	Council of the Baltic Sea States
CDC	Central American Democratic Community
CEAO	West African Economic Community
CEEAC	Economic Community of Central African States
CEFTA	Central European Free Trade Agreement
CEI	Central European Initiative
CENTO	Central Treaty Organization
CEPGL	Economic Community of the Great Lake Countries
CILSS	Permanent Interstate Committee on Drought Control in the Sahel
CIS	Commonwealth of Independent States
CMEA	Council for Mutual Economic Assistance
COMESA	Common Market for Eastern and Southern Africa
EACM	East African Common Market
ECO	Economic Cooperation Organization
ECOWAS	Economic Community of West African States
EC/EEC	European Community/European Economic Community
EFTA	European Free Trade Association
EU	European Union
GATT	General Agreement on Tariffs and Trade
GCC	Gulf Cooperation Council
IO	International Organization

IGO	Intergovernmental Organization
IGAD	Inter-Governmental Authority on Development
IMF	International Monetary Fund
IOC	Indian Ocean Commission
LAES	Latin American Economic System
LAIA	Latin American Integration Association
MERCOSUR	Southern Cone Common Market
NATO	North Atlantic Treaty Organization
NGO	Non-governmental Organization
OAPEC	Organization of Arab Petroleum Exporting Countries
OAS	Organization of American States
OAU	Organization of African Unity
OCAM	African and Mauritanian Common Organization
OECD	Organization for Economic Cooperation and Development
OPANAL	Agency for the Prohibition of Nuclear Weapons in Latin America
OSCE	Organization for Security and Cooperation in Europe
PHARE	Poland/Hungary Assistance for Economic Reconstruction
SAARC	South Asian Association for Regional Cooperation
SADC	Southern African Development Community
SEATO	Southeast Asian Treaty Organization
UDEAC	Central African Customs and Economic Union
UIA	Union of International Associations
WEU	Western European Union
WTO	Warsaw Treaty Organization

1 Democratization and international relations

Few events have captured the attention of policymakers and the public like the collapse of the Soviet Union and the emergence of independent states in Central and Eastern Europe. In the aftermath of these events, there was tremendous optimism when confronted with the prospects of how to create and preserve democracy in Central and Eastern Europe, Russia, and the former Soviet Republics. In the United States, the Clinton administration announced that the foreign policy doctrine of containment would be replaced with a doctrine of "enlargement" (Bloomfield 1994; Lake 1993; Smith 1994; Wiarda 1997). A major part of the enlargement strategy involved international support for democracy, often through regional organizations (cf. Christopher 1995). For example, the idea of regional institutions promoting and protecting democracy became a major justification for NATO expansion (cf. Albright 1997; Asmus, Kugler, and Larrabee 1993; Yost 1998).

Academic attention to the issue of transitions to and the survivability of democracy, including identifying conditions propitious for success, predated the events of 1989. The "third wave" of democratization spurred a considerable body of research examining the origins and consequences of these transitions, many of which occurred nearly fifteen years prior to the fall of the Berlin Wall (Huntington 1991; Shin 1994).[1] Based on the lessons of Latin America, Southern Europe, and to a lesser extent Africa, the research provided the foundation from which to discuss the roadblocks to democratization in Eastern Europe as well as continued challenges to the future of democracy in other parts of the world.

Unfortunately for those interested in helping to secure democracy from abroad, the weight assigned to international factors in the democratization process was quite scant. The prevailing beliefs of the democratization literature in the late 1980s is best summarized by the findings of the

---

[1] Huntington argues that transitions to democracy occur in groups or "waves" over time. According to Huntington, the third wave of democracy began in 1974 in Portugal and continued through the transitions in Eastern Europe in 1989–90. Of course, interest in movements to and from democracy predate the third wave (cf. Linz 1978; Moore 1966).

Wilson Center's multi-volume project on democratization, *Transitions from Authoritarian Rule*:

> one of the firmest conclusions that emerged from our Working Group was that transitions from authoritarian rule and immediate prospects for political democracy were largely to be explained in terms of national forces and calculations. External actors tended to play an indirect and usually marginal role . . . (Schmitter 1986: 5)

Given the absence of the study of international factors in the prospects for democracy, neither the scholar nor the practitioner could be confident in the role outside forces would play in the process of democratization. With little theoretical or empirical work on the issue, there would be no way to tell what types of strategies would succeed or fail. Indeed, many began to criticize the lack of a coherent effort to promote democracy from the US and Europe (Allison and Beschel 1992; Pinder 1994).

In light of the events of Eastern Europe, however, some scholars began to question the sweeping conclusion that external factors played only a minor role in the transition or consolidation process (Pridham 1991b; Whitehead 1996a). Unfortunately, this new literature has not developed core theories or cross-national empirical findings exploring the association of international factors with democratic transitions or democratic consolidation. Rather, it largely examines individual case studies to suggest what outside factors could influence particular nation-states. While these studies are valuable for understanding the causal processes related to democratization, from a policy and an academic perspective, such work does not allow generalizable polices or theories.

While one could turn to broader theories in international relations scholarship, theories of international institutions and organizations are also of little help. The vast majority of the international institutions literature has focused on their effect on international outcomes (war, cooperation between states, etc.) rather than their domestic ramifications (cf. Keohane 1984; Keohane and Martin 1995; Mearsheimer 1995). A small, but growing body of literature does examine the interactions between domestic and international institutions (Drezner 2003; Goldstein 1996; Milner 1997). Unfortunately, much of that research has largely focused on the developed, stable democratic systems of North America and Western Europe. In the end, neither academics nor policymakers can turn to a body of theoretical or empirical research to address questions related to the emergence or continuance of democracy around the globe.

The purpose of this book is to fill this gap by contributing a coherent theoretical framework to evaluate the association between regional organizations and democratization, while providing the first quantitative empirical results pertaining to this issue. The proposition developed and tested here is that regional organizations can facilitate transitions to democracy as well as the survival of democracy. I define regional organizations as formal institutions whose membership is limited by geography. I adopt Mainwaring's (1992: 297–8) three-part definition of democracy: (1) competitive elections; (2) broad adult suffrage; and (3) protection of minority rights and respect for civil liberties.[2]

The links between regional international organizations (IOs), transitions to and the survival of democracy arise from distinct causal processes. In the case of democratic transitions, regional institutions can pressure member states to democratize or redemocratize after reversions to authoritarian rule. In addition, IO membership can serve to reassure domestic elites that their interests will be protected in a democracy through locking in policies they value (e.g. protection of property rights or commitment to free trade). Regional IOs can be used by domestic elites to socialize other elite groups (often the military) not to intervene in the democratic process by changing their attitudes toward democracy.[3] Finally, organizational membership may help to legitimize transitional regimes, making the completion of the democratic transition more likely.

With respect to democratic longevity, I argue that domestic elites can use membership or accession to regional organizations to further democratic consolidation. Positive and negative incentives to domestic groups can be generated by accession to regional organizations. These incentives convince societal groups (including the ruling elites) to abide by democratic "rules of the game." Joining regional organizations can raise the costs of anti-democratic behavior by those outside *or inside* the regime. These costs arise out of the conditional nature of membership in the organization as well as potential audience costs created through accession to the organization. These costs serve both as a deterrent to potential anti-regime forces and provide a device for new democrats to foster credible commitments to political reform. Finally, accession to regional organizations can confer legitimacy on young democratic regimes that increases the likelihood of long-term consolidation.

One conditioning factor in this regional IO-to-democracy link, however, is that not *all* regional institutions will be associated with democratization. I contend that the more homogenously democratic a regional organization's membership, the more likely it will be to pressure

---

[2] I discuss these definitions further in Chapter 3.
[3] Empirically, this mechanism has occurred with regard to the military. For example, through involvement in regional military organizations, military officers learn the "proper" role of the military in a democratic society.

autocratic governments to liberalize, provide credible guarantees to allay elite fears, stipulate conditions on membership, and, most importantly, enforce those conditions. In short, the more democratic a regional organization (in terms of its member states), the more likely it will be to supply the political will for supporting and protecting democracy *and* the more likely the regional IO will be used by domestic groups to encourage and cement democracy.

I build my theory on two bodies of literature in international relations – theories of international institutions and work on the second image reversed. Some of the causal mechanisms have been discussed in the broader context of how international institutions facilitate interstate cooperation, none of them have previously been applied to the question of democratization. In addition, while the second image reversed family of literature does discuss how international processes create outside-in linkages that can influence domestic political processes, these theories rarely discuss regional or international organizations.[4] I first turn to this later family of theories to lay the foundation for my argument.

The second image reversed

The second image reversed literature provides an excellent starting point for thinking about the linkages between regional organizations and democratization. This framework encompasses theories that contend international factors influence domestic political outcomes. The international factors and the domestic political outcomes that fall under the second image reversed rubric span a broad number of variables and processes. Peter Gourevitch's initial survey of this literature dealt with causal factors such as military intervention, international economic trends, and the (anarchic) nature of the international system (Gourevitch 1978; see also Almond 1989). A variety of domestic political outcomes were also discussed within the framework, including electoral outcomes, trade policies, domestic coalitions, and regime change. Although a review of the corpus of second image reversed literature developed after Gourevitch's effort is beyond the scope of this work, I briefly mention a piece of this literature concerning regime change to give the overall flavor of the argument.

Gourevitch's two central discussions of regime change revolve around the influence of international economics and the nature of the international state system. In the latter realm, a litany of hypotheses concerning

---

[4] This name arises out of Waltz's typology of levels of analysis: first image (individual-level causal factors), second image (state-level causal factors), and third image (system-level causal factors). See Waltz 1959.

global economic processes has played a key role in thinking about regime type and domestic political institutions. Ranging from Alexander Gerschenkron's (1962) work on the timing of industrialization and its relationship to the centralization to James Kurth's (1979) study of the product cycle and political authority, many scholars have used international economics to explain the structure and change of domestic political institutions. Recent strands of this literature would include work in comparative politics dealing with economic crises and regime change (Gasiorowski 1995). In these works, political regimes are structured or altered to achieve the best possible economic outcomes given the constraints and the dynamic nature of the international economic system.

The anarchic nature of the international system and the resulting drive for state security also provide a link from the international to domestic sphere. Dating from the late nineteenth century, the Seeley-Hintze Law holds that the greater the insulation of a nation-state from outside influence, the less political power would be centralized within the state (Almond 1989: 242–4). More recently, William Thompson has argued that the presence of external security threats to states can inhibit and erode moves towards democracy. Democracy can suffer setbacks during security crises since leaders will often consolidate their own power in order to mobilize resources to meet (or make) external threats (Thompson 1996).[5]

Despite these potentially powerful external factors affecting regime type, Gourevitch (1978: 911) emphasizes that "[external pressures] are unlikely to be fully determining . . . Some leeway of response to pressure is always possible, at least conceptually." Thus, any theory that purports to explain how international factors influence fundamentally domestic decisions must contain references to the domestic political process. International forces create constraints and opportunities for democratization through both economic and military-security processes, yet this is only part of the picture. One must also define how the actors within the state cope with the presence of these outside influences. Unfortunately, the most developed literature on international institutions largely ignores domestic politics (Milner 1997).

Domestic actors and international institutions

With the rise of the functionalist literature over forty years ago and continuing with such works as *After Hegemony*, international relations scholars have debated the merits of international institutions (e.g. Grieco

[5] For a contrary position, see Reiter 2001a.

1988; Keohane 1993; Mearsheimer 1995; Keohane and Martin 1995; Schweller and Priess 1997).[6] Today, the institutionalist debate has moved from broad conceptual issues (e.g. do institutions matter at all?) to more focused inquiries (e.g. how and under what circumstances do institutions matter and for what outcomes?). Although little of the institutionalist debate has centered on domestic politics, the relevant literature is not an empty set.

In fact, much of the original literature on the interaction between internal and domestic forces arose out of either international political economy or comparative foreign policy. In this latter group, the work of scholars such as Jonathan Wilkenfeld (1973) and James Rosenau (1969) concerning "linkage politics" attempted to generate and test middle-range theories linking the international and national levels of analysis. Scholars such as Wilkenfeld and Dina Zinnes (1973) examined how internal and external conflict were linked, while Rosenau (1969) proposed a number of theories exploring how domestic political systems became "penetrated" by other political actors. While these scholars' work was essential in laying the foundation (theoretically and empirically) for my theory, this literature's applicability is somewhat limited due to its focus on foreign policy behavior as the dependent variable. In addition, where my theory diverges from this past work is in my emphasis that internal penetration is often a choice by elites. I argue that domestic actors allow outside influence for strategic reasons that have little to do with foreign policy cooperation.

With Robert Putnam's (1988) work examining the two-level game metaphor, scholars moved to a more formalized view of the interaction between domestic politics and international forces. In Putnam's framework, strategic actors can use international constraints at home to neutralize domestic opposition, or use domestic constraints to enhance their international bargaining strength. The implication is that domestic politics can be shaped by international forces, but can shape them as well (Evans, Jacobson, and Putnam 1993).[7]

Further work has extended this idea of strategic interaction among domestic actors and international forces, especially international institutions. Judith Goldstein (1996) shows how international trade agreements can be used by a domestic actor (e.g. the president) to constrain the behavior of other domestic actors (e.g. Congress). Specifically, she

---

[6] Although not its main impetus, the early functionalist literature also demonstrated how the construction of international institutions influenced domestic politics as well. For example, Haas (1964) and Mitrany (1966).

[7] It should be noted that some scholars have argued that while in theory these dynamics may occur, in practice they are rare (cf. Evans 1993). In addition, Reinhardt (2003) argues that the ability to tie the hands of domestic opponents can only occur under very limited circumstances.

shows how an international body with little to no enforcement capability can alter outcomes to favor one actor (the president) over another (Congress) in matters of international trade.[8] Some literature in the study of economic regionalism also discusses this international/domestic interplay. Work by Helen Milner (1997) and Marc Busch and Milner (1994) argues that domestic firms demand regional trade organizations due to the export dependence of firms, firm multi-nationality, and levels of intra-industry trade (Busch and Milner 1994: 268–70). Thus, the bond of economic conditions in concordance with the preferences of firms gives rise to regional organizations that influence international cooperation.

A similar argument is made by Etel Solingen (1994) with regard to the security arena. She argues that membership in regional non-proliferation agreements is a function of domestic political coalitions. "Internationalist" coalitions which favor domestic economic liberalization will push to join these institutions to maximize the benefits received from all international institutions, which can "bank-roll" domestic coalitions (Solingen 1994: 168). Joining regional security institutions, therefore, is driven by the domestic political concerns of liberalizing coalitions of elites. These works serve as an excellent starting point to make the broader economic and political argument I put forth. Namely, joining and creating international organizations often finds its impetus in domestic political calculations.

Most work in the international organizations field still adopts the assumption that states join IOs to pursue "common or converging national interests of the member states" (Feld and Jordan 1994: 10). International or regional organizations, for the vast majority of this literature, reflect concerns over issues in the international environment that cannot be dealt with domestically (Archer 1992: 48). Thus, institutions are demand-driven and these demands arise out of international coordination or cooperation problems (see Martin 1992).

This work speaks to the issue of when and how international institutions matter in two ways. First, it provides empirical evidence of how institutions shape state behavior. Recently, institutional theorists have called for more empirical research to outline "well-delineated causal mechanisms" to explain the impact of international institutions, especially in reference to domestic political processes (Keohane and Martin 1995; Martin and

---

[8] One challenge of this research question that limits the applicability of some models developed in the new institutionalist tradition is the issue of information. For most models of international–domestic interaction, information at the domestic level concerning the preferences of societal actors is important (cf. Milner 1997). As Chapter 2 discusses more fully, uncertainty is abundant in the transitional and the immediate post-transitional period (Whitehead 1989). There is precious little information about not only the preferences of some of the major actors, but even identifying who the important actors are can be difficult (Przeworski 1991).

Simmons 1998: 749, 757). By exploring how regional IOs influence the democratization process, this work elucidates some of the possible ways in which regional institutions interact with domestic politics to influence outcomes. Moreover, it delineates circumstances under which domestic elites may turn to international institutions to substitute for (or bolster) domestic institutions. As I show throughout the book, both membership and accession to an IO can be used strategically in the domestic arena, especially by autocratic states and states which have recently undergone a transition to democracy.

Second, by assessing how differences in the membership of institutions create varied outcomes with respect to democratization, this study shows how variations in institutions (on at least one dimension) can influence outcomes. Again, institutional theorists have lamented a lack of empirical investigation on whether differences among institutions may lead to diverse outcomes (Martin and Simmons 1998). This study makes a contribution to this question by delineating along what dimension (level of democracy within the membership) this variation matters for specific outcomes (democratization and democratic survival).

In a similar vein, this book examines the broader claim by realists that major powers are the driving force behind international institutions. If the outcomes engendered by regional organizations are simply an artifact of the preferences of major power members to support democracy, the institution can take very little credit in the success of democracy. To the contrary, I show that this argument does not hold empirically. Because most of the causal mechanisms begin with domestic elites in authoritarian or nascent democracies, it is not the institution itself that is the prime mover of the process. In those instances where regional institutions are the important first mover (in the case of external pressure) or where enforcement by the organization is the important issue, I show that this realist-oriented position is largely devoid of explanatory power. Through statistical and case material I show that regional institutions have an independent influence on the probability of regime change and regime duration. This is important not only to dispel the critique that regional organizations are epiphenomenal, but also to show that it is not the policies of one actor (e.g. the United States) within an organization that is driving the process.

The forgotten nexus

Not only does most international relations literature fail to deal with the issue of international organizations and democratization, work in comparative politics on the determinants of democratic transitions largely ignores influences external to the nation-state. This trend has begun to change, however, in response to the sweeping changes in Eastern Europe. For example, there have been at least three edited volumes discussing international factors in the politics of regime change during the past decade (Pridham 1991b; Pridham, Herring, and Sanford 1994; Whitehead 1996a). While this literature has been rich in detailed case studies, little theorizing about causal mechanisms applicable across multiple cases has taken place. Geoffrey Pridham's (1991a: 21) own frustration with the literature has centered on this shortcoming: "The main analytical problem, however, is not establishing the relevance of the international dimension of regime change . . . Rather, the main problem is one of causality, of analysing what Almond has called 'the complex dynamic process' of interaction between international factors and domestic processes." By generating and testing hypotheses about regional organizations' influence on democratization through both large-N and case studies, I hope to elucidate some of these processes linking "international factors and domestic processes."

There have, of course, been a host of causal variables posited by comparativists to explain regime change and endurance. In the following chapters, I discuss these variables in some depth, indicating how they may function in conjunction with regional IOs. In the statistical models, some variables from extant theories are found to work independently of regional IOs, while in other models, it appears that regional IOs may erode the explanatory power of variables previously championed by scholars of democratization.

Various works have also touched on the broader issue of international influences on democratization and three main groups of causal mechanisms emerge from this literature: diffusion and demonstration effects; epistemic communities and spill-over; and the use of force. Diffusion and demonstration-effect hypotheses hold that the movement towards democracy in one state will "infect" neighbors with similar motives and bring parallel moves to democracy. The rise of global trade and the ease of communications provide transmission belts for democratic ideas and movements, which can provide an impetus for democracy within states. Empirically, there have been clusters of democratization (in both space and time), which would suggest some empirical veracity to this mechanism (Huntington 1991: 100–6; Whitehead 1996c).

The epistemic communities and spillover arguments are often related to interest group activity. Non-governmental organizations (NGOs) such as human rights organizations (Sikkink 1996) or political parties (Grabendorff 1993) are the interlocutors of democracy in many of these theories. Similar to the traditional neo-functionalist arguments concerning organizations and conflict, these arguments hold that NGOs or other informal organizations transmit technical information (e.g. how to hold elections) and/or norms concerning democracy (Grugel 1999). This can lead to a move towards liberalization or can be used to solidify the norms of civil society within a new democracy.

Finally, many observers have pointed to the use of force by other nation-states as a way to begin or secure a transition to democracy (Owen 2002). Examples include the imposition of a democratic government in both Japan and Germany after World War II, or the repeated use of force by the US in Latin America to alter the regime type of governments in that region.[9] "Force" may also entail means short of physical violence. Although this work will discuss pressure from regional organizations as a catalyst for democracy, a significant body of literature discusses *unilateral* efforts to pressure for democratization. Most of this work centers on Latin America, where US attempts to foster democracy (short of armed invasion) have received attention for several decades (Drake 1998; Pastor 1989).

In the past few years, some scholars have trumpeted the belief that globalization has become a factor advancing democracy. As connections between states increase and distances reduce with the rise of virtual connections, some posit an increase in the flow of democratic ideas, and therefore regimes, across borders (cf. Hill and Hughes 1999). Often, however, the argument for globalization and democracy draws its causal link from increasing trade and economic interdependence. Such factors are not new in the international system (Keohane and Nye 2001). Moreover, these factors fall in line with much of the existing literature linking global economic conditions to domestic conditions, then to regime change. Such arguments are common in the second image reversed literature and many can be subsumed under existing causal theories.

I have chosen to concentrate on the significance of regional organizations since this is the most under-researched issue relating to democratization. The IO–democracy link continues to be asserted by academics and policymakers with little interest in specifying formal hypotheses or testing them. For example, in their article discussing IOs, interdependence, and democracy, Bruce Russett, John Oneal, and David Davis (1998) find that more democratic dyads (measured by the level of democracy in the least democratic state of the pair) are more likely to be involved in a similar set of IOs. They do not discuss this finding and the variable itself is only a

---

[9] Although in many cases it is debatable whether the end goal of the US was democratization, this was often the stated justification for intervention. In some cases, democracy did actually result (e.g. Grenada). See Pastor 1989.

control for their test of the effect of military conflict on IO involvement. Cheryl Shanks, Harold Jacobson, and Jeffrey Kaplan (1996) also link IOs with democratization, but they find that movements towards democracy are associated with a declining involvement in IOs. They speculate that democratization allows states to shed unpopular alliances and organizations joining under previous systems, yet provide no evidence or further theorizing about these findings. Finally, Russett (1998) and Russett and Oneal (2001) argue that as a part of the "Kantian triangle," IOs and democracy are inherently linked and have a complimentary effect on peace, but unfortunately neither work provides a systematic empirical test of this argument.

This dearth of research on the link between international organizations and democracy is surprising given the surge in interest among policymakers on the topic. As discussions have emerged relating to IO expansion, policymakers have increasingly turned to democracy as a *raison d'être* for enlarging international institutions. In combination with the explicit foreign policy goal of expanding and securing democracy, the purported association between international organizations and democracy seems to have gained widespread acceptance in the policy community. NATO expansion was couched in terms of "securing democracy" in the Visegrad states (Asmus, Kugler, and Larrabee 1993). Potential EU expansion is regarded in the same light (Ash, Mertes, and Mosi 1991). Proposals to expand NAFTA to the southern cone of Latin America are often justified using a similar logic (Hurrell 1994). While my findings are generally supportive of these contentions, I do find that there are instances where regional institutions may not consolidate or encourage democracy. Understanding the causal mechanisms of such a relationship is crucial if policymakers wish to utilize IOs for these ends.

A growing body of literature does exist concerning democracy assistance (Burnell 2000). Much of this literature examines the various instruments which individual states and non-governmental organizations use to enhance prospects for democracy. For example, some studies investigate the policies of NGOs in engaging civil society groups in new democracy (Mair 2000), others examine the effectiveness of election monitors (Chand 1997; Pastor 1999), while still others examine a single country's policies towards democracy promotion (Diamond 1995). Although the democracy assistance literature discusses different actors in relation to democratization, it is concerned with similar questions of conditioning benefits and legitimization of transitional regimes.

Unfortunately, much of this literature has similar shortcomings to the research on broader international influences on democracy. Most studies are single case either in terms of the promoter or the promoted.

Few works draw on well-established theories of international relations or comparative politics.[10] Nonetheless, the cases and findings of that literature are referenced in the following pages. Questions surrounding efficacy and enforcement are common within this literature and I attempt to highlight those similarities where appropriate.

Organization of the book

Chapter 2 fully lays out the theories concerning international influences on both democratic transitions and democratic endurance. I first discuss how regional IOs influence transitions to democracy, followed by a focus on their ability to assist in the consolidation of democracy. In both cases, I discuss a variety of causal mechanisms linking regional IOs to domestic change.

Chapter 3 deals with both theoretical and empirical issues. I first discuss which regional organizations are likely to be associated with transitions and endurance. I also analyze a competing hypothesis that suggests great power interests within international institutions are more accurate predictors of democratization than characteristics of the institutions per se. In addition, the chapter presents some of the basic data used in this study, including data on democracy, democratization, and involvement in regional organizations. The chapter reviews the justification for the use of certain quantitative data as well as the sample of regional organizations utilized in this work. Basic correlational statistics are also presented as an initial test of the association between involvement in regional organizations and democratic transitions as well as democratic consolidation.

Chapter 4 contains a systematic, empirical test for the association between membership in regional IOs and the transition to democracy. I find that, controlling for a wide variety of domestic factors, membership in highly democratic regional institutions increases the probability of a democratic transition by nearly 50 percent. The analyses consist of a series of maximum-likelihood models to evaluate these hypotheses.

Chapter 5 presents three case studies of democratic transitions: Hungary, Peru, and Turkey. The Hungarian case demonstrates how IOs can assist in the *completion* of a democratic transition. I find moderate support for the idea that regional organizations can have an acquiescence effect on societal elites, and stronger support for the idea of psychological legitimization benefits of membership in regional organizations. The Peruvian case illustrates how IO membership can spur political liberalization: in response to Alberto Fujimori's *autogolpe* of 1992,

---

[10] For two exceptions, see Carothers 1999 and Diamond 1999.

the Organization of American States (OAS) responded with strong condemnation, political pressure, and the threat of economic sanctions. Although critics argue that the OAS did not go far enough to pressure Peru, their actions did alter Fujimori's plans to consolidate his own authority through a national plebiscite that would have granted him near absolute power. Finally, the case of Turkey illustrates how regional institutions may pressure for redemocratization after a democratic breakdown. I show that in the aftermath of the military takeover in 1980, the European Economic Community (EEC/EC) and the Council of Europe were a potent source of pressure on the Turkish military government.

Chapter 6 consists of a quantitative test of the democratic endurance argument – democratic regional IOs will lead to increased longevity for democracies. I utilize event history analysis to investigate this claim and find support for the proposition that *joining* (rather than membership per se) certain IOs is significantly related to the duration of democracy, in some cases, increasing the longevity of democracy by over 40 percent.

Chapter 7 presents four cases to trace the influence of regional organizations in the protection of democracy: Greece, Paraguay, Guatemala, and Turkey. In the Greek case, traces of all of the causal mechanisms specified in Chapter 3 were present: assisting with credible commitments for pro-democracy groups, deterring anti-government actors from moving against the system, and bribing former regime opponents to gain the acquiescence to democracy. Paraguay and Guatemala demonstrate the strong deterrent effect that conditions on membership may have on regime opponents. Membership in the Southern Cone Common Market (MERCOSUR) for Paraguay and the OAS for Guatemala has supported those young democracies through several crises threatening to end in military coups. In both cases, the threat of punishment from the members of each organization played a large role in convincing the military to stay out of civilian politics. Finally, the case of Turkey is presented as a failed case of consolidation. Despite membership in many highly democratic regional organizations, Turkey has suffered three breakdowns of democracy, each at the hands of the military. This study explores why membership in such organizations as NATO and the Council of Europe have not created conditions conducive to the survival of democracy. I conclude that the lack of enforcement of conditions, largely due to Turkey's geostrategic importance, plays a significant role in making this a failed case for my theory.

Finally, Chapter 8 concludes with the implications for this argument for comparative politics, international relations theorists, and policymakers. I reflect on the hypothesized causal mechanisms and their presence (and absence) in the case material. I discuss how my argument impacts on the three major groups with interests in this topic: international relations theorists, comparative politics scholars, and policymakers. I conclude that more attention should be focused in international relations on domestic politics as both a causal factor (e.g. the democratic peace), but also as a dependent variable as in Peter Gourevitch's second image reversed approach (1978). For comparative scholars, I discuss the importance of external actors in the democratization process. Although these actors may not always play a determining role in the process of democratization, their presence is important and models that omit these actors risk painting an incomplete picture of the process. Finally, for policymakers, I highlight that membership in these organizations itself is important, but not enough – the incentives (both positive and negative) provided by these organizations must be credible to be effective.

2 Regional organizations, the transition to and the consolidation of democracy

This chapter outlines two distinct but related theories: how do regional organizations influence the transition to democracy and the long-term survival of democracy? While each theory discusses the unique causal mechanisms linking each concept, both draw on similar literatures. First, I outline how regional organizations can assist in the transition to democracy by encouraging domestic liberalization, by providing protection to important elite groups, by socializing key elite groups, and by helping to legitimize transitional regimes so they may complete the transition. I follow with a discussion of how regional IOs can support the consolidation of democracy by helping nascent democracies credibly commit to certain policies, by conferring international validation on new regimes, by helping to deter anti-regime forces from moving against the young regime, and by providing resources to assist leaders in gaining the acquiescence of key elite groups.

Regional organizations and democratic transitions

In the process of moving from an authoritarian system to a democracy, regional organizations may assert influence at various stages of the democratization process. I show that pressures generated from outside the state in combination with internal forces can compel autocratic regimes to liberalize, loosening control over civil society and/or political institutions. Second, I discuss how membership in a regional institution can lead certain elite groups to acquiesce to liberalization since membership can lower the risks which these groups face during the democratization process. Finally, I argue that regional organizations can function to help complete the transition process by providing a forum to signal and legitimize a transitional regime's commitment to democratic reform, assisting in completing the transition to democracy. Chapter 4 provides a statistical test of the argument, analyzing the effect of regional organizations on the probability of a regime making a transition to democracy.

*Regional IOs and transitions: pressure for liberalization
in autocratic systems*

The concept of "democratization" can encompass several dynamics. For most scholars of democratic transitions, *liberalization* is distinct from *democratization*. According to Mainwaring (1992: 298), "Political liberalization refers to an easing of repression and extension of civil liberties *within* an authoritarian regime, whereas a transition to democracy implies a change *of* regimes" (italics in original). Following this common distinction in the literature, I divide transitions to democracy into two phases: the initial decision to liberalize and the subsequent decision to move to full democracy. This section will concentrate on the former.

One common conclusion of the transitions literature is that elite schisms are an impetus for political liberalization (Kaufman 1986; O'Donnell and Schmitter 1986; Przeworski 1986). Liberalization occurs when members of the ruling coalition feel they must go outside the current cadre of elites for support (Przeworski 1991: 56). Przeworski (1991: 57) contends that liberalizers hope to "relax social tension" by incorporating new groups into the ruling elite. This process, of course, is not meant to unseat the ruling elites from power. Liberalization is meant to be a closed-ended process, a "controlled opening of political space" (Przeworski 1991: 57). This can lead directly to democratization, proceed slowly for many years, or end with more repression on the part of the regime (Mainwaring 1992; Przeworski 1986). Ideally, the authoritarian leaders hope to expand their power base through limited reform – increasing their legitimacy and forestalling calls for more significant changes in the regime.

Much of the literature, however, is mixed as to what causes the split within the elite bloc. For example, O'Donnell and Schmitter (1986) argue economic success can spur authoritarians to step down, since they can make a strong case for remaining part of a new, liberalized regime. More recent work by Haggard and Kaufman (1995b) has confirmed this notion in studies of several East Asian transitions. In a similar vein, economic crises may serve as a trigger to split a ruling coalition by creating pressures on authoritarian governments to respond to inflation or a recession (Gasiorowski 1995). Non-economic factors may also make conditions more propitious for splits in the ruling coalition leading to periods of liberalization. The failure of an authoritarian regime to legitimize and institutionalize its rule can make it more susceptible to political or economic crises (O'Donnell and Schmitter 1986: 15). The nature of the regime itself may make these splits more likely. For example, Barbara

Geddes (1999) argues that military-led authoritarian regimes are likely to split given their preference to "return to the barracks."

What many studies of the liberalization process have in common is their treatment of the impetus for liberalization as an exogenous shock. These shocks may be political or economic in nature, but either can force elites to take some action to restore the legitimacy of their regime. Disagreements then arise within the authoritarian bloc as to the prudent course of action. Some regimes may be able to weather the crisis given a variety of factors, ranging from the nature of the current autocratic regime, economic conditions, to the past performance of the regime. Other regimes may decide to liberalize in an attempt to restore legitimacy.

My contention is that a potent source of this exogenous shock can be pressure from a regional organization of which the regime is a member. This pressure can undermine authoritarian rule in two ways. First, it can create economic difficulties for the regime if part of the punishment by the organization is the suspension of trade, halting economic aid, or the imposition of economic sanctions. This can create or exacerbate economic crises undermining an authoritarian regime. Second, public condemnation and international isolation can help to delegitimize a regime at home. If allies and institutional partners treat the regime as a pariah state, this can impact on public and elite perceptions within the state. These pressures can help to weaken an authoritarian regime's grip on power. As Larry Diamond (1999: 277) notes, "concerted international pressure on authoritarian elites could reinforce domestic pressures and persuade authoritarian elites that the costs of resisting demands for democracy exceed the benefits they expect to reap."

This pressure can come in a variety of forms, ranging from overt delegitimization of the regime by members of the organization via political isolation to direct economic sanctions against the regime, even expulsion from the organization. In order to understand how this causal mechanism works, three interrelated questions will be addressed: (1) Why do member states pressure other non-democratic or semi-democratic members to undertake democratization? (2) Why is the regional IO the mechanism by which the pressure occurs? (3) What tools are used to pressure the regime in question? I address each in turn.

Why would states pressure other states to become democratic? First, as a way to boost its own international status, a young democracy may pressure former authoritarian partners to make similar moves to liberalize. In order to distance itself from former allies or autocratic neighbors, a state may become active against authoritarian regimes. As Geoffrey Pridham (1995) has argued, the act of foreign policy reorientation can lend legitimacy to new democracies.[1] Thus, new democracies will have incentives to treat autocracies (especially former political allies) as pariah states in order to establish their own legitimacy (both internally and externally). Even established democracies, such as the United States, often make the promotion of democracy a major foreign policy priority for reasons of domestic legitimacy (on the US case, see Smith 1994). In the words of Laurence Whitehead (1996d: 248), "success in supporting democracy abroad has served to reinforce the legitimation of the democratic order at home, and to boost national pride and self-confidence."

Second, if scholarly research concerning the economic and political advantages of democracies is correct, then one would expect democracies to rationally desire to have more democracies in the world. Research has shown that democracies prefer to trade (Bliss and Russett 1998; Mansfield, Milner, and Rosendorff 2000; Morrow, Siverson, and Tabares 1998; Polachek 1997), cooperate (Mansfield, Milner, and Rosendorff 2002; Russett 1993), and ally (Simon and Gartzke 1996; Siverson and Emmons 1991) with one another. In addition, democracies better promote economic growth and stability (Barro 1997; Keefer and Knack 1995, 1997). Thus, expanding the number of democracies expands interaction opportunities for such ends as trade and cooperation. Interestingly, there is evidence that policymakers actually have internalized these ideas into their foreign policies. According to Thomas Carothers (1999: 5), this was true of both Presidents Bush and Clinton who, "along with their top foreign policy advisers, repeatedly declared that in the reconfigured world, promoting democracy serves not only moral interests but also practical ones . . . Democratic governments, they asserted, do not go to war with one another, produce refugees, or engage in terrorism."

There are certainly specific instances where regime type holds little power to explain economic or political relations.[2] Nonetheless, the idea that democracies prefer to trade, ally, and cooperate with other democracies is well established. Thus, given the opportunity, a democracy will most likely push a non-democratic neighbor or trade partner to liberalize.

Why will regional IOs be the mechanism of choice for pressure against authoritarian regimes? Two factors make these institutions potentially powerful forces for change. First, regional institutions provide a forum to air complaints against member states. In essence, they provide a

---

[1] Pridham's argument is also raised in the case of consolidation, since the foreign policy reorientation may assist in the legitimization process in the post-transitional environment.

[2] There are cases where democracies have attempted to subvert other democracies if other geopolitical objectives are considered more pressing (e.g. Arbenz's Guatemala). Yet, there are also cases where geopolitical objectives have been subverted to push for political liberalization (e.g. Somoza's Nicaragua; the Shah's Iran).

low-cost "voice" opportunity for states of all sizes (Grieco 1996: 286–9). The benefits of international institutions in terms of lowering transaction costs have been elucidated elsewhere (Keohane 1984; Martin 1992). Because these institutions provide an accessible forum for public condemnation, diplomatic pressure, and economic sanctions, they provide a ready conduit for this pressure.[3]

Second, multilateral efforts will often be a favored mechanism of democracies since it minimizes the perception on the part of actors within the target state of direct violations of sovereignty. For example, the United States has been widely criticized in Latin America for its past unilateral efforts at democracy promotion (cf. Drake 1998: 79–81). Former European colonies also may remain skeptical of the intentions of their former colonizer (Burnell 2000: 35). If efforts to promote democracy are widely perceived as illegitimate or imperialistic in the target state, intervention can backfire, creating support for the authoritarian regime. Within the context of regional institutions, however, these efforts can gain legitimacy because of their multilateral nature (Farer 1989; Munoz 1998; Pastor 1989).

How do democracies use regional IOs to pressure autocratic states? Because the institution provides expanded interaction opportunities, there are a variety of possibilities. First, open and direct verbal condemnation is likely. This can be an effective tool to publicly delegitimize an autocracy to its citizens and elites within the regime. Second, if a state or group of states can build enough support within the organization, threats of sanctions or other punishments (e.g. membership suspension) can be levied against an autocratic state. These actions can provide powerful incentives, especially in combination with other domestic pressures, for a regime to liberalize.

One likely scenario for this regional pressure is the case of redemocratization after the breakdown of democracy. Regional IOs often assert pressure for the state to reinstall the democratic regime. One example of this scenario would be the Organization of American States' pressure on Guatemala after the self-coup of Jorge Serrano. In May 1993, Serrano dissolved Guatemala's legislature and courts, and announced that he would rule by decree (Halperin and Lomasney 1998: 137). Led by several of the smaller democratic members of the organization, the OAS lodged high profile protests and moved to levy sanctions against the regime (Cameron 1994: 169). After five days, Serrano was forced from office

---

[3] This skirts the collective action problems in coordinating sanctions. Since institutions are likely to help identify cheaters (for example, through the construction of focal points), concerns over free riding will be lessened within an institution (see Martin 1992). I return to this issue in the next chapter.

by the military, which reinstalled a civilian president. Many observers credit the OAS response as an important part of Serrano's calculations to step down (Cameron 1998a).[4]

In the end, regional institutions enable democracies to push non-democracies to liberalize. These institutions help to delegitimize autocratic regimes through various means including public condemnation, political or economic sanctions, even expulsion from the organization. Although this in and of itself may not be the most important determinant in convincing autocrats to loosen their grip on power, in combination with other factors, it can provide a powerful impetus for political liberalization.

Regional IOs and transitions: societal elites and acquiescence to liberalization

Besides pressure emanating from the regional organization, another causal pathway links regional IOs and liberalization. During decisions to begin liberalization and immediately thereafter, some elite groups upon which the autocratic government depends may attempt to veto this course of action, since such moves may threaten their well-being. Membership in regional organizations, however, can decrease the likelihood of this veto. First, IOs can create credible guarantees to key constituencies, assuaging these elite groups' fears of democracy. Second, IOs can lessen the probability of this veto through a socialization process. This process can make elites less inimical to the process of liberalization. This section will discuss each of these two processes as they relate to business elites and the military, respectively. Although I discuss these in the context of liberalization, these dynamics may occur later, during decisions concerning the completion of the transition to democracy.

Authoritarians (whether in single-party systems or military dictatorships) depend upon the support of other groups in society for their power. A common theory in explaining the rise of autocracies is that these regimes best protect the interests of these important groups. For example, business elites may fear that democracy will bring radical populists to power or even less-extreme movements that may not protect their property rights or financial interests. The military may fear democratic transitions because of the threat they pose to their institutional interests, especially subordination to civilian supremacy. If these groups fear their interests are threatened by political liberalization, they will likely stand in the way of liberalization efforts (Kaufman 1986: 86).

---

[4] This case is discussed more fully in Chapter 7.

Business elites   For many business elites in authoritarian systems, democracy can conjure images of populism and radicalism. Research on bureaucratic-authoritarianism in Latin America, for example, argued that business elites supported coups against democracies in the 1960s and 1970s because they felt the military would protect their interests from "the masses" (cf. O'Donnell 1973; Whitehead 1989: 85). These concerns led middle-class business interests and internationalist economic coalitions to support authoritarian takeovers, often by the military (Kaufman 1986). Even much of the democratic transitions literature of the 1980s assumes that business interests will naturally ally themselves with authoritarians who are better suited to protect their interests (O'Donnell and Schmitter 1986: 27; Payne 1994: 2).

The logic of this argument holds that business leaders fear nationalization, redistribution, and other policies that would compromise their economic position. This fear will lead business elites to have an underlying preference for autocratic regimes since these systems will better respond to their concerns. In a recent adaptation of this proposition, Leigh Payne (1994) argues that business leaders have no strong preferences for any type of government, whether authoritarian or democratic. Rather, economic elites will support any system so long as it protects their interests (see also Malloy 1987: 252–3).

When confronting a situation where liberalization could occur, economic elites will make interest-based calculations in deciding whether to support liberalization:

In some cases, the worst that an elite can expect under a strategy of toleration is an unpleasant loss of status and political power that leaves its economic base and religiocultural values secure. In other cases, the call for toleration of political opposition fuels deep-seated fears within the ruling elite about its economic viability, the continued existence of hallowed institutions, or even personal survival . . . A political elite will have some estimation of its prospective capacity to protect its basic interests both by building institutional safeguards into the emerging democratic process and by actively competing in it . . . (Marks 1992: 51)

If elites can find some way of guaranteeing their economic (or political) well-being, they are more likely to submit to liberalization. Of course, one problem faced by these elites is the difficulty in assuring that institutional safeguards are respected by reformers. If they attach a particularly low probability to the survival of these safeguards, they may refuse to liberalize at the outset (Burton, Gunther, and Higley 1992: 342). To take an extreme example from one observer of Latin America, "if open elections seriously threaten complete loss of private property, capitalists will all become authoritarians . . ." (Sheahan 1986: 163).

My contention is that membership in regional organizations can be a credible external guarantee of safeguards for elites, especially economic elites. When domestic policy violates an international agreement, the ability to change course becomes diminished. These external guarantees will lessen the perception on the part of business elites that democracy will be dangerous to their interests. In the words of Laurence Whitehead (1989: 84):

A vital element in the process of democratic consolidation is therefore to induce [business interests and propertied classes] to confine their lobbying within legitimate bounds and to relinquish their ties with the undemocratic right. External reassurance (and if possible guarantees) may provide a critical inducement at the beginning of a consolidation process, although the need for this should diminish as democratization advances.

The literature on regional cooperation agreements has long argued that these institutions perform these reassurance functions. Membership in a regional organization helps to lock in economic policies and rights enacted by domestic elites (Goldstein 1998: 143–4; Mansfield, Milner, Rosendorff 2002; Milner 1998: 24). For example, regional trade agreements codify commitments to free trade and set up a system of verification to monitor the implementation of such reform (Whalley 1998). These mechanisms help to lock in commitments among states that free trade will continue even in the face of domestic opposition (Fernández and Portes 1998; Mansfield 1998; Milner 1998: 29).

In the area of property rights, regional economic agreements also help to provide commitments that governments will not engage in opportunistic behavior. Since a common goal of many regional agreements is to lure foreign investment into the region, these institutions provide explicit guarantees about property and investment. In order to lure multinational firms to invest in a region, these arrangements must provide guarantees against opportunistic behavior on the part of host governments – guarantees that would apply to domestic firms as well (Fernández and Portes 1998; Yarbrough and Yarbrough 1992). As such, these organizations can provide important reassurances concerning property rights and investments.[5]

Laurence Whitehead has argued that these guarantees codified in the European Economic Community/European Union were essential to democratization efforts in Southern Europe.[6] Because the EEC "offered

---

[5] An example of this phenomenon can be found in the ASEAN states. See Saxonhouse 1993: 410–11.

[6] It should be noted that although Southern European states were not full members of the EC, Greece, Portugal, and Spain had association agreements.

critical external guarantees to the business and propertied classes of southern Europe . . . democracy would lose much of its sting for the rich" (Whitehead 1996a: 271). The EEC/EU insists on adequate compensation for any property taken by the state, and ensures the relatively free movement of capital and goods (Whitehead 1986). This externally monitored and enforced guarantee provided credible protection for economic elite interests, buying their acquiescence in the democratization process in Southern Europe. This was especially true in Spain (Whitehead 1986) and Portugal (Manuel 1996: 75), where economic elites had been quite hostile to democracy. For the Spanish elites who were a potential roadblock to democracy, the stipulations of the EEC "provided guarantees and reassurances to those who faced the post-authoritarian future with apprehension" (Powell 1996: 297).

These commitments to trade and property rights may persuade business leaders that even in the worst case scenario of a populist-oriented, democratic government, their interests will be protected. Of course, it is possible that any government (democratic or authoritarian) can withdraw from these international agreements, but they often pay significant costs for doing so.[7] Thus, membership in regional organizations reduces the probability of opportunistic behavior by creating an externally monitored commitment to a particular set of behaviors. This increases the chance for business elites to acquiesce to political liberalization and democracy.

The military and socialization   The other group influenced by membership in a regional organization is the military. Similar to business elites, the military is a powerful group concerned with protecting its interests and institutions (Dassel and Reinhardt 1998). Often, the military stands in the way of political liberalization out of fears for its autonomy (e.g. subjugation to civilian rule) and for the protection of its institutions (e.g. fears of reprisals for its role in past authoritarian governments) (cf. Przeworski 1991: 31–2; Whitehead 1989: 81–4). Regional IOs can help to assuage the military's resistance to democratization by providing externally supported guarantees, as well as helping to reorient military officers away from domestic politics.

Regional security organizations can assure the military of continued support either through the domestic regime or alliance partners. In order to maintain a credible military force as a part of an alliance, a state must provide adequate resources to the military and is often required by its allies to do so. These requirements of the alliance help to assure military officers their "piece of the pie." The military may also receive direct

[7] On the issue of institutional commitments, see Mitchell 2002.

financial or technical benefits from its alliance partners. This was the case for the Hungarian military. Through the Partnership for Peace (PFP) program, Hungary received technical military assistance and through NATO, it has received financial and technical assistance in the modernization process. In addition, NATO required that military spending in Hungary be stabilized and even increased. This reversed a downward spiral in the military budget that had created dissatisfaction among military officers. As I show in Chapter 5, PFP/NATO membership was important for the completion of the democratic transition in Hungary.

The stronger impact of regional military organizations, however, comes in the form of socialization. Regional alliances and military organizations, especially those which conduct joint training operations or maintain permanent consultative institutions, help to socialize military leaders in member states as to the role of the military in domestic society.

Other research on the effect of international institutions has identified this causal process in other areas (Tharp 1971: 3; Archer 1992). Martha Finnemore (1996a,b) has shown how interaction within international organizations can shape elite preferences. In addition, Strang and Chang (1993) have shown how the International Labor Organization (ILO) has influenced welfare spending through the socialization of domestic elite groups. Much of this research, growing out of sociological institutionalism, does not center on formal institutions, per se, but rather international norms (Strang and Chang 1993: 237).[8] Still, many examples in the empirical literature focus on formal organizations such as UNESCO, the ILO, or the World Bank (Finnemore 1996b). Although I identify a specific causal mechanism that is more formal than most sociological institutionalists would stipulate, the processes behind the socialization remain the same.

In this context, socialization amounts to persuading military leaders that the role of the military is not that of an internal police force involved in domestic politics, but rather to protect the state from external enemies.[9] As Pridham (1994: 196) has argued, "A more stable way for these [Southern European] governments to internationalize the military role was through integration in a European organization such as NATO." Moreover, the idea of civilian supremacy over military missions and institutions is often an issue of contention in transitional states. By interacting

---

[8] For a collection of essays discussing the sociological institutionalist view, see Thomas, Meyer, Ramirez, and Boli 1987.

[9] I make a similar argument in the context of democratic consolidation. There I contend that the threat of punishment from the IO in the case of a military coup convinces the military to stay in the barracks. Here, the argument is that during the transition process, socialization convinces the military that coups are "off-limits."

with military leaders of other states who subscribe to these types of doctrines, military elites in autocratic or recently autocratic states are likely to internalize these doctrines, making them more likely to accept full democracy. This issue may be important not only in the military's acceptance of an initial move towards liberalization, but also the removal of "reserve domains" and completing the transition to democracy.

Perhaps nowhere has this dynamic been more important than in the transition to democracy in Spain. Long excluded from NATO membership, after Franco's death and the beginning of the transition to democracy, NATO accession became a foreign policy goal of the new Spanish regime. Although Spain's transition had taken place over six years earlier, a cadre of military officers attempted a coup against the young democracy in 1981. This highlighted the need to control the Spanish military and keep it away from the domestic political process.

NATO became the vehicle to achieve this goal. According to Pridham (1991c: 228), "the belief surfaced in government circles that entry to NATO would help secure democracy as it would 'modernize' the Army through growing international contacts and direct its attention away from domestic politics" (see also Boyd and Boyden 1985; Treverton 1986: 32–3).[10] This reasoning proved correct as Spain's army did undergo significant modernization and reorientation after NATO membership (Hurrell 1996: 161). Through "joint maneuvers," "modernization," and "improvements in military technology," the Spanish military became reoriented away from domestic politics (Pridham 1994: 199–200; Tovias 1984: 167). The military alliance thus proved a powerful tool to reshape the preferences of actors, leading to the consolidation of the democratic transition in Spain.

Legitimizing transitional governments

The final mechanism linking IOs to democratization is their ability to help signal to internal and external actors that transitional regimes are committed to continuing democratic reform.[11] As states move through the second stage of democratization (from authoritarianism to democracy, after liberalization), they often spend time as a transitional regime. Also labeled "interim" governments, these regimes exist in an "undefined

---

[10] Interestingly, Spain's main opposition Socialist Party (PSOE), which had initially opposed NATO membership, acquiesced to accession after the 1981 coup attempt largely for its potential impact on the army officers (Tovias 1984: 167).

[11] The problem of making a credible commitment to democratic reform may arise at multiple stages within the democratization process. This section discusses the issue *during* the transition process. The next section makes a similar argument concerning the period *after* the transition.

period in the interval between 'the launching of the process of dissolution of an authoritarian regime,' at the outset, and 'the installation of some form of democracy . . .'" (Shain and Linz 1995: 7). For countries in this period, the democratization process is not complete and there is no guarantee that they will become a coherent democracy.

These interim regimes face unique pressures, mostly due to a "context of volatility and political vulnerability marked by uncertainty, anxiety, and high expectations concerning the future distribution of power and loyalties" (Shain and Linz 1995: 7). This creates an immediate challenge of credibility and legitimacy. Because these regimes come to power after the breakdown of autocracy, yet before elections and the completion of democracy, they must legitimize their regime. The easiest path for doing so is to make a clear commitment to democratic reform (Shain and Linz 1995: 6–9).

Making a credible commitment to reform can be difficult under these situations of uncertainty, however. This lack of commitment, in turn, can erode the legitimacy of the regime. As Mainwaring (1992: 307) argues, "Legitimacy does not need to be universal in the beginning stages if democracy is to succeed, but if a commitment to democracy does not emerge over time, democracy is in trouble." This "trouble" can arise from disloyal opposition groups during the transition or from citizens who do not trust the new, unelected regime (Mainwaring 1992: 307).

Membership in regional IOs may assist in completing the transition to democracy by helping to signal the intentions of the interim regime.[12] Specifically, membership in regional organizations will be a credible signal that the regime wishes to continue reform.[13] Geoffrey Pridham (1994: 26–7) has argued that with respect to issues such as "national pride and credibility" and "the international component of system legitimacy," membership in international institutions and the general reorientation of foreign policy can assist in the transitional process. For example, by applying to and gaining membership in such institutions as the Council of Europe and NATO, Eastern European interim regimes were able to clarify their intentions with regard to democratic reform and reassure their populace via external relations. This process was certainly in the mind of Czech President Vaclav Havel, who warned "our countries are

---

[12] This assumes that regime leaders *are* genuinely interested in completing reform, which may not always be the case. The problem arises when it is impossible to distinguish those leaders who do want to advance democracy from those who do not, which is the crux of the credibility/legitimacy problem. I assume the interim government does prefer to advance reform, but needs a mechanism to do so.

[13] Clearly not all regional organizations will serve this purpose equally well. I discuss which organizations will be tapped for this role at the beginning of Chapter 3.

Table 2.1 *Transition mechanisms*

Pressure by regional IO members
Acquiescence effect
   – Preference lock-in
   – Socialization
Legitimization of interim regime

dangerously sliding into an uncertain political, economic and security vacuum . . . it is becoming increasingly evident that without appropriate external relations the very being of our young democracies is in jeopardy" (quoted in Hyde-Price 1996: 230). As Chapter 5 discusses, this was especially true in Hungary, where the interim Nemeth regime worked feverishly to gain acceptance into European regional organizations, especially the Council of Europe (Klebes 1999; Kun 1993: 47).

Although the issue of commitment may link regional organizations to the democratization process at any stage of the transition, my contention is that this process is especially important to assist in the completion of democracy – moving from an interim government to a full democracy. In the *immediate* aftermath of the breakdown of authoritarian rule, elite groups and the general public are likely to allow some latitude in policy from a new government. As this honeymoon comes to an end, however, any signs that authoritarian tendencies could reemerge is likely to breed instability. Membership in certain regional organizations can serve as a visible commitment to continue reform, helping convince the public to invest in the new regime. Since the legitimacy issue can arise throughout the life of a democracy, I also discuss this issue in the context of the consolidation of democracy.

This section has discussed the causal mechanisms by which regional organizations may be associated with democratic transitions. Of course, none of these causal mechanisms is exclusive and each may be present in any one case. Moreover, note that only one of these mechanisms (pressure) relies on the initiative of an actor external to the nation-state. The other mechanisms arise out of desires by domestic elites to democratize. Some of these mechanisms may also help democracies to survive, after the transition has been completed. To that end, I now turn to the issue of regional organizations and democratic longevity.

Regional organizations and democratic consolidation

This section develops a theory linking regional organizations to the longevity of democracy. I begin by discussing the nature of the consolidation problem and the dynamics of domestic politics that can threaten the stability of young democracies. I then show how regional organizations can assist in consolidation by helping to commit domestic actors to post-transitional reform by raising the cost of anti-democratic action on the part of elites. In addition, these organizations provide both positive and negative incentives for regime opponents to abide by emerging democratic institutions. Finally, joining regional organizations can help legitimize the new regime, increasing the likelihood that the common citizen will invest in the new system, furthering the consolidation process. Chapter 6 tests the argument using event history analysis to analyze whether regional IOs increase the endurance of democracies, while Chapter 7 investigates four cases of whether state ties to regional IOs helped to protect democracy.

The perils of consolidation

There are many ways to conceptualize democratic consolidation (Burton, Gunther and Higley 1992; Gunther, Puhle, Diamandouros 1995; O'Donnell 1996; Schedler 1998; Shin 1994). Various factors, including elite unity, economic stability, and mass attitudinal support for democracy, have been proffered as definitions and operationalizations of consolidation. Rather than review these multiple conceptualizations at length, I will follow the advice of Giuseppe Di Palma (1990: 31): "when it comes to consolidation, we should try to avoid the impulse to take refuge behind questions of definition . . . The task, on the contrary, is to focus on the theories . . ."

The crux of the issue confronted by this chapter is, what factors contribute to the duration of democracy? Can young democracies overcome challenges to their nascent institutions posed by anti-democratic forces that previously benefited from authoritarianism? For democracy to become consolidated, it must overcome these short-term challenges. Pridham (1995: 169) has labeled the short-term obstacles to democracy "negative consolidation," which "includes the solution of any problems remaining from the transition process and, in general, the containment or reduction, if not removal, of any serious challenges to democratization."[14] Other scholars have labeled this immediate issue of regime durability "democratic breakdown" (Schedler 1998).

I have chosen to concentrate on this short-term aspect of consolidation, ignoring the long-term aspects of democratic legitimization. While

---

[14] This view is in contrast to positive consolidation, which is a long-term attitudinal shift in society towards democratic norms.

some would object to my characterization of democratic "endurance" as "consolidation," this view does have adherents in the existing literature (Power and Gasiorowski 1997). Moreover, because there are no widely accepted criteria for democratic consolidation (McClintock 1989: 133), I limit my use of the term "consolidation" in most of this work to minimize conceptual confusion. I use the term here only to give the reader an anchor point to the existing democratization literature. I prefer to label the issue endurance, survival, or durability. While democratic endurance may not equate directly with consolidation (Shin 1994), it is at a minimum, a necessary condition.

New democracies face a high risk of failure (Mainwaring et al. 1992: 8). Empirically, the survival rate of democracies in their infancy is quite low: one-third of all new democracies fail within five years (Power and Gasiorowski 1997). Why are democracies so susceptible to failure in the immediate post-transitional period? Two factors help explain this vulnerability: (1) change in the composition and structure of domestic institutions, and (2) increased uncertainty about both the durability of these institutions and the identity of the relevant actors which influence them (Whitehead 1989: 78–80).

By their very nature, institutions have distributional consequences (Knight 1992). As old institutions are cast aside and new institutions are formed, new "winners" and "losers" arise (Przeworski 1991). Regardless of whether the change is political or economic, some groups suffer, while others improve their lot. As J. Samuel Valenzuela (1992: 71) notes, these distributional squabbles flowing from institutional change are the essence of the consolidation process: "while democratic consolidation is basically about the elimination of formal and informal institutions that are inimical to democracy, it takes the form of a struggle between actors who benefit – or think they could benefit at a certain point – from those institutions' existence, and those who do not." Both the winners and losers of this struggle can pose a threat to the new democracy – a threat exacerbated by the uncertainty of the transitional period.

Losers and the threat to new democracies

Distributional losers often pose the most visible threat to nascent democracies. Unhappy with their new status, some groups may focus only on their short-term deprivations rather than the prospect of future gains under a democratic system (Valenzuela 1992). Any group may fall into this category, but the same two groups which may veto initial moves to liberalize often stand out as potential spoilers in the consolidation effort: the military and business elites.

The military can provide the largest roadblock to democratic consolidation, especially if it was an integral part of the previous authoritarian government (Aguero 1995; Linz, Stepan, and Gunther 1995). There are generally two dynamics that lead the military to move against a nascent democracy. Either domestic institutions are contested and the military feels its leadership is needed to protect its own institutions, or a new democracy can attempt to subjugate the military to civilian control, leading to a crisis in civil–military relations.

Haiti is one example of the military moving against a regime in a post-transitional environment. Less than seven months after Haiti's first elections, President Jean-Bertrand Aristide was toppled by a military-led coup in September 1991. A three-person junta took power amidst massive violence in the small island nation. The leader of the coup, General Raoul Cedras, claimed that the new democratic government had not effectively established itself after elections justifying the coup: "What we need to do now is reestablish the state and control the country" (Inter Press Service 1991).

If the military feels its interests are threatened during a time when institutions are contested, it is more likely to move against its opponents at home (Dassel 1998). Moreover, the military may feel that society has become too polarized and that strong central leadership is necessary to protect "the state" (Huntington 1968: 194–6). General Cedras' first post-coup pronouncements summarize this view quite succinctly: "The Army is steering the ship of state into port."[15] In these cases, democratization suffers a clear set-back. In some instances, the military offers to return control of the state to civilians. Its track record is mixed in fulfilling this promise,[16] but even in cases where power is returned to an elected government, the very political fabric of a society suffers (Finer 1962) and the probability of recurrent coups increases (Londregan and Poole 1990).

The military may also move against a young democracy if it feels threatened by attempts to establish civilian supremacy. The government is placed in a difficult position vis-à-vis the military and its proper role in the new regime. On one hand, it is widely recognized that democracy requires civilian supremacy over the military (Linz and Stepan 1996; Valenzuela 1992: 87). Attaining this supremacy can prove a difficult task since the regime must simultaneously try to keep the military loyal to the

---

[15] *Christian Science Monitor*, "Haitian President Flees Country After Coup," 2 October 1991, 3.

[16] In Turkey, the military has a strong track record of "leaving" government (see Chapter 7). In Haiti, it took an invasion of US troops to convince the military government to leave power.

new democratic regime during this process (Aguero 1992). In the post-1983 return to democracy, Argentina faced such a dilemma. Attempts by President Raúl Alfonsín to impose civilian authority on the military had taken great strides in the first part of his administration (Aguero 1995). Eventually, as budget cuts grew deeper and prosecutions for human rights offenses expanded, the military began to oppose reform. After a series of revolts by mid-level officers, Alfonsín limited the state's prosecution of officers for human rights crimes, weakening his own as well as the subsequent Menem administration (Pion-Berlin 1991). Although subsequent military uprisings failed against the Menem administration, this example illustrates the delicate balance between controlling a post-authoritarian military force while simultaneously holding their loyalty to the new regime.

The military, however, does not often act alone. Other groups may exert similar pressures against the new regime, even pressuring the military for action (Dassel and Reinhardt 1998). Specifically, business elites can be a salient source of these threats (Kaufman 1986: 101; Whitehead 1989: 84). As discussed in the previous section, lack of protection for property rights, poor economic policy and performance, or excessive regulation can spur economic elites to not only withhold support from a regime, but actively work against it.[17] In addition, business elites may decide that they do not want to "share the stage with a wide range of other political interests" and may desire to return to the "comfort and shelter" of authoritarian rule (Whitehead 1989: 85). While these business elites may not possess the resources to directly overthrow the regime, they can sow the seeds of discord, undermining the regime or allying with a group that does possess the power to depose the government, such as the military.

Under what circumstances is one likely to find such an alliance between the military and business interests? Existing literature sheds some light on this question. First, the military must feel there is an alternative to the current regime before it acts (Przeworski 1986: 52). According to Aguero (1995: 126), elite behavior is important to this perception of alternatives. Given a poor economic environment, economic elites may begin to turn against the existing regime. Contested institutions function as an enabling factor for military action, while poor economic policy and performance by the new regime may push business elites to ally with the military. With a

---

[17] Recall the previous section's discussion of the appeal of authoritarianism to business interests. If these ideas of the bureaucratic-authoritarian model are correct, business leaders may be hostile towards democracy after the transition. Of course, if regional organizations provide guarantees *ex ante*, this opposition may be less of a problem for the new regime.

support base of economic elites, the military would perceive a clear alternative to the existing regime, heightening its propensity to move against democracy. This dynamic explains the findings of Londregan and Poole (1990) that economic growth is a key determinant to military coups.

It is important to remember that losers do not necessarily suffer losses before they move against the system. Merely the perception that they will suffer losses under the new government may be enough to spur them to action. Recall Valenzuela's earlier quote discussing the calculus of potential coup perpetrators: "actors who benefit – *or think they could benefit at a certain point*" (emphasis added). Actual losses are not a necessary condition for an anti-regime stance.

For democracy to survive, these potential anti-regime forces need to accept democratic institutions and work within the institutions rather than despite them. This issue was discussed in the previous section in reference to elites' *pre*-transition behavior (the acquiescence effect), but similar problems can arise in the *post*-transition environment as well, especially in the early tenure of democracy. Mainwaring (1992: 309) expresses this idea in the context of consolidation: "In many cases, the actors who supported authoritarian rule remain equivocal at best about democracy as a form of government . . . In the early phases of a new democracy, it is more feasible to induce these actors to abide by the democratic rules out of self-interest, by creating a high cost for anti-system action, than to transform their values." I argue that membership in regional organizations can help to alter the cost–benefit calculations of potential anti-regime groups through increasing the costs for overturning the democratic system. Before elucidating how IOs perform this task, however, I will focus on an equally problematic group for the consolidation of democracy – the "winners" in the new regime.

Winners, credible commitments, and the threat to democracy

Winners in new democracies could attempt to turn their (often newfound) power into a permanent political advantage. As Lane (1979) and Przeworski (1991) have argued, political power gives rise to increasing returns to scale – political power begets more political power. This "temptation of power" could result in biased institutions, the exclusion of some groups from the democratic process, a freezing of the pace of reform, even a reversal of earlier liberalization (Hellman 1998). The major difficulty comes when winners must convince other elites (e.g. losers) and the public that they are committed to reform. If either group (elites or the masses) does not perceive this commitment, consolidation will be unlikely.

Committing to reform is an important issue for winners in newly democratic regimes, which face several hurdles in convincing observers that their reform is credible.[18] The problem can be cast as an information-related issue. Some regimes (democratic and authoritarian) can and do begin reform which they have no intention of completing. Tempted by the ability to bias the system in their favor, new leaders freeze or even reverse liberalization and reform. Partial reform can halt the democratic consolidation process in its tracks. For example, "electoral rules may be deliberately designed . . . to under-represent grossly significant sectors of opinion, while over-representing others" (Valenzuela 1992: 67). The problem is that it is difficult to know *ex ante* whether new regimes will engage in opportunistic behavior or pursue genuine reform.

The uncertainty over the intentions of the regime arises from at least two factors. First, there are certain benefits that accrue to those who make liberalizing political reforms (loans, increased investment, etc.) which give non-committed governments an incentive to appear as reformist (Frye 1997). Earnest reformers would benefit from sending a credible signal to distinguish themselves from fraudulent reformers.

Second, and most importantly, new regimes lack a reputation for self-restraint and honoring commitments (Diermeier et al. 1997; Linz 1978). Given that the regime is relatively new, external and internal actors have even less information about the true intentions or motivation of the government (Crescenzi 1999). According to Valenzuela (1992: 66), "it is not at all clear that those who take power in such convulsed situations will be committed to building a genuine democracy." Established governments are much more likely to have built a reputation as honoring commitments to political reform. New regimes have no track record and thus foster few expectations that commitments to reform will be credible.

Adding to this problem is that during many transitions, existing institutions are cast aside by the winners.[19] Thus, any reputation that may exist for those in power will be negative: "After any transition from authoritarian rule, the emergent democracy will be a regime in which not all significant political actors will have impeccable democratic credentials" (Whitehead 1989: 78). Since winners' past behavior consisted of gutting or severely altering domestic institutions, their ability to signal credible commitments in the post-transition period will be limited.

---

[18] Here, I focus on credibility problems that are largely political in nature. Other credibility problems exist, especially in the realm of economic reform. For a discussion of additional credibility problems in economic liberalization, see Rodrik 1989.

[19] One could cite the findings of Londregan and Poole (1990: 175) that coups tend to beget coups as evidence of this problem. They find that once a coup occurs in a state, "it has a much harder time avoiding further coups."

Finally, these problems are compounded by the uncertainty arising from the transition process itself, when elites will often be unsure about the "identity, resources, and intentions of those with whom they are playing the transition game" (O'Donnell and Schmitter 1986: 66). In addition, although winning groups may remain winning groups, there is often high turnover in leadership of elite groups in the post-transition environment (Whitehead 1989: 79). This uncertainty over the type of government (sincere versus dissembling) can limit how much losing elites or the general public will invest in democracy.

In mature democracies, a common strategy to signal sincerity of reform is the creation of new institutions. Unfortunately, the option is not wholly credible in this particular political environment. Theories of "endogenous institutions" hold that domestic institutional arrangements can arise because of the preferences of important political and economic actors (North and Weingast 1989; Root 1994). Institutions (such as constitutions) bind these actors to certain courses of action since their initiation and consequences reflect the *ex ante* preferences of the actors themselves. This binding occurs to confront the problem of credible commitment – namely a fear that *ex post* opportunism will lead to a collapse of an agreement. Formalized arrangements in the form of institutions can create a self-enforcing equilibrium. This option, however, faces two major obstacles in new democracies.

First, as previously discussed, the vast uncertainty of the transitional period can obscure information about the preferences of other actors (Przeworski 1991: 87). Although this information is not a strict requirement for demand-driven institutions to arise, North and Weingast (1989: 806) note that institutions must match "anticipated incentive problems" to be self-enforcing. Without knowledge of the basic preferences of actors, this task could prove to be troublesome. In some cases, it may not even be clear who the relevant actors are (Whitehead 1989). For example, will labor emerge as a powerful interest group to oppose reform or will it be marginalized? Institutions that do not account for such groups are unlikely to be stable. Given this uncertainty, it is difficult to imagine the natural emergence of institutions to instantiate credible commitments.

Second, any commitment to these new institutions will be suspect because of reputation issues. Again, elites in the new regime have a reputation for using extra-legal means to achieve their goals. This is especially devastating since reputation can be as important as institutions themselves in securing a credible commitment (North and Weingast 1989). Unlike states where institutions have survived for years and are only dissolved by lengthy political and legal processes, transitional states have recently gutted existing institutions. In sum, even though institutions may arise because of the demand for credibility or to enhance efficiency, the perception of *commitment* to these institutions is lacking in the post-transitional environment.

This inability to create credible commitments can spell disaster for the consolidation of democracy. From both an elite and mass perspective, a perception of weak commitment on behalf of the winners in a new democracy can lead these groups to withhold their support from the new regime, potentially undermining democracy. Elites often have a deep mutual distrust for one another in the transitional period (Burton, Gunther, and Higley 1992). This absence of trust flows directly from the lack of reputation for keeping agreements and is compounded by the uncertainty of the transitional environment. Those who "lose" in the transition agree to abide by democratic rules since, once elected, they can attempt to change policies they dislike (Przeworski 1991). If these elites do not believe political reform efforts are sincere, they will not lend support to the new regime, since they will heavily discount their future probability of gaining power. They may also turn against the regime, utilizing violent measures, especially if alternatives to the democratic regime exist.[20]

This lack of support on the part of elites can itself undermine democratic consolidation (Mainwaring 1992). It can also lead to reactions on the part of the regime further undermining the new democracy: "if each political sector concludes that the democratic commitment of the other is lukewarm, this will reduce the motivation of all, and so perpetuate the condition of fragility" (Whitehead 1989: 94). Stephan Haggard and Robert Kaufman (1995b: 8) allude to this dynamic when they argue that "the fact that so many leaders in new democracies have acted autocratically in crisis situations implies that such behavior cannot be explained simply in terms of personal ambition or lack of concern for democratic institutions." As Gunther, Puhle, and Diamandouros (1995: 9) note, this lack of respect for the governing elite's authority, "could be compatible with an abridgement of democracy that might ultimately culminate in its transformation into a limited democracy or authoritarian regime." The key issue is that the bias in institutions does not result from the preferences or greed of the new regime per se, but is a consequence of the lack of a credible commitment to democracy. In a sense, the non-credible commitment becomes a self-fulfilling prophecy.

One outcome of this process is the self-coup (*autogolpe*), where democratic leaders suspend democracy to "protect" it (Cameron 1998a). An

---

[20] As previously discussed, alternatives to the current regime are often a prerequisite for any group to attempt an overthrow of the system.

important example was the suspension of democracy by Peruvian president Alberto Fujimori in 1992. Faced with an armed opposition group as well as a judicial and legislative branch he felt could not trust, Fujimori suspended the legislature and installed his own government. He justified the coup on the grounds that he needed more power to fight "legislative and judicial corruption" (Galvin 1992), and to improve democracy by making it more "direct, authentic, and, above all, efficient" (Cameron 1998a: 125). A major reason the legislature had become so opposed to Fujimori was its worry over his potentially dictatorial style: dubbed the "Little Emperor" by many Peruvian observers, he often accused "special interests" of making too many demands on the state (Hayes 1992). The distrust among Peruvian elites was a major reason for Fujimori's action (Gunther, Puhle, and Diamandouros 1995: 9).[21]

For democracy to endure, the masses must also be convinced that there is a commitment to democracy. Citizens must vote and become politically active for democracy to take root, especially early in the reform process. Because political activity is not costless, the masses must be convinced that their efforts are not in vain, i.e. that democracy will continue and the process will remain open to them. If citizens do not perceive this commitment on the part of elites, they will themselves remain uncommitted to the process. This is similar to the previous dynamic concerning elites:

> Although commitment to democracy is especially critical for the political elite, common people and especially leaders of popular groups may also care more about preserving democracy than some of the literature suggests. Caring about this issue, of course, may not always lead to an effective ability to contribute to democratic consolidation. But a society in which there is limited support for democracy does not bode very well for this form of government. (Mainwaring 1992: 310)

Shin (1994: 154) also notes that this can spell disaster for the new regime since "it appears that democracy can still be created without the demand of the masses, yet cannot be consolidated without their commitment." In some cases, this lack of commitment on the part of the masses can combine with elite dissatisfaction to threaten the regime (Mainwaring 1992: 307).

Citizens need to see clear commitments that the reform process will continue. This will help to establish the legitimacy of the reform effort for the masses and encourage their participation in the system. Similarly, elites need to be reassured that liberalization is credible so they will support (or at least acquiesce to) the system. Winners would benefit from either a way to guarantee their own commitment to reform or a credible

---

[21] This case is discussed more fully in Chapter 5, in the context of redemocratization.

signal that they were serious about reform. Either or both of these strategies would increase the commitment of the regime to reform, lowering the probability that either the masses or the elite will turn against the regime. Again, the irony is that a failure of consolidation is consistent with elite preferences to consolidate their own power or to advance reform. If one cannot make credible commitments, the outcome is the same.

How might regional organizations assist new democracies in furthering negative consolidation? The next section outlines how this process can occur.

Regional organizations and democratic consolidation

I argue that regional organizations can facilitate deterring anti-regime behavior by losers as well as credible commitments in order to enhance the longevity of new democracies. Regional IOs can assist young democratic regimes in the consolidation process in several ways. First, IOs serve as an external commitment device through which winners can bind themselves to political liberalization. Membership in regional organizations can be made conditional upon democratic institutions, which can instantiate a credible commitment on the part of the regime. This conditionality is credible since regimes would incur significant political and economic costs by joining regional IOs then violating the conditions of their membership, making reversals of democracy costly to winners. Second, these new memberships also provide a public and highly visible external validation of the new regime that increases the probability that the masses will commit to the new democracy. This external validation can legitimize the new regime in the eyes of citizens, making their support for anti-system actors less likely.

Third, IOs bind distributional losers through the same commitment mechanism since a reversal of democracy at the hands of *any* domestic actor will incur punishment from the organization. Losers must calculate whether the costs imposed by reneging on IO membership will undermine attempts to consolidate their power after a coup. If these costs, which can include a loss of trade, economic aid, military assistance, international status, or military protection, are significant, losers are more likely to remain loyal to existing democratic rules and institutions. Finally, IOs can provide positive incentives to "bribe" losers into complying with democratic institutions. Bribes can occur through a direct transfer of resources (economic assistance) or an expansion of the range of resources that can be utilized as side-payments to opponents. The remainder of this section reviews each of these arguments and provides illustrative examples drawn from several cases.

Regional IOs and consolidation: binding winners by creating credible commitments

IOs provide a commitment to existing reform efforts by creating mechanisms to increase the cost of anti-regime behavior while simultaneously publicly signaling a commitment to reform. Both mechanisms arise from conditions imposed by the organization for new members or for material assistance. These conditions raise the costs of limiting reform since any reversal of reform will bring an end to the benefits of the IO as well as audience costs.

Membership and/or assistance from some IOs are conditional upon domestic liberalization. The European Union (EU) requires all members to be liberal, free-market democracies as does the Council of Europe (Klebes 1999; Schmitter 1996). These requirements are highly publicized and rigorously enforced. For example, Greece left the Council of Europe after the 1967 military coup.[22] Turkey has been continually frustrated by the EU's refusal of admission, which stems from that state's questionable record of democracy (Whitehead 1993: 159–61). This phenomenon is not limited to Western Europe: the Southern Cone Common Market (MERCOSUR) also contains a clause in its founding treaty (the Treaty of Asunción) which requires all members to have a democratic polity (Schiff and Winters 1998). The OAS, in 1991, created the Santiago Commitment to Democracy, which calls for an immediate meeting of OAS members if any state suffers a reversal of democracy (Acevedo and Grossman 1996: 137).

Conditionality is not a black-and-white issue. Some IOs are vague as to their conditions of membership. Although the NATO preamble contains references to democracy as a underlying principle, one of its founding members was a European dictatorship (Portugal) and military coups in member states never resulted in major changes within NATO, nor pressure to end authoritarian rule (Greece and Turkey). The North American Free Trade Act (NAFTA) is another example of imprecise conditionality – the implicit US criteria for NAFTA expansion seem to include democracy, although there are no formal written conditions (Whitehead 1993).

The presence of membership criteria implies (often explicitly) a system of negative sanctions if the conditions are violated. If a regime were to undergo a democratic breakdown, the benefits of membership

---

[22] The fact that Greece left rather than being expelled was a technicality. The resolution to expel Greece was on the table when the military colonels defiantly declared they no longer wished to be a part of the organization.

could be suspended, including the state's membership in the organization. Any financial assistance from the organization, preferential trade arrangements, monetary policy coordination, military protection, even international status brought by membership would all be put at risk by a democratic reversal. These potential costs serve as a deterrent to winners who would undermine liberal reform. At best, violating conditions of membership or agreement will lead to a suspension of benefits. At worst, a violation can bring expulsion from the organization. Given these costs, there is a strong incentive for domestic actors to work within the rules of the system rather than work against them (Hyde-Price 1994: 246).[23]

This conditionality imposed by the regional organization is not the only source of credibility for reform for winners who utilize these institutions. An IO can require costly measures that assist in making accession a credible signal, by demonstrating that the action is anything but "cheap talk." Fulfilling the initial condition of membership can require policy changes and non-trivial financial outlays. In addition, membership in many regional institutions requires either the creation of additional bureaucracy, membership dues (to fulfill the IO's budget obligations), economic or monetary reform.[24] For example, upon joining the EU, Spain was forced to implement a value added tax (VAT), which required a large restructuring of the domestic tax system (Pridham 1995: 181). Such costs can be a clear signal of the state's commitment to the organization and its conditions.

Even if the conditionality policy of the IO is unclear (e.g. NATO) or there is a possibility of non-enforcement by the organization itself (discussed in Chapter 3), the process of joining regional organizations can assist in legitimizing the democratic reform process to common citizens. Accession itself can be a form of "international recognition of a country's democratic credentials" (Klebes 1999: 3). The domestic political audience is likely to be attuned to these issues since association with a highly democratic IO is an early chance to break with the vestiges of an authoritarian past (Pridham 1994: 26–7). As Pridham (1995: 177) discusses, there is a symbolic element to regime transitions and joining an international institution: "There is an evident link . . . between recasting the national self-image and opening the way for consolidating democracy." He goes on to argue that acceptance into these organizations plays an important role in legitimizing reform amongst the public: "Undoubtedly, the citizens of [Southern Europe] felt gratification over being treated

---

[23] I discuss how these costs can deter distributional losers in the next section.
[24] This is not to suggest that states do not gain benefits from the creation of additional bureaucracy which can serve as an additional source of patronage.

as equals by international partners . . . We may say that external policy practice has *confirmed the credibility of the democratic decision-making structures*" (Pridham 1995: 191; emphasis added).

Again using the example of Spain, both EC and NATO membership supplied external validation that its isolation during the Franco regime was over and Spain would be accepted into the international community of nations (Story and Pollack 1991: 134; White 1986). In the words of the *Financial Times* (White 1986: S1), "The impact of entry for Spain is mainly psychological, but is by no means a negligible one. Achieving membership was the political equivalent of a doctor's certificate – a sign of acceptance of recognition of Spain as a 'normal' country." This psychological benefit was important to both elites and the masses (Pridham 1995: 174).

Reneging on international agreements can thus bring heavy reputational and domestic audience costs on the regime. Making international agreements places a state's relatively new reputation on the line. This domestic loss of face can have electoral ramifications for those in power in a democracy (Fearon 1994; Richards et al. 1993).[25] These audience costs are potentially high and flow from the fact that these young democracies are attempting to establish a reputation as upstanding members of the international community and regional organizations. Losing this membership thus risks a backlash from both elite and mass publics who would no doubt blame regime leaders for ruining their chances at international acceptance.

Regional organizations can serve as a device for winners to signal a commitment to democratic reform through the imposition of financial and reputational costs if conditions of the IO are violated. By making international commitments tying their own hands, winners send a costly signal to both domestic elites and common citizens. This can move the consolidation process forward as these groups will be more likely to invest in the new system. Just as important, however, these IO memberships also raise the costs to losers who would attempt to reverse liberalization *ex post*.

Regional IOs and consolidation: binding and bribing losers

Those who lose or perceive they might lose under the new system face a temptation to overthrow or undermine the regime. IO membership

---

[25] Note that there may or may not be a loss of *international* reputation. What is important is that domestic agents perceive or fear that a young democracy's credibility will be tarnished. This will have potential electoral consequences for a government that blemishes the reputation of the state.

provides both negative and positive incentives for these groups to support the new democratic system. The negative incentives flow from the same costs imposed on winners who would move against their own democratic system. The conditions imposed by IOs increase the costs to *any* elite who would move to overthrow the regime. Any military junta or economic elite allied with the military would think twice before embarking on a policy that would cost its economy valuable links, including trade and economic assistance from multilateral organizations. These potential costs may serve as a deterrent against coups, even for elites that do not necessarily buy into the concept of democracy. According to Miles Kahler (1997: 308), "Even elites that are not imbued with democratic norms may choose to follow democratic rules of the game in order to win the economic benefits of membership."[26] Because the conditions are monitored and enforced by third parties, this threat of punishment gains credibility and becomes "an external anchor against retrogression to authoritarianism" (Huntington 1991: 87–8).

One example of this scenario was played out in April 1996 in Paraguay. While attempting to replace a powerful military general early that year, Paraguayan president Juan Carlos Wasmosy found himself the target of a potential coup.[27] The general, Lino Oviedo, not only refused to resign as requested by Wasmosy, but called for Wasmosy to step down and threatened to foment massive unrest in Paraguay. Immediately a host of international actors condemned the act, led by MERCOSUR ministers from the neighboring states of Uruguay, Brazil, and Argentina. The crisis ended with Oviedo stepping down in disgrace after mass demonstrations in support of democracy. Many observers have noted the importance of MERCOSUR in enforcing its democracy condition: "But for Mercosur, Paraguay would this year almost certainly have gone back to military rule, setting a dangerous precedent for Latin America."[28] The threat of economic isolation and the costs imposed by this expulsion helped turn the tide in favor of democracy.

Regional IOs can also provide positive incentives to support young democratic institutions and governments. They can provide direct material resources to groups or help create credible side-payments in the form of new policies that would otherwise be difficult to guarantee. Why would

[26] Note this is the exact scenario of credible commitments previously discussed. *Ex ante* there is no way to determine how long elites will follow the "democratic norms." Regional IOs provide an anchor against abandoning those norms for personal gain.

[27] The factual details of this example are drawn from Valenzuela 1997. This case is discussed in more detail in Chapter 7.

[28] "Survey: MERCOSUR," *The Economist*, October 12, 1996, S6. See also Dominguez 1998; Feinberg 1996.

a regime turn to external means of bribing a group over internal measures? Internal policy could achieve similar ends at a potentially lower cost. In fact, new democracies frequently do employ these domestic side-payments after a democratic transition (e.g. power-sharing agreements). There are two potential problems with such payments, however. First, a regime may not possess the requisite resources to effectively bribe the groups in question. Regimes emerging from transitions are usually not flush with excess resources to distribute to whomever they chose (Haggard and Kaufman 1995a). Second, because of the new democracies' diminished capacity to make credible commitments, it is difficult for those in power to commit to any particular policy as a side-payment. Newly established governments often lack the "institutional structure which supports policy continuity" (Karp and Paul 1998: 335), which implies that any promise of a specific policy is vulnerable to change *ex post*. Essentially, the same commitment problems that plague a new regime's liberal political reforms can hinder its ability to make credible promises for internal side-payments.

Some organizations such as the European Union and NATO provide direct resource allocations to states. These resources can be used to mollify groups threatening the regime. One example is the EC/EU's policy towards Greece after its accession in 1981. The rural sector of Greek society was traditionally susceptible to the call of authoritarian movements (Tsingos 1996). To complete the consolidation of democracy, the government needed to garner the support of this segment of society. EC development assistance was used to improve the quality of life for the agricultural sector and "facilitate the full and managed incorporation of the countryside's rural population into the new democratic regime" (Tsingos 1996).[29]

Regional institutions can also help provide a commitment to certain policies that benefit disaffected groups.[30] For example, regional trade associations or regional economic associations provide a guarantee that trade and economic liberalization will proceed despite domestic pressures for reversal (Mansfield 1998; Milner 1998). Thus, if trade liberalization is enacted to "pay off" export-oriented groups, IO membership assures these groups that reform is much less likely to be reversed. Without the IO and its attendant credible commitment, the regime would be unable to guarantee this side-payment. This is a form of increasing the policy latitude of a regime by increasing policy options. In other words, IOs can

[29] The case is discussed in more detail in Chapter 7.
[30] This argument mirrors the acquiescence argument, but applies to situations where groups threaten the consolidation of, rather than the transition to, democracy.

increase the range of policy resources to a regime which can be used to placate opposition groups. In many ways, this mechanism mirrors the acquiescence effect found in the transition period, but can function long after the transition period has come to an end. A major issue area where IO membership can assist with consolidation in this manner centers on civil–military relations.

As previously discussed, the military can be a large hurdle to democratic consolidation. As in the Argentina example, attempts to establish civilian supremacy over the military can be fraught with danger.[31] IOs, in the form of military alliances, can provide assistance in this area. Not only did Spain's membership in NATO help that country *complete* their transition to democracy, but it assisted in the consolidation process as well. One impetus to NATO membership was to socialize Spanish military officers to accept civilian control by integrating them with military officers from democratic states. In addition, joining NATO was seen as a way to divert the military's attention away from internal Spanish politics (Pridham 1995: 199), while providing the military with access to more resources than had previously been available: "Not only did NATO membership contribute in redirecting Spain's military mission away from previous domestic concerns, it also accelerated military modernization, including participation in supranational technological development projects" (Aguero 1995: 162).

Although many observers have noted that there is no NATO equivalent in South America to serve a similar function (Linz and Stepan 1996: 219–20), current efforts under the auspices of MERCOSUR, including joint training exercises between Brazil and Argentina, may pay similar dividends.[32] Without the regional organization, subjugating the military to civilian control by refocusing the military's attention away from domestic politics would have been more difficult, especially in Southern Europe. This process can be valuable in both the transition and the consolidation process.

This section has attempted to construct a theory of how domestic actors might use international organizations to enhance the prospects for long-term democracy by constraining the behavior of potential domestic opponents. A commitment to IO membership raises the cost of reneging on political liberalization by any domestic actor, providing a deterrent to the

---

[31] Many comparativists have labeled the problem of de facto military power one of "reserve domain." That is, the military still possesses an unquestioned position of privilege over some issues within the state. For a complete discussion of reserve domains and their relation to the military see Linz and Stepan 1996: 67–9.

[32] "Survey: MERCOSUR," *The Economist*, October 12, 1996, S1–S33. See also Grabendorff 1993: 342.

Table 2.2 *Consolidation mechanisms*

Binding: deters losers
  – Conditions on membership
Binding: deters winners
  – Conditions on membership
Psychological legitimization and audience costs
Bribery of societal groups

reversal of this reform. This may arise because of conditions on membership in the regional IO or because of the psychological legitimization processes that arises from accession to a regional organization. Finally, membership may serve as a bribe towards opposition groups who are apprehensive about potential losses under the new government. In effect, regional IOs can "underwrite" democratic consolidation.[33]

In the end, of course, the "carrots" and "sticks" provided by regional organizations are no guarantee of democracy's survival. If regime opponents are determined and supported by large segments of society, there may be little any external (or internal) actor can do to dissuade them from moving against the regime. Still, if regional organizations can increase the costs of this behavior for both winners and losers, it increases the likelihood of regime survival. This type of dynamic was discussed by Carlos Westendorp, the secretary-general of EC affairs in Spain:

You can never prevent an adventurer from trying to overthrow the government if he is backed by the real economic powers, the banks and the businesses. But once in the [European] Community, you create a network of interests for those banks and businesses, the insurance companies, and the rest; as a result, those powers would refuse to back the adventurer for fear of losing all those links. (Quoted in Pridham 1991c: 235)

However, not all regional IOs are likely to serve these purposes adequately. To this point, I have only examined the demand for regional organizations in the post-transitional context. Will all IOs pressure nondemocratic member states to democratize? Do all international organizations provide the resources and commitment to help consolidate democracy? Clearly, the answer to these questions is no. Regional institutions may lack both the resources and the political will to serve as an external promoter or supporter of democracy. After all, organizations such as the Council for Mutual Economic Assistence (CMEA) or the Warsaw Pact will not be willing to condone democratic transitions or encourage

---

[33] I borrow this term from Tsingos 1996.

democratic longevity. With this in mind, the next chapter turns to the "supply-side" (enforcement) part of the argument.

The next chapter deals with a related concern: that regional organizations are merely a fig leaf for the interests of their large members. This realist-oriented argument is a strong counter to the theory presented here. If regional organizations are simply serving as tools for the major powers to promote democracy, there is little room left for influence by the organization itself. If the story is one of major power politics, democracy promotion and protection does not thrive through a community effort, but by the dictates of a great power. In the next chapter, I discuss why this argument does not hold in this case – the regional institutions themselves are essential for the causal mechanisms to function.

3   The supply-side of democratization, realist theories, and initial tests

Chapter 2 discussed how regional organizations encourage and protect democracy. This chapter continues the argument in three ways. First, I discuss the supply-side part of the argument: why we should expect only certain regional organizations to assist in the transition to and the consolidation of democracy. I then turn to *which* regional organizations are more likely to fulfill this role. Second, I examine the alternative hypothesis that great power preferences could be behind the relationship between regional institutions and democracy. Finally, I formally operationalize the two key concepts discussed so far: regional organizations and democracy. While doing so, I present descriptive statistics as well as some initial statistical tests of my hypotheses.

The supply-side of democratization

Chapter 2 discussed the variety of causal mechanisms linking regional organizations to democratization, and while the testing of the particular causal mechanisms will be left to case studies, it would be helpful to understand whether these processes occur in the aggregate. That is, across a variety of regions and time periods, does membership in regional organizations promote democratization and/or consolidation? While one could undertake a simple test of whether membership in a regional organization is associated with the transition to or the consolidation of democracy, since almost every state in the world is a member of multiple organizations, this proves to be difficult (Pevehouse, Nordstrom, and Warnke 2004). Moreover, intuition tells us that only some organizations are likely to perform any or all of the functions discussed in the previous chapter.

My argument is that those organizations with a higher democratic "density" are more likely to be associated with both transitions and consolidation. By democratic "density" I refer to the percentage of permanent members in the organization that are democratic.[1] There are a

---

[1] Note that this measure does not refer to the level of democracy within the organizational structure or procedures. From this point forward, any reference to "democratic" IOs

variety of theoretical reasons to expect more homogenously democratic regional organizations to be more likely to "supply" the causal mechanisms linking regional IOs with democracy.

First, homogenously democratic regional organizations are more likely to place conditions on membership, since such a requirement requires a high degree of shared interests.[2] This is not to say that IOs composed of only democracies are completely harmonious, but compared to a mixed-regime IO, however, the range of shared interests will be larger. For example, recent research by Erik Gartzke has shown that democracies tend to have similar underlying preference structures (Gartzke 1998, 2000; see also Weart 1998). One of these shared interests is likely to be democracy promotion. Although common interests are no guarantee that a regional organization will promote democracy, this should bode well for the setting and enforcement of political conditionality (assisting in consolidation). In addition, it should increase the probability that an organization will exert pressure on an authoritarian regime (assisting in transitions).

Second, the more democratic an IO, the higher the probability that conditions will be enforced. Enforcement of these conditions is a key part of the ability of regional organizations to promote democracy (Bloomfield 1994; Halperin and Lomasney 1998). These organizations may choose not to enforce conditions by turning a blind eye toward autocracies (in cases of transition) or democratic breakdown (in cases of consolidation). If the members of the organization deem the costs too high or if other "strategic considerations" mitigate the likelihood of enforcement, IOs may do little to promote or protect democracy (Whitehead 1986: 13).

One incentive of democracies to overcome this collective action problem in enforcement was discussed in the previous chapter (rational expectations about trade, peace, or cooperation with other democracies). Another factor increasing the likelihood of enforcement is that democracies are more transparent (Schultz 1998; 1999; Smith 1998). This transparency means that democratic states are less likely to openly shirk on enforcing conditions of an IO. If a state is deciding on whether to help enforce a conditionality clause (e.g. suspending free trade or imposing trade sanctions), it is easier to witness the behavior of fellow democratic members than autocratic members, *ceteris paribus*. If one member state attempts to circumvent the external pressure applied by the organization

---

should be understood as the aggregate level of democracy among the members rather than a trait of the organizational structure.

[2] Not all of the causal mechanisms linking IOs to transitions or consolidation are based on conditions imposed by the organizations. This eliminates the possibility of coding only the level of conditions in a given organization. In addition, this would still not confront the issue of enforcement of the conditions.

by working with the offending state, other members may be less likely to push for punishment. Since cheating is easier to detect in more homogenously democratic organizations, members will have fewer fears of cheating, increasing the odds of enforcement.

Closely related to this argument is the contention that democracies are more likely to fulfill their international commitments. This is important not only for the enforcement of democratic conditionality, but for the operation of the reassurance and legitimation mechanisms as well. Elites contemplating liberalization will be especially reassured by regional IOs composed of democracies, because of this ability to instantiate more credible commitments. Scholars have pointed to two mechanisms that enhance the credibility of democratic commitments. First, some scholars have argued that since democratic leaders face potential audience costs for not following through on their international obligations or for reneging on these commitments, this increases the likelihood of fulfilling these promises (Fearon 1994; Leeds 1999). Brett Leeds (1999) provides empirical support for this proposition, showing that democracies are more likely to complete cooperative initiatives with one another. Thus, audience costs can make commitments by democracies inherently more credible.

Another factor making democracies' commitments inherently more credible is the nature of executive constraints. A variety of scholars have argued and shown empirically that either because of separation of powers, divided government, or other institutional factors, democracies can more credibly commit to international agreements (Cowhey 1993; Gaubatz 1996; Martin 2000). For elite groups within states facing liberalization pressures, assurances offered by IOs composed mainly of democracies will be preferred over assurances by "mixed" organizations, since there will be an *ex ante* perception that democracies are more likely to uphold their commitments.[3]

In fact, highly democratic regional IOs do inflict punishment on those who break conditions of agreements. For example, the EEC suspended the Greek association agreement in 1967 after the colonels came to power (Whitehead 1993: 154). Turkey has been continually frustrated by the EU's refusal of admission, which stems from that state's questionable record of democracy (Whitehead 1993: 159–61). In addition, the Council of Europe suspended Turkey's involvement in that organization after the September 1980 coup (Karaosmanoglu 1991: 162). The OAS threatened Guatemala with punishment after a coup by its president (Cameron 1998a).

---

[3] For a specific empirical application, work on regional trade agreements has found that democracies are more likely to join these arrangements with one another for reasons of commitment (Mansfield, Milner, and Rosendorff 2002).

The ability to uphold commitments is important on a variety of levels. It provides reassurances to other member states concerning the enforcement of political conditionality. It provides reassurances to nervous elites that their rights will be respected during and after the transition. It also provides important signals to mass publics that the transitional regime (or first elected regime) is truly committed to democratic reform, increasing the probability of the completion of the transition as well as democratic consolidation.

In addition, if one of the key mechanisms by which IOs consolidate democracy is through credible commitments and signaling to domestic audiences that a state is serious about democracy, highly democratic organizations should provide the clearest signal. Joining a regional institution made up of semi-democracies and autocracies does little to assure citizens that there is little risk of reversal in the future. Joining a homogenously democratic organization is the easiest way to make a clear break with the authoritarian past (Pridham 1994: 26–7).

Finally, if the socialization influence of the regional IO is the causal process linking these institutions with democratization, these processes will be more common the more democracies exist in the organization. That is, the more interactions with democratic actors occur, the more likely the transmission of values and norms about the democratic process.

Regional versus non-regional organizations

In both the large-N analysis and the case studies, I limit the investigation to regional organizations. By considering only regional IOs, I exclude non-regional (or universal) organizations from this study. I define regional organizations similarly to Nye (1987), as organizations made up of geographically proximate states. For the purposes of this book, regions are limited by physical boundaries. While I have chosen to define regions from a strictly geographic perspective, Katzenstein and Hemmer (2002) remind us that conceptions of regions need not be fixed in time (see also Russett 1967: 168). They argue that regions are social and cognitive constructions that vary according to the perspective of state actors. While this is no doubt true, I adopt Nye's (1987: 8) position that "it seems clearer to apply the term 'regional' to selective organizations which restrict membership on the basis of geographical principle."[4]

---

[4] A handful of the organizations included in this study have members that are "extra-regional." Most of these exceptions are cases where the US or Canada is a member of an otherwise "European" institution (e.g. NATO). Nye (1987: 8) defines these organizations as "quasi-regional."

I focus my empirical investigation on regional IOs for several reasons. First, regional organizations are the most common type of IOs in the world system (Jacobson, Reisinger, and Mathers 1986: 143; Shanks, Jacobson, and Kaplan 1996). Examining the most ubiquitous type of organization has obvious advantages in terms of inferences drawn from statistical findings. Second, recall from Chapters 1 and 2 that regional political, military, and economic organizations such as the EEC/EU, the Conference on Security and Cooperation in Europe (CSCE), MERCOSUR, and the OAS have been the most heavily discussed organizations in the context of democracy assistance (see Pridham 1991a; Whitehead 1996a).[5] The small literature that exists on this topic focuses on regional organizations since, according to Whitehead (1996b: 395), "the importance of such international dimensions of democratization seems much clearer at this regional level than at the world-wide level of analysis."

Third, from a theoretical perspective, one expects the causal processes to function more readily in regional organizations. Because regional IOs tend to operate with small numbers and with higher levels of interaction than global organizations, causal processes such as socialization, binding, monitoring, and enforcement are more likely in regional organizations (McCormick 1980: 79; Nye 1987). In addition, regional IOs are more likely to possess the economic and political leverage to pressure member states to democratize as the vast majority of economic and military agreements are made under the auspices of (or create) regional organizations. These economic and military benefits are key to the functioning of the causal mechanisms. For these reasons, as the first systematic cut at this question, I exclude non-regional organizations from the discussion and analyses.

A second group of international organizations excluded from this analysis are international and regional financial institutions (IFIs). Although there is tremendous speculation and debate over the impact of these organizations (such as the IMF and regional development banks) on democratization, little systematic research exists on this topic (for exceptions, see Haggard and Kaufman 1992; Kahler 1992; Santiso 2000). My justification for the exclusion of these institutions is twofold. First, IFIs are likely to influence democratization through fundamentally different causal processes. For example, although the *assistance* from IFIs is often conditioned, *membership* is rarely conditional on anything other than

---

[5] The one exception to this is the United Nations. A handful of authors have examined UN efforts to promote democratization – see Russett (1998); Russett and Oneal (2001) and White (2000) for discussions. The vast majority of academic and policy discussion, however, centers on regional organizations such as the Council of Europe, the OAS, and NATO.

paying the costs associated with membership.[6] It is this aid conditionality that is discussed in the context of political liberalization, yet the conditions are almost always economic in nature. While these economic conditions may have clear political implications, transitions to democracy (as measured here) would be a second-order effect. An empirical test of this IFI-democratization proposition would be different than the one undertaken here and should reflect the multi-stage processes linking economic and political liberalization.

Another difficult issue in testing the IFI-democratization proposition is that IFI activity could merely be an intervening variable for economic crises. That is, IFI activity may correlate with democratization because such activity is often spurred by economic crises – which can have an independent effect on the prospects for democracy. One would need to disentangle the influence of economic crises from that of IFI policies. Again, this would entail a different empirical test than the one undertaken here.

These practical and theoretical issues concerning non-regional IOs and IFIs aside, I do rerun the statistical analyses including membership in several non-regional organizations (e.g. the United Nations) *and* IFIs (e.g. the World Bank, the IMF, and regional development banks). Their inclusion should weaken the results, since these organizations influence consolidation in different ways. By adding IOs that may or may not influence the process of consolidation to the data, the observed relationship should attenuate. As I discuss in both Chapters 4 and 6, the inclusion of these organizations does alter the statistical estimates. For the transition models (Chapter 4), the estimated relationships are weaker, yet still within conventional bounds of accepted statistical significance. Yet for the consolidation models (Chapter 6), their inclusion occasionally undermines the statistical relationship between IOs and the endurance of democracy. In each chapter, I discuss these alternative models, and the estimates themselves may be found in the appendices.

Foundation or fig leaf? A realist account of regional
institutions and democracy

One counter-hypothesis to my argument is that regional institutions have no bearing on the prospects for democracy. This hypothesis accepts that external factors are important, but places the emphasis of this influence

---

[6] Regional organizations condition membership – rarely do regional IOs condition a specific benefit while allowing full membership. Rather, regional IOs tend to create various levels of membership – observer status, associate membership and full membership – each of which carries different obligations and benefits. I include associate memberships in these analyses.

not in regional institutions but democratic great powers. This is a very important argument, arising largely out of a realist understanding of world politics. The important variable in predicting outcomes, according to this position, is the preferences of the powerful states in world politics, not the status of regional institutions.

Realists largely believe that international institutions play minor roles in world politics. While they may influence outcomes at the margins or on issues of minor importance, most realists see states as the driving force behind international outcomes. This position is eloquently summarized by John Mearsheimer (1995): "What is most impressive about institutions, in fact, is how little independent effect they seem to have had on state behavior." Such a position has a long history in international relations, certainly predating the end of the Cold War (Carr 1946; Morgenthau 1967).

A more nuanced version of this realist-inspired critique is found in the institutionalist literature. George Downs, David Rocke, and Peter Barsoom (1996) argue that institutions are typically associated with "shallow cooperation." Rather than foreclosing *any* role for international institutions, these authors suggest that while states will work through institutions to accomplish goals, they will only do so in cases where cooperation is in the state's interest in the first place. Thus, the fact that many institutionalists have noted that compliance with international agreements is the rule rather than the exception, does not necessarily bode well for cooperation. State strategies vis-à-vis institutions are endogenous – states will only sign agreements or join organizations where they foresee that compliance will be in their interest. Downs, Rocke, and Barsoom (1996: 383) argue that institutions may be associated with certain outcomes, but these outcomes would have occurred with or without the institution. To demonstrate the importance of institutions, one must show that outcomes would have differed without them.

These arguments have important implications for my theory and hypotheses. If democratic transitions and durability are driven by the powerful members of regional organizations, institutions themselves are of little value. The better focus would be on the policies of the democratic great powers and their influence on the politics of liberalization and the survival of democracy. The key question is what drives an association between regional organizations and democracy – the institutions or great power interests? The counterfactual question in this case is quite clear: would great power preferences and policies alone account for the outcome?

I answer this question with a resounding no – regional institutions play a vital role in the democratization process. Although there are some isolated examples of great power (usually American) preferences also playing an important role, the vast majority of the evidence points away from the great power explanation. There are several reasons to doubt the realist-based explanation.

Most importantly, this critique is not applicable to one of the major theoretical contributions of this study – that regional organizations are used by elites within nascent democracies to encourage transitions and democratic durability. Indeed, it is important to remember that the outcomes in question are democratic transitions and endurance. While I argue that international factors are extremely important in shaping these outcomes, recall from Chapter 2 that most of the causal mechanisms associating regional IOs with democracy rely on actors within the state. Indeed, the causal process relating regional institutions to democracy belies the unitary actor cast of the realist hypothesis. My argument is that in many instances, regional institutions work through domestic politics to shape outcomes. Most of the causal mechanisms discussed in Chapter 2 are not about regional IOs imposing democracy on states. Rather, domestic elites use these institutions to engender and cement democracy.

The key question in this case is not what are the preferences of existing IO members, but of societal elites in transitional states. As discussed in Chapter 2, in some cases (psychological reorientation and binding winners) key elite preferences are for democracy, but domestic elites lack a mechanism to make credible commitments to democracy. In these cases, although preferences do align closely with outcome, because of the uncertainty of the transition, the regional institutions are *essential* to the outcome. Domestic elites do not work through regional institutions because they are sure to comply, but to tie their hands since compliance itself is uncertain *even though compliance is consistent with their preferences*. Regional organizations provide a vehicle for credible commitments to compliance.

In other cases (acquiescence effect and binding losers), it is less clear if elite preferences favor democracy. In these cases, the institution is important to *changing* elite preferences (acquiescence) or at least placing restrictions on the actions to achieve those preferences (binding). Here, regional organizations play a clear role in shaping outcomes by assuring or deterring potential regime opponents whose preferences are not for the creation or continuation of democracy. For these reasons, the realist challenge simply does not apply to a key contribution of this study.

The place where great power preferences could be important in my argument is in the realm of the pressure mechanism or the realm of enforcement. It could be the case that external pressure on domestic elite groups, for example, may only arise if great power members of the organization have a desire to supply that pressure. Similarly, enforcement of membership conditions may be lax if the powerful democratic members of the organization do not feel such a strategy is in line with their interests. Indeed, here is where evidence of the realist claim surfaces. In response to Peru's domestic problems, the United States placed key pressures on the Fujimori government to restore democracy. The United States also pushed Haitian military leaders to step aside and return the island to democracy, even sending military forces to achieve this goal. When discussing the pressure mechanism and membership condition enforcement, is it more meaningful to focus on great power preferences rather than regional institutions?

Again, I answer no. The realist hypothesis has a clear, observable implication – that international organizations (IOs) with democratic great powers should be more successful in promoting democracy than IOs without these types of states. Moreover, the presence of a democratic great power should be stronger than the influence of other measures of regional organizations, such as the level of democratic homogeneity. As I show in Chapters 4 and 6, however, controlling for the presence of democratic major powers in highly democratic regional organizations is almost never a significant predictor of democratic transitions or democratic endurance.[7] In addition, I control for a host of domestic factors thought to be related to democratic transitions and endurance. This approach is similar to Simmons' (2000) strategy of controlling for the other plausible explanations that may be correlated with both my outcome (democracy) and my key independent variable (regional institutions). This strategy and the attendant statistical results are powerful evidence that the institutions themselves matter, rather than simply the presence of a democratic major power in the organization or other domestic political variables.

There is also strong case evidence to suggest that regional institutions matter apart from their democratic great power members. As I discuss in Chapter 5 in the case of Peru, although US condemnation of President Fujimori's *autogolpe* was important in assisting the Organization of American States (OAS) to pressure the Peruvian government, even US decision-makers knew that efforts to restore democracy would be more successful through a multilateral institution such as the OAS. In the case of Turkey's 1980 military coup, large democratic members of the European Union and Council of Europe changed their bilateral behavior towards Turkey to match their position coordinated through regional

---

[7] The variable tapping democratic great powers achieves statistical significance in only one out of ten tests.

organizations. In the final chapter of the book, I discuss the case of Venezuela, where in the spring of 2001, the OAS pressured coup perpetrators to restore the elected government, *despite* the fact that US officials regarded the coup as in America's interests. I show that in each of these cases, pressure from the multilateral organizations (versus great power members) was essential to the outcome. In none of these cases (nor, I contend, the cases of Paraguay, Hungary, or Guatemala) would the outcome have been the same had the regional organization not been the central actor.

Even if the promotion of democracy is in the interests of the democratic great powers, multilateral institutions can still be essential to achieve the outcome. As discussed in Chapter 2, unilateralism in democracy promotion often backfires since these efforts will be viewed as imperialism. This is especially true for the United States, given its history in Latin America. Even democratic great powers cannot go it alone in promoting democracy. Does this relegate the regional institution to a ceremonial position only? Although the realist might answer in the affirmative, the statistical and case material here suggests that is not the case. If smaller states felt they were simply serving as tools for the interests of the great powers, why would they be willing to serve this role? Parallel theories in international relations suggest that great power cooperation with regional institutions is not just a one-way street.

For example, G. John Ikenberry shows how great powers build international institutions to support postwar orders, yet although the parties are asymmetric in terms of power, small states still receive something in the bargain (2001: 258–9). Institutions, for Ikenberry, represent a credible commitment on the part of strong powers to restrain their arbitrary use of power. Small states do not suffer what they must at the whims of great powers. Given the need for legitimacy in post-war orders, small states can influence the policies of the large states. The same dynamic occurs in the context of democratization given the need of *all* parties (democratic great powers and smaller state members) to provide legitimacy to the process of supporting democracy. Indeed, the OAS's Declaration of the Defense of Democracy (the Santiago Declaration) provides an example of opposition to a great power.

In 1991, several Latin American states, as well as the United States, proposed to institute a formal legal procedure that would require economic and political sanctions against any member state which fell victim to a coup. This strong proposal, pushed by the US, was stopped by both Mexico and Brazil (Gonzalez 1991). Both states argued that such a legal commitment was a violation of state sovereignty and as a compromise proposed mandatory summit meetings in response to coups. This weaker version of the resolution passed the OAS Twenty-first General Assembly. Despite US preferences for a stronger defense of democracy regime, politics within the OAS worked against US wishes and denied the US its preferred policy. Interestingly, this opposition continued as the US spent the 1990s attempting to strengthen the Santiago Declaration (see DeYoung 2002; Downes 1994; LaFranchi 1999). Rather than go along with US efforts, Latin American states resisted American policies that they felt could lead to violations of sovereignty. Instead of demonstrating a lack of resolve to protect democracy, this example illustrates that OAS member states balanced (for over ten years) the demands of a great power with their own desires to protect democracy. Instead of rolling over for the US, smaller states fought for their own system of enforcement for the Santiago Declaration (LaFranchi 1999). Although this is only one case, it is an important illustration that regional organizations are more than vessels that are filled or emptied by great powers.

A final version of the "shallow cooperation" argument is discussed in Chapter 6. In this version of the argument, only states that are likely to be successful democracies are allowed to join democratic regional organizations, endogenizing the selection of member states. This strategy falls in line with the realist argument since institutions themselves do very little. In this scenario the nascent democracies allowed into the organizations would have succeeded anyway. As I discuss in Chapter 6, however, there are theoretical and empirical problems with this argument. Most notably, the idea that regional IOs admit only consolidated or near-consolidated democracies receives no statistical support.

The issue of the efficacy of regional institutions is important to my argument. Through both statistical and case analysis, however, I argue that these organizations have an *independent* influence on the outcomes in question – democratic transitions and survival. Rather than serving the whims of the democratic great power members, these organizations assist domestic elites in making credible commitments to democracy.

The dependent variables: democratic transitions and
democratic consolidation

Having established the scope of the study, I now discuss the data used in this work. To conduct these analyses, it is necessary to choose a definition of democracy and operationalize the concept. I adopt Mainwaring's (1992: 297–8) three-part definition of democracy: (1) competitive elections; (2) broad adult suffrage; and (3) protection of minority rights and respect for civil liberties.

I use Mainwaring's definition because it includes the procedural aspects of democracy (elections, universal suffrage), as well as the substantive (or outcome) aspects of democracy (civil liberties). While this definition does not emphasize economic rights or social justice, common substantive aspects of democracy, few scholars, however, argue that these latter issues are central to basic definitions of democracy (Mainwaring 1992; Shin 1994).[8]

Unfortunately, there is no single measurement of democracy which fully incorporates Mainwaring's three criteria, although there have been many attempts to operationalize democracy to facilitate its measurement (Alvarez et al. 1996; Dahl 1971; Gurr et al. 1990). Various authors have emphasized elections or "contestation" (Dahl 1971), institutions (Gurr 1990), as well as civil liberties (Gastil 1990). The one consensus reached is that none of these operationalizations is entirely adequate. The problem becomes more acute when one attempts to differentiate among democracies. Is it possible to classify one democracy as more "democratic" than another? Clearly, most scholars, policymakers, and even the casual observer would want to distinguish Great Britain from Russia or Argentina, where freely elected leaders who "bypass their parliaments and rule by presidential decree" are often labeled as "illiberal democracies" in the eyes of some observers (Zakaria 1997: 23).[9]

In an attempt to deal with these measurement issues, I use two different data sets employed in quantitative research on democracy and democratization. These data sets are familiar to many scholars and one of them (Polity) has become something of the "coin of the realm" in quantitative research on democracy. Thus, using these data sets has the benefit of making any findings from this statistical investigation comparable with past work on related topics such as the democratic peace (cf. Russett 1993; Russett, Oneal, and Davis 1998), democratization and war (Mansfield and Snyder 1995), democratic consolidation (Power and Gasiorowski 1997), and external influences on democratization (Reiter 2001a).

The first measure of democracy and democratization I utilize is from the Polity98 data set (Marshall 1999), an updated version of the Polity III data (Jaggers and Gurr 1995). The Polity data is widely used in cross-sectional research in international relations and comparative politics

---

[8] For more on the differences between substantive (or outcome) versus procedural definitions of democracy, see Shin 1994: 141–2.

[9] Of course this also leaves aside the historical context of democracy. For example, was the US a democracy before the Civil War or the enfranchisement of women? Standards of "democracy" may change over time. The data used in this work helps to confront the problem of spatial comparisons of democracy in their coding, it also attempts to address this intertemporal issue as well by varying the levels of regime type year-by-year.

(Farber and Gowa 1995; Mansfield and Snyder 1995; Oneal and Russett 1996). For most states in the international system, the Polity data codes "authority patterns" within each state (Gurr 1990). Eckstein and Gurr (1975: 41) define these authority patterns as the nature of relations among "superordinate and subordinate" political entities at the national level. Most of their measures of authority patterns tap the nature of political institutions within each state. Specifically, they define seven variables measuring authority patterns through political institutions: (1) regulation of chief executive recruitment, (2) competitiveness of executive recruitment, (3) openness of executive recruitment, (4) monocratism, (5) executive constraints, (6) regulation of political participation, and (7) competitiveness of political participation.

The first three measures tap patterns in executive recruitment. These variables show "the ways in which superordinates come to occupy their position" (Eckstein and Gurr 1975: 150). The ease in rising to a leadership position within the state is an important quality of democracy, while most observers would identify a routinized and open process for promotion to societal leadership positions (in legislatures, executive branches, or courts) as an important part of democracy. Thus, these three variables are included to capture authority patterns relating to who may become the executive as well as the regulation of the process of promotion.

The fourth and fifth variables measure the responsiveness of national leadership. These two indicators measure the extent to which leaders "must take into account the preferences of others when making decisions" (Gurr 1990: 13). Monocratism refers to whether executive decision-making in a state takes place within a collective group or by one individual. In addition, the variable measuring executive constraints gauges the official institutional restrictions on the executive's decision-making authority. The final two variables measure the extent of political competition. These two variables measure whether participation in political life is regulated as well as whether "alternative preferences for policy and leadership can be pursued in the political arena" (Gurr 1990: 18).

The seven variables are coded using an ordinal system. Each variable has a different number of categories, ranging from three to seven. Gurr (1990) provides an algorithm to aggregate the seven component variables to create yearly measures of autocracy and democracy for each country (Gurr 1990; Jaggers and Gurr 1995). The resulting autocracy and democracy measures range from 0 (least autocratic; least democratic) to 10 (most autocratic; most democratic).

Note that the Polity98 data captures two aspects of the Mainwaring definition quite well. First, Polity98's emphasis on the regulation of executive recruitment and the competitiveness of political participation measures the extent to which elections help govern the political process. Second, the variables measuring openness of executive recruitment as well as the regulation of participation tap the universal suffrage dimension of the definition. Those states with elections and universal suffrage will be scored as a democracy according to the Polity98 coding rules.

One common practice in research using this data is to take each state's yearly democracy level minus its autocracy level ($DEMOC_{it}$-$AUTOC_{it}$) to create a single measure of democracy. The resulting democracy score runs from -10 (complete autocracy) to $+10$ (complete democracy). Figure 3.1 shows this continuum of democracy scores, giving examples of countries and years coded at several levels of democracy. Using this single measure of democracy, scholars often set "cut-points" or threshold values for labeling regime type. Any regime at or above a certain positive number is labeled a democracy, while any regime at or below a certain negative number is labeled an autocracy. States in between these cut points are commonly labeled anocracies (cf. Jaggers and Gurr 1995). For the purposes of this study, I define the threshold values of -6 for autocracy and $+6$ for democracy.

Figure 3.2 shows the distribution of these three types of governmental systems over time. A visual inspection of this graph shows that the general trends towards and away from democracy are captured by this measure. First, it is interesting to note that at the beginning of the time period, the distribution of the three systems is relatively equal. Starting in the 1960s, with the decolonization of Africa, the number of autocracies begins to rise steadily as many postcolonial democracies give rise to single-party and sultanistic systems (Linz and Stepan 1996). Beginning in the late 1970s, however, the number of democracies begins a steady rise, while the number of anocracies begins to fall. This reflects the beginning of the "third wave" of democratization, as many Latin American and Southern European states begin the move away from military-led and bureaucratic-authoritarian systems to multiparty democracies (Huntington 1991; O'Donnell and Schmitter 1986). As the 1980s progress, democracy levels continue to rise, now at the "expense" of authoritarian systems, as African and Eastern European states move towards democracy. In 1989, the number of democracies in the world surpasses the number of authoritarian regimes. Note also that very late in the data set, the number of anocracies begins to rise as well. This is no doubt due to those states that did not complete their transition to democracy or have suffered slides away from democracy since their initial transition.

To create data pertaining to transitions (democratic or autocratic), one examines the variation in democracy scores over time. Any time a state

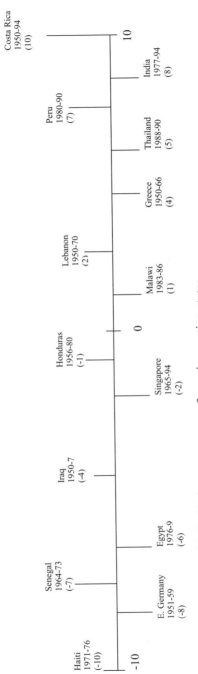

Figure 3.1 Examples of Polity98 democracy scores for various nation-states

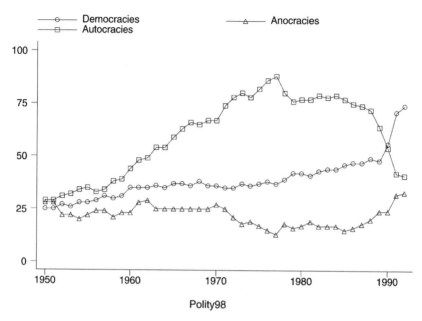

Figure 3.2 Polity 98 distribution of regime type over time

passes a threshold ($+6/-6$) in a given year, a regime change is coded. A set of six dummy variables can be created to describe any of the possible changes in regime type.[10] Thus, a set of transitions data can be generated using changes in the Polity scores over time.

A transition to democracy is coded when a state moves to or above the $+6$ threshold. If a state moves from autocracy to anocracy, it is *not* included as a transition. I combine these transitions with autocracy-to-democracy transitions and label them "liberalization." They are analyzed separately in Chapter 4. Thus, only movements from autocracy or anocracy to democracy (at or above the $+6$ threshold) are treated as "democratization."[11]

Since one hypothesis to be explored is what makes democracy last, it is also necessary to define a variable indicating when a democracy ends. I

[10] There are three types of democratic transitions: autocratic to democratic, autocratic to anocratic, and anocratic to democratic. Likewise, there are three types of autocratic transitions: democratic to autocratic, democratic to anocratic, and anocratic to autocratic.

[11] In Chapter 4, I also label anocracy-to-democracy shifts as democratic completions in order to break them out of the general "transitions" data. They are also analyzed as a distinct political process. If there is missing data during a transition itself, the year in which the transition is completed is coded. For example, if state i begins a transition in 1985 and Polity data is missing for 1986 and 1987, but the 1988 data shows the state above $+6$, state i is coded as undergoing a transition in 1988.

thus define a variable dealing with the movement *away* from democracy, or democratic breakdown. This dummy variable is coded 1 if a regime moves from the +6 level or above to a level below this threshold; otherwise, the variable is coded 0.

As the second source of democracy measures, I use data on democracy and regime change from Mark Gasiorowski's (1993; 1996) Political Regime Change data set. Gasiorowski codes transitions for only the developing world (Latin America, Africa, Middle East and Asia) from 1815–1992. He distinguishes among four types of regimes: authoritarian, semi-democratic, democratic, and transitional.[12] Gasiorowski's definition of democracy includes three main components: competition for political offices, a highly inclusive level of political participation, and a "sufficient level" of civil and political liberties to "ensure the integrity of political competition" (Gasiorowski 1996: 471). Countries are coded as undergoing a transition to democracy if they move towards a "highly competitive, highly inclusive, liberal ideal embodied in the definition of democracy" (Gasiorowski 1996: 471).[13]

This conception of democracy closely matches Mainwaring's on all three dimensions. Gasiorowski's measure captures the process of elections, suffrage, as well as civil and political liberties. Less emphasized in Gasiorowski's measure are the institutional arrangements of the regime (e.g. checks on executive power, openness of the recruiting process for the executive). Gasiorowski's conception of democracy emphasizes civil and political liberties more heavily than the Polity98 data.

There are two reasons for using the Gasiorowski data. First, it will provide a robustness check on the results using the Polity data. Recall that the Polity98 data differs in its measurement of democracy, concentrating on institutional factors to classify regime type. Because the Polity data taps two aspects of our definition of democracy, it is adequate for my purposes, especially since a major focus of this work will be domestic changes in institutions essential for democratization. Still, using the Gasiorowski data allows one to say whether the relationship between IOs and transition and/or endurance is based only on issues of institutional change. Since Gasiorowski emphasizes other factors such as civil liberties, it provides variation on the measurement of democratization. Comparing these two measures will tell us how robust these results are with respect to the definition of democracy.

---

[12] For Gasiorowski (1993: 2), "transitional" does not necessarily imply democratic transition. It is applied to any regime in which "top government officials . . . engineer a change from one . . . regime type to another."

[13] Gasiorowski's own definition of democracy is drawn mostly from Diamond, Linz and Lipset (1989) as well as Dahl (1971).

Second, Gasiorowski excludes most of North America, all of Europe (East and West), as well as Japan, Australia, and New Zealand from his data set. There is not complete spatial overlap between the Polity98 and Gasiorowski data, which presents problems in comparing the results of the models. It does, however, provide a check against the criticism that those who extol the virtues of international institutions focus too much on Western Europe. Since the estimates of the models using the Gasiorowski data do not include the transitions of Southern or Eastern Europe, this provides a powerful robustness check against the influence of the EU. This guards against the possibility that the findings are driven by a handful of Western cases.

Gasiorowski codes specific transitions for every country, which makes generating the transition variables much simpler. I code a state as undergoing a democratic transition if any of the following movements occur: transitional to democratic, semi-democratic to democratic, and autocratic to democratic.[14] In a similar way to Polity98, I code a dummy variable 1 if any of these types of democratic transitions occur and 0 otherwise.

As with the Polity98 data, I also code a variable for the breakdown of democracy. Again, Gasiorowski describes these autocratic transitions in detail. I code a dummy variable 1 if a movement from democracy to autocracy or anocracy occurs. In addition, since in some instances I include "partial" democratization with this data set, some movements from anocracy to autocracy are coded as breakdowns as well. If no break-down occurs, the variable is coded 0.

Figure 3.3 shows the distribution of Gasiorowski's coding from 1950 to 1992. Again, a visual inspection of this graph provides preliminary evidence for the general accuracy of Gasiorowski's coding with regard to the trends to and away from democracy in the world. Recall that this data excludes many countries that would be labeled by most as democracies (e.g. the US, UK, Japan, France, the Benelux states, Australia, etc.). It is not surprising that this data set shows comparatively higher levels of autocracy than democracy for the majority of the time period under inspection. As with the Polity98 data, the number of democracies and anocracies remain similar over time, yet in this data set, the number of democracies does not surpass the number of autocracies. This is no doubt due to the exclusion of the many Eastern European transitions in

---

[14] For Gasiorowski, I also include three cases of authoritarian to "transitional" as democratization since those three states made the transition to full democracy later in the year. I also include shifts from "transitional" to semi-democracies in the general transitions measure when the states were previously authoritarian. I do not include their initial liberalization from authoritarian to "transitional" since, in many cases, they immediately revert to authoritarianism.

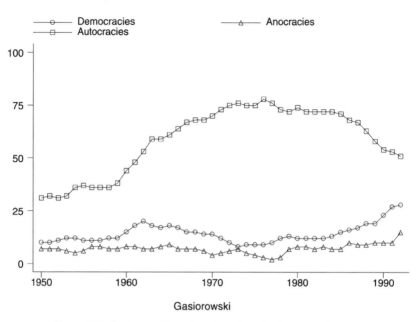

Figure 3.3 Gasiorowski regime type distribution over time

Gasiorowski's data set. Nevertheless, the level of democracy does begin to rise steadily in 1974 (the "Third Wave"), as corresponding levels of autocracy fall.[15]

Before moving to some descriptive statistics of this data, I note that the data set begins in 1950 largely because of data availability issues on some of the control variables. Although data on regime characteristics extends back as far as 1800 for Polity98 and 1815 for Gasiorowski, comparable economic data does not exist. Given the importance of these economic factors in accounting for regime transitions and duration, I felt it would not be prudent to rely on the poor economic data before 1950. The data analysis ends in 1992 for similar reasons. Much of the data pertaining to internal and external conflict used as controls in the models is not measured past 1992.

Descriptive statistics: democratic transitions and
democratic consolidation

Utilizing the preceding coding criteria for democratic transitions, the Polity98 data contains 52 transitions between 1950 and 1992, while the

---

[15] Other data sets emphasize civil liberties such as Freedom House (Gastil 1990). I have chosen Gasiorowski over Freedom House because of limited temporal coverage in the latter (coded only since the mid 1970s).

Table 3.1 *Correlation among regime type variables*

	Democracy P98	Democracy Gasior.	Anocracy Polity98	Anocracy Gasior.	Autocracy Polity98	Autocracy Gasior.
Democracy Polity98	1.00					
Democracy Gasior.	0.816*** (3404)	1.00				
Anocracy Polity98	−0.359*** (6120)	−0.359*** (3404)	1.00			
Anocracy Gasior.	0.031* (3404)	−0.140*** (3554)	0.345*** (3404)	1.00		
Autocracy Polity98	−0.675*** (6120)	−0.538*** (3404)	−0.447*** (6120)	−0.322*** (3404)	1.00	
Autocracy Gasior.	−0.681*** (3404)	−0.712*** (3554)	−0.153*** (3404)	−0.481*** (3554)	0.659*** (3404)	1.00

NOTE: First line of each cell is calculation of Pearson's r. Second line is the number of overlapping observations used to generate the statistic. ***$p < .01$; **$p < .05$; *$p < .10$

Gasiorowski data contains 69 for the same time period. Likewise, Polity98 contains 32 instances of democratic breakdown, while Gasiorowski contains 64. Tables 3.1 through 3.3 reveal the statistical similarities and differences between these two data sets.[16]

The correlation between these two data sets is not high.[17] Table 3.1 shows the correlations among the basic regime type variables. The highest agreement between the data sets comes on their categorizations of democracies. A statistically significant correlation of r = 0.82 shows some agreement between the two data sets. Their measures of autocracy agree much less, yielding a statistically significant correlation of r = 0.66. The least agreement comes in what each data set considers an anocracy. Comparing across this category yields a low, yet statistically significant correlation of r = 0.35. The varied operationalizations in each data set explain the low correlation among the coding of regime type. These differences will serve as an excellent robustness check for the models of both democratic transitions and endurance.

[16] A transition from democracy to a transitional government would be considered a breakdown as well, but only occurs once in the data (Uruguay 1973), and in that same year, the transitional government gives way to a pure authoritarian government. It is thus coded as a democratic breakdown.

[17] These correlations apply only to those cases where both data sets code a particular nation-state. Those cases (e.g. Eastern Europe) where there is no spatial overlap are excluded for the correlation statistic. This explains why the N for the correlations among the Polity98 data is around twice that for the Gasiorowski–Polity correlations.

Table 3.2 *Correlation among regime transition variables*

	Polity98	Gasiorowski
Polity98	1.00	
Gasiorowski	.53***	1.00

NOTE: N = 3250; ***p < .01; *p < .05; *p < .10

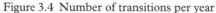
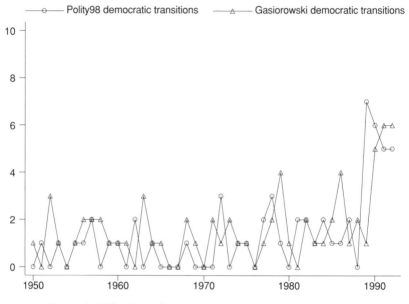

Figure 3.4 Number of transitions per year

The correlations presented in Table 3.2 compare the dummy variables marking transitions to democracy for both data sets. In coding transitions to democracy, these two data sets show less agreement than their coding of regime type. The correlation, while statistically significant, is a modest r = .53. Again, this should not be entirely surprising given each data set's varying operationalization of democracy. For example, expanding protection of individual rights may lead Gasiorowski to code a transition to democracy, but without attendant institutional change, such reform would not qualify the state as a democracy given Gurr's measure. Figure 3.4 shows the number of transitions plotted over time for the two data sets. Each line tracks very closely with the other, yet they are clearly not identical. As such, using both data sets will provide

Table 3.3 *Correlation among democratic breakdown variables*

	Polity98	Gasiorowski
Polity98	1.00	
Gasiorowski	.83***	1.00

NOTE: N = 596; ***p < .01; **p < .05; *p < .10

an excellent robustness check for the results in Chapters 4 and 6. Finally, Table 3.3 shows the correlation between each data set's coding of democratic breakdown. This correlation of r = 0.83 is statistically significant.

If the findings of the models of democratic transition and democratic survival are divergent across each data set, this difference could be traced to the different standards and measurement of democracy. They could also result from the lack of spatial overlap between the two data sets. Again, because of this difference in definition and coverage, the use of both data sets will serve as an excellent robustness check.

The independent variable: regional international organizations

The key independent variable of concern is regional organizations. For a definition of IOs, I follow Banks who defines international organizations as "composed of more than two states, whose governing bodies meet with some degree of regularity, and which possess permanent secretariats or other continuing means for implementing collective decisions" (Banks and Mueller 1998: viii). Based on this definition, I choose a sample of the population of IOs to include in this study. I code state membership in IOs based on Banks' *Political Handbook of the World* (various years). The sample of IOs I have chosen to include is also based on this source, augmented with a few additional organizations (a complete list of these organizations is shown in Table 3.4).[18] Alternative sources of this data do exist, namely, the *Yearbook of International Organizations* published by the Union of International Associations (1996). This later source lists far more organizations and includes thousands of

---

[18] These additional organizations are used in Mansfield and Pevehouse 2000. I add regional organizations that meet Banks' criteria, but were excluded from his publication. Most of these were regional economic arrangements in the developing world not notified to the GATT/WTO (General Agreement on Tariffs and Trade/World Trade Organization).

Table 3.4 *International organizations included in the primary analyses, 1950–92*

ACC (Arab Cooperation Council)	1989–90
Andean Pact	1969–92
ANZUS	1952–92
APEC (Asia-Pacific Economic Cooperation)	1989–92
ASEAN (Association of Southeast Asian Nations)	1967–92
ASPAC (Asian and Pacific Council)	1966–75
Benelux Union	1950–92
BSEC (Black Sea Economic Cooperation)	1992
CACM (Central American Common Market)	1961–92
CARICOM (Caribbean Community and Common Market)	1966–92
CBSS (Council of the Baltic Sea States)	1992
CDC (Central American Democratic Community)	1982–92
CEAO (West African Economic Community)	1959–92
CEEAC (Economic Community of Central African States)	1984–92
CEI (Central European Initiative)	1989–92
CENTO (Central Treaty Organization)	1955–79
CEPGL (Economic Community of the Great Lake Countries)	1976–92
CILSS (Permanent Interstate Committee on Drought Control in the Sahel)	1973–92
CIS (Commonwealth of Independent States)	1991–2
CMEA (Council on Mutual Economic Assistance)	1950–91
Colombo Plan	1951–92
COMESA (Common Market for Eastern and Southern Africa)	1993–2
Council of Europe	1950–92
Council of the Entente	1959–92
EACM (East African Common Market)	1967–77
ECO (Economic Cooperation Organization)	1965–92
ECOWAS (Economic Community of West African States)	1975–92
EFTA (European Free Trade Association)	1960–92
ESAPTA (Eastern and South African PTA)	1981–92
EU (European Union)	1958–92
GCC (Gulf Cooperation Council)	1981–92
IGAD (Inter-Governmental Authority on Development)	1986–92
IOC (Indian Ocean Commission)	1982–92
LAES (Latin American Economic System)	1975–92
LAIA (Latin American Integration Association)	1961–92
Maghreb Union	1989–92
Mano River Union	1973–92
MERCOSUR (Southern Cone Common Market)	1991–2
NATO (North Atlantic Treaty Organization)	1950–92
Nordic Council	1953–92
OAPEC (Organization of Arab Petroleum Exporting Countries)	1968–92
OAS (Organization of American States)	1951–92
OAU (Organization of African Unity)	1963–92
OCAM (African and Mauritanian Common Organization)	1965–85
ODECA/SICA (Central American Integration System)	1951–92

Table 3.4 (*cont.*)

OPANAL (Agency for the Prohibition of Nuclear Weapons in Latin America)	1969–92
OSCE (Organization for Security and Cooperation in Europe)	1973–92
SAARC (South Asian Association for Regional Cooperation)	1985–92
SADC (Southern African Development Community)	1980–92
SEATO (Southeast Asian Treaty Organization)	1955–77
SPC (South Pacific Commission)	1950–92
SPF (South Pacific Forum)	1971–92
UDEAC (Central African Customs and Economic Union)	1961–92
WEU (Western European Union)	1955–92
WTO (Warsaw Treaty Organization)	1955–91

non-governmental organizations.[19] I have chosen to use Banks' data over the *Yearbook* because of his selectivity. Banks' IOs generally consist of regional political organizations such as military alliances, trade groups, and economic organizations.[20]

Regional organizations that are technical, cultural, or environmental organizations are excluded from this study. While these organizations may serve very useful purposes for the international community, they possess very few resources to contribute to transitions to democracy. It should be noted that some organizations that appear to be environmental in nature, such as the CILSS (Permanent Interstate Committee on Drought Control in the Sahel), are included since they often provide or monitor development assistance both to and between member states. In addition, the CILSS and a handful of other environmental IOs list the promotion of economic development and trade as key areas of work. These organizations are included in the sample.

Table 3.4 presents the list of organizations included in these analyses. Although I have chosen to exclude certain classes of international organizations from this study, most of the ubiquitous international organizations are included in this sample. Excluding many of the UIA (Union of International Associations) organizations has the effect of excluding such groups as the International Studies Association, the International Postal Union, and the Association of the Chocolate, Biscuit and Confectionery Industries of the EEC/EU.[21] Although limiting the focus of this research

---

[19] Banks in his 1998 edition lists 88 IOs, while the 1992 version of the *Yearbook* lists approximately 1,690.

[20] Banks selectivity also helps control for emanations from extant IOs. As Shanks, Jacobson, and Kaplan (1996) discuss, most of the increase in IOs over the 1980s and 1990s have been organizations set up by existing IOs.

[21] The UIA (1996) adopts the broadest possible standards for IOs (which include both IGOs and NGOs) so that individual researchers may "make their own evaluation in the light of their own criteria."

to regional political, economic, and military organizations may provide an incomplete picture of the interaction between IOs and democracy, as the first cut at this, I feel this limitation is necessary. I now turn to how state memberships in these organizations are coded.

Coding IO membership

As previously discussed, simple dichotomous variables are inadequate for conducting an analysis of IOs' effects on democratization and democratic endurance since every state is a member of at least one IO. One must then devise a coding scheme to differentiate IOs along some dimension, which can be quite difficult (Nierop 1994: 100). Many quantitative studies of IOs measure only on the number of shared memberships between dyads (Russett, Oneal, and Davis 1998) or the number of memberships for each state (Jacobson, Reisinger, and Mathers 1986). Yet, the theory discussed in the first section of this chapter stresses the importance of the "democraticness" of a regional organization.

To this end, I compute a variable to measure the most democratic IO of a state's IO memberships as well as changes in that membership including accession to IOs that are highly democratic. First, I construct a data set of IO membership using the sample of IOs (shown in Table 3.4) found in Banks and Mueller (1998) and Banks (various years). For each state i, I then compute the average level of democracy of all members in the organization *except state i*.[22] I use the Polity98 democracy scores to determine the level of democracy in each member state.[23] Now for each state i, which is a member of k IOs, there are a total of k IO weights equal to the average level of democracy of the member states of those k institutions.[24] In Chapters 4 and 6, the variable $IOScore_{it}$ is equal to the largest value of k for each state i in year t. This variable represents the average level of democracy in the most democratic IO of which state i is a member.

I use only the most democratic organization to measure each state's IO involvement (versus an average of all IOs) since it should take only one membership to supply any of the causal mechanisms posited by my theory. To this end, in both Chapters 4 and 6, I also utilize a measure of

---

[22] This is essential since if state i is included, it is possible that an organization would become democratic because of a transition to democracy in that state.

[23] I use the Polity98 data rather than Gasiorowski data since the Polity98 data provides a continuous score of democracy. This makes creating an aggregate measure easier since the resulting IO score could have the same "cut points" as the regime scores.

[24] I scale the Polity98 scores by adding 11 to each IO's score, moving the scale from -10 to $+10$ to $+1$ to $+21$. Thus, a state with no IO memberships is coded as 0.

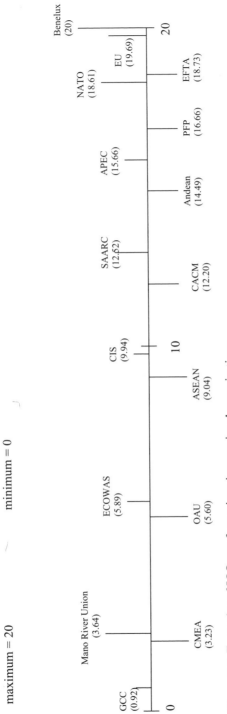

Sample statistics for IOScore_{it}

mean = 10.9   median = 10.2
maximum = 20   minimum = 0

Figure 3.5 Examples of IOScore for various international organizations
NOTE: IOScores are averaged over the life of the organization.

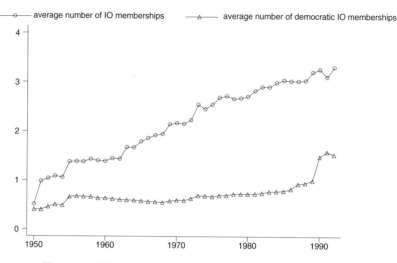

Figure 3.6 IO involvement over time

the number of regional IOs of which state i is a member. As discussed in those chapters, this measure is not statistically associated with the transition to or the survival of democracy, nor does the presence of this variable erode the statistical significance of the $IOScore_{it}$ measure. This suggests that membership in merely one highly democratic IO is enough for the causal processes to function.

Figure 3.5 provides some basic descriptive statistics and some case examples for $IOScore_{it}$. Note that the scores for each IO in the figure represent the average of all members over the life of the organization. For example, the Benelux Union is composed of all democracies for the duration of the organization. At the other end of this continuum, the GCC (Gulf Cooperation Council) is composed of autocracies over its life span. In general, it is true that most of the "democratic" international organizations in this figure are European-based. Still, non-European organizations such as APEC (Asia-Pacific Economic Cooperation), the CACM (Central American Common Market), and MERCOSUR (Southern Cone Common Market – not listed in the figure, but with a score of 17.94) are quite democratic in their membership profile.

Figure 3.6 tracks membership and the democratic nature of IOs over time. "Democratic" IOs are those organizations whose aggregate IOScore is above the +17 (recall I have re-scaled the Polity scores by adding 11) threshold set for individual nation-states. Thus, if in any given year, the average level of IOScore$_{it}$ for all member states is above +17, the IO is

Table 3.5 *Descriptive statistics of IOs and democratization*

IOScore for . . .	N	Mean	Student's t[a] (p of t)
Polity98			
Regimes undergoing transitions to democracy . . .	52	13.35	2.08
Regimes undergoing democratic breakdown . . .	31	10.92	(0.041)
All anocratic regimes . . .	947	9.85	3.96***
Regimes in transition from anocracy to democracy . . .	27	14.18	(>0.001)
All autocratic regimes . . .	2581	6.79	6.48***
Regimes in transition from autocracy to anocracy . . .	54	11.38	(>0.001)
All autocratic regimes . . .	2581	6.79	5.48***
Regimes in transition from autocracy to democracy . . .	25	12.46	(>0.001)
Gasiorowski			
Regimes undergoing transitions to democracy . . .	67[b]	11.49	2.00**
Regimes undergoing democratic breakdown . . .	639	83	(0.05)
All anocratic regimes . . .	306	9.61	2.14***
Regimes in transition from anocracy to democracy . . .	31	11.57	(0.033)
All autocratic regimes . . .	2514	7.45	4.84***
Regimes in transition from autocracy to anocracy . . .	36	11.50	(>0.000)
All autocratic regimes . . .	2515	7.46	2.27***
Regimes in transition from autocracy to democracy . . .	8	11.46	(0.023)

[a] Equal variances are assumed for these t tests. The absolute value of the t statistic is taken since the sign of the statistic is only an artifact of whether the larger or smaller number is designated as "sample #1."
[b] In years where both a transition and a breakdown occur, the breakdown only is counted.

coded as "democratic." Figure 3.6 shows the average number of memberships in democratic IOs for all states in the sample per year. Thus, a "1" on the graph would mean that the average state in the data set was a member of at least one democratic IO. The other line tracks the overall number of memberships in IOs, regardless of their "democraticness." Note that the number of IO memberships grows steadily over time, while membership in democratic IOs stays fairly steady until the end of the sample period.

General statistical trends: IO membership and democratization

Before moving on to the first chapter of statistical analysis, I will briefly outline some of the general statistical trends between IOs and democratization. To this point we have discussed the coding criteria for the major dependent and independent variables. Tables 3.5–3.6 present a series of

Table 3.6 *Successful consolidation and IO involvement*

IOScore for a country in which . . .	N	Mean	Student's t[a] (p of t)
Polity98			
the democratic transition breaks down	20	10.94	2.963***
the democratic transition does not break down[b]	32	14.86	(0.005)
is a democracy	1664	15.58	4.32***
undergoes a democratic breakdown	31	10.92	(>0.000)
Gasiorowski			
the democratic transition breaks down	37	10.39	2.30**
the democratic transition does not break down	32	12.91	(0.025)
is a democracy	609	11.61	2.51**
undergoes a democratic breakdown	63	9.83	(0.012)

[a] Equal variances are assumed for these t tests. The absolute value of the t statistic is taken since the sign of the statistic is only an artifact of whether the larger or smaller number is designated as "sample #1."
[b] This pair of lines compares only those states who undergo a transition to democracy during the observation period (1950–1992), while the next pair of lines compares all states who undergo a democratic breakdown, even if their transition preceded the observation period.

four basic tests (two for each data set) of the relationship between democratic transitions or democratic endurance and involvement in regional organizations.

Table 3.5 first outlines the number of transitions and democratic breakdowns in the data along with the average level of IOScore across those cases. Recall that IOScore is the average level of democracy in the most democratic IO of which state i is a member. Some common patterns emerge across both data sets. Note that regimes undergoing a transition to democracy, on average, belong to more democratic IOs than those that are in the process of democratic breakdown. In both data sets this is statistically significant using the student's t-test for equivalence of means, indicating a systematic difference between IO memberships for states in each circumstance.

For both the Polity98 and Gasiorowski data, states which are "finishing" their transitions (moving from anocracy to democracy) maintain memberships in many more democratic IOs than their stable anocratic counterparts. In the Polity data, this difference is over four points higher and is statistically significant. Although the equivalent comparison in the Gasiorowski data yields a less dramatic difference, it is nonetheless statistically significant. Thus, states concluding their transitions to democracy after spending time as an anocracy belong to more democratic IOs than those states that remain anocracies.

Moreover, in both data sets, those regimes in transition from autocracy to democracy or autocracy to anocracy belong to more democratic IOs than their stable autocratic counterparts.[25] For the both the Polity98 and Gasiorowski data sets, this difference is statistically significant. Similar trends are evident for partial transitions (autocracy to anocracy). Here the differences are smaller than in the autocracy to democracy case, yet in both data sets the differences in IOScore between these two groups is statistically significant. These figures all provide preliminary evidence of the association between membership in democratic IOs and democratic transitions.

Table 3.6 examines the fate of those states that undergo a transition to democracy. The average level of IOScore for a state whose transition will eventually give way to democratic breakdown is much smaller than a state that maintains its democracy in both the Polity98 and Gasiorowski sample. For the Polity98 and Gasiorowski data, this difference is statistically significant. Controlling for no outside factors, membership in a democratic IO after the transition seems to bode well for the survival of democracy. The next lines consider a similar comparison, but examine all cases of democratic breakdown whether the transition occurred in the sample period or not. Again, for both data sets the difference in the IO membership for each group is statistically significant.

Although these tests are preliminary in nature, they are quite suggestive of some general trends in the data. Regimes that undergo transitions to democracy are members of regional organizations that are much more homogenously democratic than states not making the transition. One conclusion is that democratic organizations do effectively pressure and facilitate the transition to democracy. This is true no matter which data set is used to measure democracy and transitions. Similarly, in states that have recently undergone a transition to democracy, membership in a democratic regional organization bodes well for democracy. New democracies who are members of these organizations appear to be less likely to suffer a breakdown of democracy. Taken together all of these results suggest that there is an empirical link between membership in homogenously democratic regional organizations and democratic transitions and democratic endurance.

---

[25] The sum total of transitions for the Gasiorowski data (the three transition categories) exceeds the total number of transitions since multiple transitions can take place in the same year in the Gasiorowski data.

Conclusion

This chapter began by examining the supply-side of the argument. My contention, derived from extant international relations theory, is that more homogenously democratic regional organizations are more likely to be associated with democratization. Thus, we should not expect all IOs to assist in this process. I also examined an alternative hypothesis that the true causal process behind the regional IO–democracy link was the interest of great power members of regional organizations. While it is essential to evaluate this position in order to assess the true impact of regional IOs, I argue that this hypothesis only undermines part of the argument made here. Namely, if regional IOs influence democracy because of decisions of domestic elites in nascent democracies to use international institutions as commitment devices, the opportunities for great powers to use regional institutions is limited. In a similar vein, I preview the empirical findings throughout the next four chapters that suggest regional IOs do play an independent role in the democratization process.

I then discussed the coding criteria for the two key concepts in this work: democracy and international organizations. As a first systematic, quantitative empirical cut at the question of IOs and democratization I have kept these tests relatively focused. Examining only regional institutions, for example, is a way to find out if certain types of organizations can assist in the transition to and consolidation of democracy. In addition, the theories discussed in Chapter 2 yield hypotheses that lead us to expect that only certain types of regional IOs will be associated with democratization. These coding criteria (both choosing the sample and measuring IO involvement) are meant to reflect these hypotheses.

The general statistical trends presented in this chapter provide preliminary support for the theory. These tests, however, are not meant as the final word on the veracity of my claims. They establish, in a very broad way, an association between democratic IOs and democratic transitions and democratic endurance. Now that we have discussed the coding of the dependent variables, the major independent variable, and noted the general associations within each data set, we move to the first chapter that more fully tests the theory linking regional organizations and democracy.

4 Regional organizations and the transition to democracy

A major set of variables often discounted in studies of democratization concerns international factors. Comparative scholars have traditionally chosen to concentrate on the internal dynamics of the nation-state in transition, embracing such concepts as *virtu* (the influence of specific individuals) and *fortuna* (the influence of unexpected events) – representing the importance of random chance and situational factors, respectively (O'Donnell and Schmitter 1986: 5). This approach not only eschews international variables but domestic structural variables as well.[1] Much descriptive and choice-theoretic work on transitions continues this perspective (cf. Przeworski 1991; Schmitter and Karl 1991). While this approach is extremely useful if the goal is to discuss a single transition, it is less useful when building a broader theory of transitions.

Recently, domestic structural explanations have reemerged in the study of transitions (Gasiorowski 1995; Haggard and Kaufman 1995a; Ruhl 1996).[2] This emerging literature (re)focuses on factors such as economic conditions or financial crises and their propensity to constrain or compel the democratization process (or the process of democratic breakdown). In addition, factors such as collective action problems (Clemens 1998), modernization (Diamond 1992), and ethnic homogeneity (Linz and Stepan 1996) have been emphasized in recent work. Still, with a few exceptions (Kadera, Crescenzi, and Shannon 2003; Reiter 2001a; Whitehead 1996a), even most structural-oriented theories still ignore influences that arise outside the state. Those that do discuss international influences on the transition process tend to examine isolated case studies. While this approach is important for discovering particular causal paths, it does not allow us to think about the broader nature of the links between the international system and domestic politics. For purposes of

---

[1] In fact, this represented a move away from the structural orientation of modernization theory (see Lipset 1959). For a review of modernization theory work, see Diamond 1992.

[2] By "structural," I refer to variables or processes constraining or conditioning the probability of an event taking place. See Clemens 1998 and Ruhl 1996.

generalizability and even policy formulation, discovering these links is essential.

Chapter 2 presented a theory linking regional organizations to democratic transitions in an attempt to bring an external-structural perspective to the study of transitions.[3] By adopting this approach, however, I do not wish to minimize the importance of domestic factors in the transition process. To the contrary, I argue that regional organizations shape the incentives and constraints of individual agents during democratic transitions. The causal mechanisms linking regional IOs to democratization allow a variety of choice on the part of individual agents at the state level and are not incompatible with unit-level explanations of democratization. In detailing the factors which shape the context in which domestic agents act, I hope to paint a more complete picture of the transition process by including factors external to the nation-state.

In this chapter, I undertake a statistical evaluation of the theory presented in Chapter 2. The theory discussed how regional organizations could influence domestic regime choice through several mechanisms including pressure emanating from the organization, creating credible commitments to protect interests of key elite groups though the acquiescence effect (including socialization), and helping to signal intentions to domestic political audiences (legitimization). These mechanisms influence the cost–benefit calculations of domestic actors as they consider beginning the liberalization process or supporting the transition process to completion. In particular, regional organizations which are made up predominantly of democracies are likely to supply these causal mechanisms The first section of this chapter evaluates this basic argument – that membership in regional organizations of predominantly democracies should be associated with transitions to democracy. I examine all movements from either authoritarianism or anocracy to democracy.

The second and third sections of this chapter present more narrow tests that examine particular causal mechanisms relating regional organizations to regime change. I break down the process of democratization into two phases: liberalization and the completion of the transition. As discussed in Chapter 2, the first two mechanisms (pressure and acquiescence) should play a larger role in the liberalization process, while the third (legitimization) should be closely linked with completing the transition to democracy. By liberalization, I refer to a movement away from authoritarianism to anocracy or democracy, while I define completion of

---

[3] I should note that it is possible to do each separately as well. Haggard and Kaufman (1995a) represent an extensive attempt to emphasize the importance of structural variables in the democratization process. Grabendorff (1996) represents an attempt to highlight external influences as a non-structural variable.

the transition as movement from anocracy to full democracy.[4] Finally, to ensure that the results are consistent across a variety of transition types, I model those transitions moving from highly authoritarian systems to full democracies.

The chapter also includes a variety of tests of competing hypotheses and robustness checks of the initial results. In each section of the chapter, I include an auxiliary regression to test for the influence of major powers in regional organizations. I also show that the inclusion of additional non-regional organizations and international financial institutions does not alter the inferences drawn from these statistical models.

Testing the argument: general transitions

If the theoretical argument is correct, a statistical association should exist between membership in democratic regional organizations and democratization. To test this hypothesis, I use the data on democracy and regional IOs described in Chapter 3. Recall that I have coded transitions to democracy based on both the Polity98 data and Mark Gasiorowski's regime transitions data set. This section tests for an association between democratic regional organizations and general transitions (a movement to democracy from autocracy or anocracy).

To begin, I estimate the following statistical model:

$$
\begin{aligned}
(4.1) \quad \text{DemTransition}_{it} = &\; \alpha_0 + \beta_1 \text{IOScore}_{it-1} + \beta_2 \Delta \text{IOScore}_{it-1} \\
&+ \beta_3 \text{pcGDP}_{it} + \beta_4 \Delta \text{pcGDP}_{it} + \beta_5 \text{RegContagion}_{it} \\
&+ \beta_6 \text{PastDemocracy}_{it} + \beta_7 \text{RegConflict}_{it} \\
&+ \beta_8 \text{InternalViolence}_{it-1} + \beta_9 \text{MilitaryRegime}_{it} \\
&+ \beta_{10} \text{Independence}_{it} + \beta_{11} \text{MAR}_i + \mu_{it}
\end{aligned}
$$

The dependent variable in Model 4.1, *DemTransition$_{it}$* measures the probability that state i completes a transition to democracy in year t. The coding of this transition variable for both data sets is described in Chapter 3. The first independent variable, *IOScore$_{it-1}$* is also discussed in Chapter 3. It represents the average level of democracy in the most democratic IO of which state i is a member in the year $t - 1$. My theory suggests we should expect existing membership in democratic IOs to make the probability of a democratic transition more likely. Thus, the coefficient estimate for this variable should be positive and statistically significant.

---

[4] The second and third dependent variables in this chapter are almost subsets of the first. The first dependent variable essentially includes all transitions ending in democracy, the second can include transitions ending in anocracy (partial transitions), while the third includes transitions ending in democracy, but starting only as anocracies.

The second independent variable, $\Delta IOScore_{it-1}$, is the one-year difference of $IOScore_{it-1}$. This variable is included to isolate the effects of joining a regional organization since this could be an important impetus to make the transition to democracy. If a state joins an IO that is more democratic than any previous IO to which it belongs, the value of $\Delta IOScore_{it-1}$ will be positive. Including this change variable as well as the level variable will allow a comparison of the effects of joining a democratic organization versus the overall level of "democraticness" in the IO.[5] The expectation is that the estimate for this coefficient should be positive.

While these two variables will answer the question of whether regional organizations are associated with transitions to democratization, a wide variety of other factors inside and outside the state have been hypothesized to influence this process. First and foremost, the status of the domestic economy has long been thought to influence the prospects for regime change. The variables $pcGDP_{it}$ and $\Delta pcGDP_{it}$ are intended to capture those economic factors which may be relevant to democratization. The link between economic development and democracy has been a controversial one for almost fifty years. Beginning with Seymour Martin Lipset's (1959: 75) observation that "Perhaps the most widespread generalization linking political systems to other aspects of society has been that democracy is related to the state of economic development," the idea that economic wealth fosters democracy has become widespread (Dahl 1989). This theorized relationship has been supported in a variety of quantitative empirical tests as well, including work by Bollen (1983), Bollen and Jackman (1985), Burkhart and Lewis-Beck (1994), and Londregan and Poole (1996). In fact, the idea that economic well-being creates demands on the part of citizens for responsive government has been described by some as "almost beyond challenge" (Burkhart and Lewis-Beck 1994: 903).

Some have challenged this conclusion, mostly on statistical grounds. Two studies have found only a weak statistical relationship between economic development and democracy (Arat 1988; Gonick and Rosh

---

[5] Change in the level of democracy could represent a change in the level of democracy of the same IO. That is, $\Delta IOScore_{it-1}$ may have a positive value because of democratization in other member states rather than a new membership for the state in question, although increases of this nature will probably be smaller since the change is averaged over all members. Increases of this type, however, still yield the same prediction. As a regional IO becomes more democratic, it is more likely to encourage transition through the increased supply of the causal mechanisms. In addition, because the $RegContagion_{it}$ variable will control for surrounding states' democratization, any influence of regional IOs will not be through the demonstration effect.

1988).[6] Recently, Przeworski and Limongi (1997) have shown that economic development may not be related to transitions to democracy, but to sustaining democracy.[7] Nonetheless, it is possible that the status of the economy may still play an indirect role in bringing the downfall of *autocracies*. Haggard and Kaufman (1995b) stress the importance of poor economic performance in the breakdown of authoritarian regimes. Thus, economic development may not lead directly to democratization, but could facilitate the decline of an autocratic regime that could be replaced by a democracy.

Despite the occasionally inconsistent empirical results found in existing literature, it is essential to include factors such as wealth and changes in wealth in any model of democratic transitions. Whether the question is phrased as the breakdown of autocracy or the transition to democracy, scholars have consistently noted the importance of economic factors in influencing domestic politics. To this end, I include both per capita income ($pcGDP_{it}$) and changes in per capita income ($\Delta pcGDP_{it}$) in the model. The first variable captures the influence of wealth, while the latter taps the influence of economic growth rates within the state. While it is possible that this measure can overstate the average level of wealth and development in a country (if wealth is extremely concentrated in a few hands), it should generally reflect the level of income for a particular state. I expect $pcGDP_{it}$ to be positively associated with transitions to democracy, based on theory and the findings of previous research.

The expectation of $\Delta pcGDP_{it}$ is less clear. While growth and modernization are hypothesized to bring pressures for democratization, low economic growth is likely to hit authoritarians very hard, perhaps causing a breakdown of their regime. Phrased differently, high growth may give rise to a politically active middle class, but these same growth rates may add to the legitimacy of the authoritarian regime, especially if that regime came to power on the promise of better economic performance. Both $pcGDP_{it}$ and $\Delta pcGDP_{it}$ data are taken from Gleditsch (2002).

The variable $RegContagion_{it}$ controls for possible diffusion effects from other established democracies (Huntington 1991; Whitehead 1996c).[8] The theory argues that the presence of democracies located in close geographic proximity is likely to encourage democracy in authoritarian

---

[6] Burkhart and Lewis-Beck (1994) contend that these studies suffer from statistical problems that undermine their conclusions. Their own study finds support for the development–democracy relationship.

[7] I discuss this theory more fully in the next chapter, which focuses on the consolidation of democracy.

[8] Of course, IOs' effect on democracy could take this form as well. By controlling for this phenomenon independently, however, it will parse out any contagion effect independent of IO membership.

states. The actual causal mechanism often differs, but usually includes the transmission of norms via the modern media or epistemic communities (O'Loughlin et al. 1998).[9]

RegContagion$_{it}$ is the percentage of geographically contiguous neighbors to state i in year t that are democracies.[10] Depending on which data set is used to measure the dependent variable, however, the value of *RegContagion*$_{it}$ may vary since each data set differs on which states are democracies. This variable is measured on a yearly basis and should be positively associated with democratic transitions, since a higher percentage of democratic neighbors should lead to a more hospitable environment for democratization.

Many who study transitions to democracy have argued that past experience with democracy makes a transition to democracy more likely. Past development of civil society can often survive a period of autocracy and can reemerge as a foundation for democracy. Interestingly, Przeworski and his colleagues (1996: 43–4) point out that a past history of democracy in an authoritarian regime also means a past history of democratic *breakdown*, so it is not clear whether this factor works for or against the likelihood of a democratic transition. To control for either of these dynamics, I include *PastDemocracy*$_{it}$, which measures a nation's past experience with democracy. The variable is coded as a 1 if state i has previously been a democracy, otherwise, the variable takes on a value of 0.[11] Despite Przeworski's argument, I expect this variable to be positive in sign – a past history of democracy should increase the likelihood of a democratic transition.

The next two independent variables tap the level of external and internal conflict experienced by a nation-state. *RegConflict*$_{it}$ measures the number of Militarized Interstate Disputes (MIDs) in state i's region in year t (Jones, Bremer, and Singer 1996).[12] Some scholars have argued that regional instability and international conflict will not augur well for the development of democracy (Thompson 1996; Reiter 2001a). The argument, often couched in terms of the democratic peace, is that states

---

[9] This "active" version of contagion differs from a more "passive" theory that holds that the number of democracies at any given time sets an important structural limitation on democratization (Przeworski et al. 1996).

[10] Contiguity is defined as sharing a border with a state (i.e. contiguous by land).

[11] The state must have been a democracy between 1950 and year t. States suffering democratic breakdowns before 1950 are coded as 0. The value of this variable is dependent on which data set is used, yielding a different variable for each data set.

[12] I follow the Correlates of War coding of regions: North America, South America, Africa, Europe, Asia-Pacific, Asia, Middle East. See Small and Singer (1994). Although Small and Singer consider the Oceania area as an independent region (Australia, New Zealand, Fiji, etc.), I combine these few states with the Asia region. This makes no substantive difference in any of the models, since in all but a small handful of cases this Pacific dummy is thrown out as no country in that region experiences democratization or liberalization.

require a peaceful international environment to democratize. Democracy can suffer setbacks during crises since leaders will often consolidate their own power in order to mobilize resources to meet (or make) external threats. In more peaceful times, leaders have no need to control the reins of the state for security purposes, giving democracy a chance to flourish.[13] I thus expect this variable to have a negative effect on the probability of democracy – the more disputes within a region (which may or may not involve state i), the less likely a transition to democracy.

To measure the effect of internal violence, I include the variable *InternalViolence$_{it-1}$* in the model. This variable, taken from Banks (1994), is coded 1 if state i suffers from anti-government riots, strikes, guerilla insurgencies, or assassination attempts on major government officials in year $t - 1$.[14] I expect this variable to be negatively related to transitions to democracy, since internal violence is unlikely to give way to democracy in the short run (recall that the dependent variable takes on a value of 1 if a transition is completed that year). Although violence is often required to unseat an autocrat, it will be rare for democracy to arise given the civil and economic upheaval accompanying large-scale internal violence (Linz and Stepan 1996: 107–8).

Some scholars have argued that different types of autocratic regimes (military dictatorships, one party systems, etc.) are more or less susceptible to democratization. Most recently, Barbara Geddes (1999) contends that military regimes "carry with them the seeds of their own disintegration." Her argument is that since returning to the barracks is always a fairly attractive option for some set of military leaders within a country, when faced with a crisis, military regimes are more likely to collapse than other forms of autocracy. Past quantitative research has not provided support for this argument. Specifically, Gasiorowski (1995) finds that military regimes are less likely to undergo transition to democracy in his sample of 75 developing countries from 1950–92. To control for this dynamic, I include *MilitaryRegime$_{it}$* which equals 1 if state i is controlled by the military in year t. This data is taken from Banks (1994).[15] Given the past empirical findings, I expect this variable to be negatively related to the probability of a transition to democracy.

The next independent variable, *Independence$_{it}$*, measures the length of time state i has been an independent nation-state. As an extension of

---

[13] A more complex causal story could exist: if peace means prosperity, then the economic development and democracy link again becomes important. I do not attempt to evaluate this theory, per se, and leave the question of causal mechanisms aside.

[14] Banks (1994) provides a description of his coding criteria for each type of event for the duration of his data set. I have lagged this term to avoid endogeneity, since violence may be the result of a breakdown of democracy.

[15] Banks' data is coded only through 1989. I have updated the data through 1992, relying on Banks and Mueller (1998) as well as the CIA Factbook (1999).

the idea that past experience with democracy may be correlated with democratization, I hypothesize that longer periods of political independence should be positively related to the probability of a transition to democracy. Longer periods of political independence will increase the probability that civil society and independent political parties will develop. The dates of independence are taken from Small and Singer (1994).[16]

The final independent variable, MAR_i, measures number of major minority groups residing within the state. Juan Linz and Alfred Stepan (1996) have argued that a key roadblock to finishing democratic transitions is the issue of "stateness." They argue that states that have large communities of ethnic minorities create "competing nationalisms within one territorial state" (Linz and Stepan 1996: 16). By undermining the very legitimacy of the state itself, this factor can make completing a transition difficult. They contend that under authoritarian systems, issues of citizenship and the legitimacy of the state are less salient, thus these problem arise only under fragile democratic systems. The expectation is that this variable will be negatively associated with democratization. The data is taken from the Minorities at Risk project (Gurr 1993). Finally, μ_{it} is a stochastic error term.

I should note that the sample for this model does not include the entire data set. Existing democracies cannot experience a transition to democracy. Thus, only states that can undergo a democratic transition (autocracies and anocracies) are included in the estimation of Model 4.1.[17] This explains why the N of each model is smaller than the N of the entire data set and why the estimates using different data sets have different sample sizes (since their definition of democracy differs). Moreover, it is important to remember that Gasiorowski's data examines only developing states, excluding Europe, Japan, the United States, and Canada.

Statistical results: general transitions

Because the observed value of the dependent variable is dichotomous, I utilize logistic regression to estimate Model 4.1.[18] The estimates of the

---

[16] Small and Singer trace the origin of the international state system to 1815 and thus, for all nations who were independent before this date, their date of independence is set to 1815.

[17] Autocracies and anocracies at $t-1$ are included in the sample. That is, if a state is a democracy in year t because of a transition, it is included, since in the prior year it was either an autocracy or anocracy. Transition years, those years where the outcome of the transition is uncertain, are also included.

[18] In each specification of the model, I have checked for the inclusion of a correction for temporal dependence (see Beck, Katz, and Tucker 1998). In each case, a cubic spline function and one to three knots are never statistically significant. This indicates

model for each data set are presented in the first two columns of Table 4.1. For both data sets, membership in democratic international organizations is positively related to the likelihood of a transition to democracy. In addition, both coefficient estimates are highly statistically significant. Thus, membership in democratic regional organizations, while controlling for a variety of other domestic and international factors, is significantly correlated with the transitions to democracy. The other independent variable of interest, $\Delta IOScore_{it-1}$, is inconsistent in its influence on the probability of transition. For the Polity98 data, this variable is barely statistically significant, yet for the Gasiorowski data, the variable is not statistically related to transitions to democracy. Given these results, I conclude that existing memberships in homogeneously democratic regional organizations play a stronger role in democratization than accession to these organizations.

To gain some understanding of how important the IO variable is to the prospect of experiencing a transition to democracy, Table 4.2 presents the changes in predicted probabilities of a transition based on the statistical results of Table 4.1. These percentage changes represent the change in the probability of a transition from the probability established by the modal case in the data set. This "baseline" likelihood of a democratic transition is computed by taking the mean value of all continuous variables, setting each dichotomous variable to their modal value.[19] The value of a variable is then varied to yield the percentages in Table 4.2. Initially, note the change in probability of a transition where $IOScore_{it-1}$ is increased by one standard deviation from its mean value. For both the Polity98 data set, the likelihood of a transition increases by over 60 percent, while the estimates based on the Gasiorowski data yield a nearly 40 percent increase.

The second line of each table presents the predicted probability of a transition in the case where the state is not a member of an organization included in the regional IO sample.[20] These results are quite striking. For the Polity98 data, membership in an IO with the mean level of $IOScore$ increases the odds of a transition over a state with no IO memberships by 50 percent. For the Gasiorowski data, the comparable change is nearly 40 percent. Thus, regional organizations have a very strong impact on the likelihood of a democratic transition and this impact grows as the organization's membership becomes more democratic.

that temporal dependence is of little concern for these models and, thus, no corrective measures are taken.

[19] For both data set estimates, $PastDemocracy_{it}$ and $MilitaryRegime_{it}$ are set to zero, while $InternalViolence_{it-1}$ is set to 1.

[20] Examples of states party to no international organizations over *some periods* of time in the data are Israel, North Korea, Cuba, North Vietnam, Taiwan, and China.

Table 4.1 *Estimates of the determinants of the transition to democracy,*
1950–92

	Polity98	Gasiorowski	Polity98	Gasiorowski
$IOScore_{it-1}$	0.091***	0.064**	0.090**	0.067***
	(3.45)	(2.41)	(3.40)	(2.58)
$\Delta IOScore_{it-1}$	0.083*	0.046	–.–	–.–
	(1.80)	(0.96)		
$MajPowerIO_{it-1}$	–.–	–.–	0.142	0.097
			(1.07)	(0.66)
$pcGDP_{it}$	2.70×10^{-5}	-2.77×10^{-5}	2.62×10^{-5}	-2.64×10^{-5}
	(0.83)	(−0.65)	(0.76)	(−0.60)
$\Delta pcGDP_{it}$	−0.0004	0.0006*	−0.0004	0.0006*
	(−1.58)	(1.78)	(−1.44)	(1.64)
$RegContagion_{it}$	0.810*	0.665	0.921**	0.772*
	(1.75)	(1.57)	(1.96)	(1.73)
$PastDemocracy_{it}$	1.542***	0.600**	1.501***	0.568**
	(4.80)	(2.29)	(4.89)	(2.24)
$RegConflict_{it}$	−0.469***	−0.158	−0.484***	−0.168
	(−2.85)	(−1.32)	(−2.87)	(−1.41)
$InternalViolence_{it-1}$	2.341***	1.016***	2.326***	0.929***
	(4.13)	(2.90)	(4.14)	(2.59)
$MilitaryRegime_{it}$	−1.992***	−1.739***	−1.965***	−1.745***
	(−2.88)	(−3.27)	(−2.87)	(−3.27)
$Independence_{it}$	0.006*	0.005	0.005*	0.004
	(1.83)	(1.35)	(1.73)	(1.20)
Constant	−7.176***	−5.137***	−7.1204***	−5.102***
	(−12.32)	(−12.74)	(−12.31)	(−12.31)
N =	3291	2722	3364	2776
Log likelihood	−207.67	−272.61	−208.88	−277.67
Chi-square	98.96***	66.06***	101.01***	68.14***

Figures in parentheses are asymptotic z-statistics computed using Huber/White/sandwich
standard errors.
*** − p <= .01; ** − p <= .05; * − p <= .1; two-tailed tests.

Table 4.2 *Percentage change in probability of transition*

	Polity98 estimates	Gasiorowski estimates
Increase IOScore 1 standard deviation	+62%	+37%
State is a member of no regional IOs	−50%	−39%
Past experience with democracy	+300%	+78%
Military regime	−86%	−83%

These estimates confirm the theory that membership in democratic regional IOs is associated with the transition to democracy. While the discussion of each causal mechanism in Chapter 2 provided illustrative case material to this end, this cross-national statistical examination provides more systematic evidence on the veracity of these ideas. Although these estimates show the importance of one set of external factors, I make no claim that these variables are determining or even the most important in terms of democratic transitions, only that they are significant factors in that process. Other domestic political and economic factors are clearly important as well.

Past experience with democracy and a previous military regime has substantial impacts on the probability of a transition. For both data sets, these variables are consistently statistically significant. This finding concerning $MilitaryRegime_{it}$ is in accord with past empirical literature which finds that these regimes are more difficult to overthrow than single-party or personalistic regimes (Gasiorowski 1995), yet contradicts Geddes' (1999) argument that military regimes may be more susceptible to transitions to democracy. In addition, past experience with democracy ($PastDemocracy_{it}$) is positively related to the propensity for a transition. This is in accordance with the expectations that a history of democracy bodes well for the probability of future transitions to democracy. Both of these variables also have an enormous effect on the predicted probability of a transition. As seen in the third line of Table 4.2, past experience with democracy increases the probability of a transition dramatically for both data sets (in the case of the Polity98 data from .02 to .08 – over 300 percent). Similarly, the final line of the table shows that the presence of a military regime lowers the likelihood of a transition by over 80 percent for both data sets. Clearly, internal characteristics are quite important for the prospects of regime change, even when controlling for the influence of regional organizations.

The estimate of the effect of regional conflicts ($RegConflict_{it}$) on the prospects for democracy are statistically significant in the Polity98 data, but not for the Gasiorowski data. The estimates have the predicted sign across both data sets – increasing regional hostilities lowers the probability of democracy. Again, the difference in spatial coverage may account for the fact that only in the Polity98 data is this variable significant. Europe experiences the highest number of militarized disputes during the vast majority of the period under analysis, largely because of incidents arising out of the Cold War. The lack of democratization in Eastern Europe coincided with a high rate of disputes. Given that these cases are absent in the Gasiorowski data, this relationship is much weaker in the models estimated using his data.

Many of the control variables are of the expected sign, but not all of the estimates achieve statistical significance. One variable with inconsistent estimates, however, is $pcGDP_{it}$. Depending on the data set (and thus the sample) utilized, the influence of wealth differs, but in all cases, the estimate of this influence is not statistically significant. For the Polity data, wealth has a positive effect on the likelihood of transition, yet the opposite seems to hold using the Gasiorowski sample. One implication, given the difference in sample coverage of the two data sets, is that higher economic development *lessens* the probability of democratic transitions when examining only the developing world, but the lack of statistical significance of these estimates should instill caution when interpreting these results. The safest conclusion to draw is that the overall level of development in a country has little direct impact on the likelihood of transitions. This finding is consistent with the Przeworski and Limongi (1997) argument that higher levels of development are associated with the continuation of, rather than the transition to, democracy. The same conclusion can be drawn from the estimates for change in per capita GDP, which shows little influence on the probability of a democratic transition. Recent economic performance seems to have little bearing on the likelihood of a democratic transition, a finding not in accord with past statistical research (Gasiorowski 1995). As I discuss later in this chapter, economic forces seem to play only a minor role in any of the various types of democratic transitions, suggesting that political, societal, and regional variables are more important factors in regime change.

Domestic violence appears to be a clear harbinger of regime change. Recall that this variable is lagged in order to avoid spurious correlations (in violent transitions, the transition could precede the violence). Nonetheless, the presence of domestic violence in the previous year has a positive and statistically significant influence on prospects for democratization. This finding holds across both data sets and suggests that domestic violence is a strong predictor of regime transitions. This finding is surprising given the perception that many regime transitions in the third wave were non-violent. The Banks data, however, includes a wide variety of events in the counts of domestic violence including large-scale strikes and large anti-government demonstrations. If this type of behavior occurs for multiple years before the breakdown of authoritarianism, even though the variable is lagged, an association will still exist between domestic violence and transition.

In consonance with the diffusion and/or contagion hypotheses, the higher proportion of contiguous states that are democracies (higher values of $RegContagion_{it}$), the more likely a state's transition to democracy. This result, however, is only moderately statistically significant in the

Polity98 data. The measure of years since independence (*Independence$_{it}$*) is statistically significant in the Polity98 data, but again, not with the Gasiorowski measures. Finally, the level of ethnic heterogeneity appears to have no bearing on the prospects for transition, as the estimates of *MAR$_i$* are never statistically significant.

Overall, these models provide firm evidence that involvement in democratic regional organizations can encourage the process of democratization. This is strong initial support for the theory, especially since other factors associated with transitions are controlled for in this analysis. Again, several domestic factors seem to play a larger role than regional organizations, yet external forces still play an important role in shaping the likelihood of transition.

Additional tests: assessing possible omitted variables and simultaneity

To ensure that there is no alternative explanation behind the association between regional IOs and democratization, I undertake a specification check on the model, the results of which are reported in Table 4.1. This model evaluates the competing hypothesis that regional organizations reflect the preferences of major power members and that what accounts for transitions to democracies are not the organizations, but the large, democratic major powers that are members. Recall from the discussion in Chapter 3 that only one of the causal processes could be the result of this dynamic, yet it is still an important test to ensure that the institutions are indeed performing as specified by my theory.

To test this alternative hypothesis, I code an additional variable named *MajPowerIO$_{it-1}$* and replace $\Delta IOScore_{it-1}$ in Model 4.1 with this new variable.[21] This codes the number of democratic major powers that are in the most democratic regional organization – the same organization used to generate *IOScore$_{it-1}$*.[22] If the alternate hypothesis is correct, one observable implication is that regional IOs with democratic great powers will be a better predictor of democratization than the *IOScore$_{it-1}$* variable. If these large states use regional organizations as facilitators to pursue their interests in promoting democracy, this new variable should capture this effect. Organizations with no democratic great powers should have no

---

[21] The inclusion of $\Delta IOScore_{it-1}$ makes no difference in the results.

[22] To compute this variable, I determined which particular organization was the most homogenously democratic regional IO of which state *i* was a member in year *t* − *1*. I then counted the number of democratic major powers. For the time period under consideration, this consisted of France, the US, and the UK. Major-power status is determined by Small and Singer 1994. Democratic status was determined by the Polity98 data.

ability to promote democracy, even if they are completely homogenous with reference to regime type. This new variable should be positively associated with transitions, since the key predictor of whether IOs help democratization will be the presence of a major power willing to do the heavy lifting of asserting pressure on authoritarian states to democratize, rather than the nature of their membership.

As the estimates of columns 3 and 4 of Table 4.1 indicate, there is no support for this alternative hypothesis. While the estimate of this new major power variable is positive, meaning a larger chance of transition, the estimate is not statistically significance. Moreover, the estimates of $IOScore_{it-1}$ remain positive and highly significant predictors of democratization. The insignificance of this variable in the Gasiorowski sample is especially telling. Since that sample excludes European states undergoing transition to democracy, much of the variance in $MajPowerIO_{it-1}$ will arise due to US membership in regional organizations. This is an especially critical test since it yields no statistical evidence that the US is playing a dominant role in shaping democratization. Thus, there can be little doubt that in the sample of states analyzed here, there is little systematic influence of major powers on the prospects for democratization. I return to this issue in the next chapter as well.

The final two tests for the influence of omitted variables for the transition model are reported in more detail in the appendix, but I briefly review the results here. The first model adds region-specific fixed effects to the original model test whether there are systematic differences in the probabilities for transitions across each region. By introducing a dummy variable for each geographic region, one can account for factors that may be important in particular regions that are not included in the model.[23] Of course, controlling for these unspecified factors may eliminate any association between IOs and democratization, since the measurement of regional organizations could be serving simply as a proxy for the geographic region. Thus, these estimates will help ensure that our results are not an artifact of omitted variables at the regional level.

---

[23] On the use of region-specific dummies see Feng and Zak 1999. I have chosen to use the region as the unit of analysis for two reasons: one substantive, one methodological. The substantive reason is that in much of the transitions literature, the region is the relevant unit of analysis. Although most studies concentrate on individual countries, these studies are almost always grouped in terms of regions (cf. O'Donnell and Schmitter 1986; Huntington 1991). The methodological reason is that if one moves down a level of analysis to the individual nation-state, much of the data will be lost since any country that does not experience a transition will be excluded from the data set. While this is not a problem econometrically, it does introduce potential bias in the results since one is summarily excluding "the dog that doesn't bark."

The estimates of this model are presented in full in the appendix to this chapter (first and second columns of Table A4.1). In brief, the estimates do not change substantially based on the addition of these region-based variables. The key independent variable of interest, $IOScore_{it-1}$, remains statistically significant in both data sets. It is also important to note that the chi-square test for inclusion of the fixed effects rejects the hypothesis that they should be included in the model, indicating that they are providing little new information.[24]

As another check on the robustness of these findings, the basic model is reestimated with new $IOScore_{it-1}$ and $\Delta IOScore_{it-1}$ variables. As discussed in Chapter 3, only regional IOs are included in the initial computation of these variables. These new models are estimated with revised IO variables that include non-regional organizations, including several universal organizations (United Nations, the Commonwealth, etc.) and the major international and regional financial institutions (IMF, World Bank, African Development Bank, etc.).

The estimates of the model using non-regional IOs are shown in the appendix (columns 3 and 4 of Table A4.1). Note that there are few differences in these results. The sign of the $\Delta IOScore_{it-1}$ variable is in the opposite direction, but as the estimates are not statistically significant, this is not an important issue. The other variable of interest, $IOScore_{it-1}$ remains positive and statistically significant in estimates using both data sets. Although these findings suggest that *both* regional and non-regional IOs may assist in the process of democratization, the theory spelled out in Chapter 2 was more oriented to regional organizations. Thus, I would argue that one should not extrapolate too much from these estimates as one may conceive of different causal theories linking universal organizations and/or financial organizations to democratization. This test is simply meant as a check to ensure the stability of the previous results.

Finally, it is important to ensure that these results are not undermined by simultaneity bias. If countries first undergo transitions to democracy, then join highly democratic regional organizations, a statistical association may exist even though the causal process is reversed. To guard against this possibility, I have lagged the value of *IOScore*. This is the best insurance against a simultaneity problem, since during the year of transition, the *IOScore* from the *previous* year is utilized. Thus, the causal process must begin with a high *IOScore*, followed by democratization. Second, I estimate a model identical to 4.1, but I reverse the dependent

---

[24] Note that the estimates of the control variables remain highly similar to the original model. This is not surprising given that none of the new variables is statistically significant.

and major independent variable (*IOScore*).[25] To show no reverse causation, I measure *IOScore* in year *t*, and the democratic transition in year *t* − *1*. In this model, the estimate of the democratic transition variable is not statistically significant, indicating that democratic transitions have little influence on *IOScore*.[26]

Testing the argument: modeling political liberalization

One implication of the theory as outlined in Chapter 2 is that membership in democratic regional organizations should be associated not only with the prospect of transitions generally, but political liberalization as well. One should be able to break down the democratic transition to see if democratic regional organizations are related to initial political liberalization. In particular, I hypothesize that membership in democratic regional organizations, through either the pressure mechanism or the acquiescence effect, should be associated with initial political liberalization. This section directly tests this proposition by estimating the following model:

$$
\begin{aligned}
(4.2) \quad \text{Liberalization}_{it} = {} & \alpha_0 + \beta_1 \text{IOScore}_{it-1} + \beta_2 \text{pcGDP}_{it} \\
& + \beta_3 \Delta \text{pcGDP}_{it} + \beta_4 \text{Contagion}_{it} + \beta_5 \text{PastDemocracy}_{it} \\
& + \beta_6 \text{RegConflict}_{it} + \beta_7 \text{InternalViolence}_{it-1} \\
& + \beta_8 \text{MilitaryRegime}_{it} + \beta_9 \text{Independence}_{it} + \beta_{10} \text{MAR}_i + \mu_{it}
\end{aligned}
$$

Model 4.2 is nearly identical to Model 4.1.[27] The only difference is the dependent variable. *Liberalization*$_{it}$ measures those transitions where a state moves from an autocracy to either a semi-democracy or a full democracy. For the Polity98 data, this means a state must go from below

---

[25] In addition, $\Delta IOScore_{it-1}$ is excluded. Its inclusion makes no difference in the results.

[26] Two additional specification checks are performed to assess alternative hypotheses. First, I estimate a variant of Model 4.1, substituting NIO_{it-1} for $\Delta IOScore_{it-1}$. This variable measures the number of IOs of which state i is a member in year $t − 1$. If *any* regional organization can fulfill the functions outlined in my theory, regardless of the "democraticness" of the members, this new independent variable should be positive and statistically significant, while $IOScore_{it-1}$ would become statistically insignificant. This is not the case in either data set – while the new variable is positive and nears statistical significance, $IOScore_{it-1}$ remains positive and highly significant. The second model variant substituted a measure of the average level of democracy across *all* regional organizations of which state i is a member. Although this variable always was of the predicted sign, it never attained statistical significance. This is further corroboration that only one democratic IO is needed to supply the functions linking IOs with democratic transitions.

[27] I exclude $\Delta IOScore_{it-1}$ in the remaining models since it was not statistically significant in many of the previous models. Its inclusion in the following sets of models makes no difference in the estimates of the $IOScore_{it-1}$ variable.

the −6 threshold to between the −6 and +6 cutoffs (i.e. from an autocracy to an anocracy) or above the +6 cutoff (i.e. from an autocracy to a democracy).[28] For the Gasiorowski data, this includes transitions from autocracy to semi-democracy, an autocracy to a transitional state, and a semi-democracy to a full democracy.[29] If the state is already an anocracy or democracy, the variable is coded as missing and is excluded from the analysis, since these states cannot experience the event. Otherwise, this variable is coded 0.

This new dependent variable is meant to capture the process of liberalization in autocratic states by measuring movements towards democracy whether they end in partial or full liberalization of the political system.[30] If liberalization "consists of measures which, although entailing a significant opening of the previous bureaucratic-authoritarian regime, remain short of what could be called political democracy" (O'Donnell 1979: 8; see also Przeworski 1991), then partial transitions captured by the $Liberalization_{it}$ variable should adequately measure this process. There is also reason to believe that similar dynamics occur in movements from autocracy to full democracy as well. If the "opening" of the regime moves quickly or goes beyond what its proponents intend, a transition to full democracy can result. Since there is no *a priori* ground on which to exclude these regime changes, they are included in this analysis as well. Given the theory presented in Chapter 2, highly democratic regional IOs should be associated with these political "openings" since fellow members of the organization may push for political opening and/or elites previously opposed to such policies will now acquiesce to these changes.

Statistical results: liberalization

Table 4.3 presents the estimates of Model 4.2. Across both data sets, membership in democratic international organizations is positively associated with political liberalization and this association is statistically

---

[28] Note there is some overlap between these transitions and the ones modeled in the previous section. This section excludes "completion" transitions (from semi-democracies to full democracies), but includes partial transitions, which were not included in the previous section.

[29] I exclude movements from transitional states to full democracies since Gasiorowski's definition of a transitional state requires that some liberalization has already taken place. Even so, the inclusion of these transitions makes little difference in the statistical results.

[30] States which begin as autocracies and become "anocracies" or semi-democracies, for both Gurr and Gasiorowski include polities which have "mixed authority traits" (Gurr 1990: 38) and in which "electoral outcomes, while competitive, still deviate significantly from popular preferences" (Gasiorowski 1993: 2).

Table 4.3 *Estimates of the determinants of liberalization, 1950–92*

	Polity98	Gasiorowski	Polity98	Gasiorowski
IOScore$_{it-1}$	0.111***	0.062**	0.104**	0.060**
	(5.05)	(2.28)	(4.68)	(2.10)
MajPowerIO$_{it-1}$	–.–	–.–	0.111	0.046
			(0.84)	(0.22)
pcGDP$_{it}$	-1.36×10^{-5}	5.11×10^{-6}	-1.46×10^{-5}	1.81×10^{-6}
	(−0.43)	(0.01)	(−0.45)	(0.05)
ΔpcGDP$_{it}$	−0.0001	0.0003	−0.0002	0.0002
	(−0.51)	(0.53)	(−0.53)	(0.52)
RegContagion$_{it}$	0.856**	0.844**	0.935**	0.850**
	(2.08)	(1.99)	(2.23)	(1.99)
PastDemocracy$_{it}$	0.848	0.864***	0.877	0.861***
	(1.48)	(2.71)	(1.63)	(2.68)
RegConflict$_{it}$	−0.314*	−0.236**	−0.316*	−0.240**
	(−1.79)	(−2.08)	(−1.87)	(−2.13)
InternalViolence$_{it-1}$	1.343***	0.434	1.352***	0.430
	(4.24)	(1.35)	(4.27)	(1.35)
MilitaryRegime$_{it}$	−0.693*	−0.126	−0.693*	−0.123
	(−1.74)	(−0.37)	(−1.74)	(−0.36)
Independence$_{it}$	0.001	0.007**	0.0002	0.007*
	(0.20)	(1.97)	(0.08)	(1.97)
Constant	−5.042***	−5.047***	−5.034***	−5.052***
	(−14.36)	(−12.92)	(−14.19)	(−12.71)
N =	2447	2399	2447	2399
Log Likelihood	−303.50	−251.20	−303.20	−251.18
Chi-square	85.40***	78.34***	87.71***	77.49***

Figures in parentheses are asymptotic z-statistics computed using Huber/White/sandwich standard errors.
*** − p <= .01; ** − p <= .05; * − p <= .10; two-tailed tests.

significant. These results largely corroborate the theory that democratic regional organizations are associated with political liberalization.[31]

Table 4.4 shows the predicted probabilities of liberalization based on the coefficient estimates in Table 4.3. For the Polity98 data, membership in a democratic international organization with an *IOScore* one standard deviation higher than the mean increases the likelihood of liberalization over 80 percent. For the Gasiorowski data, the increase is a more modest 30 percent. In addition, as shown in the second row of each table, a state with no IO memberships has a greatly reduced propensity to undergo

---

[31] As in the previous section, the estimates of Δ*IOScore* are not statistically significant. I have chosen to eliminate this term from the model. Its inclusion makes no difference in any of the estimations in this section.

Table 4.4 *Percentage change in probability of liberalization*

	Polity98 estimates	Gasiorowski estimates
Increase IOScore 1 standard deviation	+82%	+32%
State is a member of no regional IOs	−55%	−37%
Past experience with democracy	+136%*	+126%
Military regime	−45%	−13%*

* = estimate is not statistically significant.

political liberalization (55 percent lower for Polity98 and over 35 percent lower for Gasiorowski). These tables illustrate the substantive importance of membership in regional organizations with respect to the domestic liberalization process.

Most of the control variables yield similar findings as the general transition estimates of the previous section, although some vary in their statistical significance. Specifically, $RegContagion_{it}$ now is highly significant in both the Polity98 and Gasiorowski estimates, suggesting demonstration effects are more salient in initial moves towards liberalization. $RegConflict_{it}$ is now also negative and statistically significant in the Gasiorowski data, while it no longer achieves significance in the Polity98 data. This is limited evidence in support of Thompson's (1996) hypothesis that peace is a prerequisite for democracy.

In three cases, variables lose their statistical significance in one data set suggesting they play smaller roles in the liberalization process. The $PastDemocracy_{it}$ variable loses statistical significance in the Polity98 estimates, while $InternalViolence_{it-1}$ and $MilitaryRegime_{it}$ are not statistically significant in the Gasiorowski estimates. In the Gasiorowski data, the influence of $PastDemocracy_{it}$ is still quite strong, as seen in the third line of Table 4.4. This finding does not accord with Przeworski's insights that the presence of a past breakdown may not bode well for future democratization.

The estimate of $InternalViolence_{it-1}$ is highly statistically significant in the Polity98 estimates. This is not entirely surprising given that a common explanation for attempts to open the political sphere in an autocracy is to respond to domestic pressures against the government (O'Donnell and Schmitter 1986; Przeworski 1991). Thus, when confronted with mass uprisings, domestic elites may turn to liberalization to quell this violence.[32] While the estimate of this variable is positive for the Gasiorowski data, it does not achieve statistical significance.

[32] A less pleasant alternate explanation could be that movements towards liberalization create patterns of domestic violence. This violence could be part and parcel of the process

Additional liberalization tests: omitted variables and simultaneity

As with the previous model, I also estimate a variant of Model 4.2, which tests for the influence of major powers in regional IOs and its effects on political liberalization. As in the previous section, I add $MajPowerIO_{it-1}$ to the existing model. These estimates are presented in the third and fourth columns of Table 4.3. As in previous tests of the major power hypothesis, these results yield little evidence that democratic major powers drive these democratization dynamics. The estimates of the control variables remain largely consistent with previous findings.

Two additional sets of estimates are reported in the appendix (Table A4.2). The first set of models includes region-specific fixed effects. As in the previous section, I include dummy variables for each geographic region in addition to the nine original variables. The estimates of $IOScore_{it-1}$ remain stable even with the inclusion of these fixed effects. This is very important since the chi-square test for the inclusion of the region-specific effects rejects the hypothesis for their exclusion. Thus, these variables add a significant amount of information to the model.[33] Finally, the measurement of $IOScore_{it-1}$ is adjusted to include non-regional organizations and international financial institutions. Similar to the results for general transitions, a strong positive association still exists between IO membership and liberalization. Still, these results should be treated as simply a robustness check rather than the final say as to the influence of universal IOs and IFIs on transitions. Taken together, these models all point to the conclusion that democratic regional IOs can enhance the prospects for initial movements towards political liberalization.

Testing the argument: completing the transition to democracy

The second part of the theory relating democratic IOs to transitions involves the effects of IO membership on the probability that a regime moves from the liberalization stage to full democratization. To test this implication of the theory, I use a variant of the general transitions model, labeled Model 4.3:

---

itself or a result of the electoral process that accompanies democratization (Snyder and Ballentine 1996 and Snyder 2000).

[33] The only control variable to change in significance is $Independence_{it}$, which is now not statistically significant in the Gasiorowski estimates.

(4.3) $\text{CompTrans}_{it} = \alpha_0 + \beta_1 \text{IOScore}_{it-1} + \beta_2 \text{pcGDP}_{it}$
$+ \beta_3 \Delta \text{pcGDP}_{it} + \beta_4 \text{Contagion}_{it} + \beta_5 \text{PastDemocracy}_{it}$
$+ \beta_6 \text{RegConflict}_{it} + \beta_7 \text{InternalViolence}_{it-1}$
$+ \beta_8 \text{MilitaryRegime}_{it} + \beta_9 \text{Independence}_{it} + \beta_{10} \text{MAR}_i + \mu_{it}$

Again, the only difference between this and the previous two models is the dependent variable. *CompTrans*$_{it}$, represents changes from anocracy (for Polity98) or semi-democracy (for Gasiorowski) to a full democracy.[34] The relevant sample also changes, since we are now only concerned with anocracies or semi-democracies, since they are the only states which can undergo such transitions. If the theory is correct, involvement in democratic regional IOs should be positively related to the probability of a finishing transition. All independent variables are identical to those in Models 4.1 and 4.2.

Statistical results: completing the transition

Table 4.5 presents the estimates of Model 4.3. In these models, involvement in IOs shows a weaker association with democratization as this variable is statistically significant only in the Polity98 model. My hypothesis that membership in IOs can help complete transitions to democracy by signaling the intent of reformers and/or the acquiescence effect receives very limited support. It is notable that in the following chapter, the only case that finds this causal mechanism at work is an Eastern European transition (Hungary). If this is the only realm where regional IOs (such as the EEC/EU, Partnership for Peace, or the Council of Europe) fulfilled more of a signaling function, then it is not surprising that there is no association between regional IOs and the completion of democracy in the Gasiorowski data, which excludes Eastern Europe. Given these estimates, one can conclude that regional IOs have less influence on completing the transition to democracy compared to general transitions or liberalization.

Table 4.6 presents the predicted probabilities of this type of transition, based on the Polity98 estimates in Table 4.5.[35] The first line of the table shows the increase in the predicted probability of completing a transition to democracy when a state is a member of a regional IO with an IOScore one standard deviation above the mean. The prediction is an impressive 55 percent increase in the likelihood of completion. Moreover, when a

---

[34] In the case of Polity98, the variable represents a movement from between the $-6/+6$ range to the $+6$ threshold or above.

[35] No predicted probabilities are computed for the Gasiorowski data since few variables achieve statistical significance.

Table 4.5 *Estimates of the determinants of democratic completion, 1950–92*

	Polity98	Gasiorowski	Polity98	Gasiorowski
IOScore$_{it-1}$	0.085***	0.049	0.041	0.051
	(2.68)	(0.98)	(1.21)	(0.95)
MajPowerIO$_{it-1}$	–.–	–.–	0.596***	−0.051
			(2.98)	(−0.15)
pcGDP$_{it}$	0.0001	−0.0001*	0.0001	−0.0001*
	(1.46)	(−1.76)	(1.64)	(−1.75)
ΔpcGDP$_{it}$	−0.001*	0.0002	−0.001*	0.0002
	(−1.77)	(0.32)	(−1.85)	(0.34)
RegContagion$_{it}$	0.413	0.498	0.712	0.472
	(0.53)	(0.63)	(0.83)	(0.54)
PastDemocracy$_{it}$	1.913***	−0.748	1.786***	0.760
	(4.61)	(−1.60)	(4.36)	(1.61)
RegConflict$_{it}$	−0.295	0.448**	−0.308	0.455**
	(−1.60)	(2.21)	(−1.49)	(2.22)
InternalViolence$_{it-1}$	1.160	0.630	1.070	0.628
	(1.55)	(1.12)	(1.42)	(1.12)
MilitaryRegime$_{it}$	−1.146	−1.512	−1.266	−1.505
	(−1.43)	(−1.64)	(−1.51)	(−1.63)
Independence$_{it}$	0.007	0.004	0.008*	0.004
	(1.47)	(0.52)	(1.81)	(0.53)
MAR$_i$	−0.074	−0.434*	−0.135*	−0.428
	(−0.86)	(−1.70)	(−1.65)	(−1.60)
Constant	−6.291***	−2.123***	−6.168***	−2.133***
	(−8.68)	(−2.94)	(−8.67)	(−2.90)
N =	864	405	864	405
Log likelihood	−98.52	−93.35	−95.16	−93.33
Chi-square	81.14***	22.46**	62.84***	23.17***

Figures in parentheses are asymptotic z-statistics computed using Huber/White/sandwich standard errors.
*** − $p <= .01$; ** − $p <= .05$; * − $p <= .10$; two-tailed tests.

state is a member of no regional institution, it is far less likely to move from an anocracy to a full democracy.

Unfortunately, only a handful of variables in either model are statistically significant. For the Polity98 data, past experience with democracy seems to bode well for the probability of competing the transition, while for Gasiorowski the opposite holds true, although this latter estimate is not statistically significant. It is also interesting to note that ethnic/racial diversity seems to have little influence on the completion process. This runs counter to the hypothesis of Linz and Stepan (1996) that a high

Table 4.6 *Probabilites of completion of democratic transition*

	Polity98 estimates
Increase IOScore by 1 standard deviation	+55%
State is a member of no regional IOs	−59%
Past experience with democracy	+450%
Military regime	−68%

amount of ethno-linguistic diversity does not bode well for completing a transition to democracy. MAR_i is always negative, yet achieves statistical significance only in the Gasiorowski estimates.

For the Polity98 data, increases in the growth rates of per capita GDP do not bode well for completing the transition. The interpretation of this result is similar to that of this finding in Model 4.1. Namely, in good economic times, there are few complaints about the limited nature of democracy or the remaining vestiges of authoritarian rule (see Haggard and Kaufman 1995b). Thus, completing the transition to democracy becomes a less pressing issue.

Overall, these models provide limited support for the idea that regional institutions are related to the completion stage of democratization. While this association is strong in the Polity98 data, the relationship does not exist in the Gasiorowski estimates. Unfortunately, even the finding in the Polity98 data proves to be fairly fragile, as shown in the next section.

Additional tests on completing the transition: omitted variables and robustness checks

As with the previous two models, it is essential to test for the alternate realist-based hypothesis that democratic great powers drive the relationship between regional IOs and democracy. Once again, I include $MajPowerIO_{it-1}$ to control for the influence of democratic major powers in the most democratic regional institutions for each state i. As shown in the third and fourth columns of Table 4.5, the results show some support for the major power argument.

The previous association between regional IOs and the completion of democracy in the Polity98 data disappears with the addition of this new variable. The new variable is itself positive and statistically significant, suggesting great powers in regional organizations make the end-stage of the transition more likely. The influence of $IOScore_{it-1}$ remains positive, but loses statistical significance. This same pattern does not hold in the

Gasiorowski estimates – neither measure of regional institutions achieves statistical significance.[36]

Why would major powers play a role only with the completion of democracy and only in one of the data sets? This is the only instance where the major power variable achieves statistical significance. An analysis of the data in this model sheds some light on this finding.[37] Since the relevant area of non-overlap between the Gasiorowski and the Polity data is Europe, one can examine which completion cases are creating this finding. Four cases of completion exist in the Polity data that are not included in the Gasiorowski data – France 1969, Poland 1990, Hungary 1990, and Russia 1991. Three of the cases are post-Cold War Eastern European transitions. The relevant organizations for these states have high IOScores, but they also contain multiple democratic great powers (the EU, OSCE [Organization for Security and Cooperation in Europe], Council of Europe, NATO).

A realist could also make a case that all the democratic major powers had strong preferences for democratic completion in Eastern Europe and that this preference was more important than the presence of regional organizations themselves. The US, France, and Great Britain were each important actors attempting to cement the post-1989 trend to democracy in that region. Does this mean the regional institutions themselves were less important than the interests of the major powers? I contend that the balance of evidence in the case of Hungary (one of the cases accounting for the major power result), which I analyze in the next chapter, suggests that the answer is no. Regional institutions were important for the completion of the transition in Hungary, independent of the efforts of the large democratic states. The major causal mechanisms at work were socialization and legitimization – each of the mechanisms is difficult to imagine in a bilateral context. The legitimization factor was especially important as the case evidence indicates that the multilateral nature of the European Union, the Council of Europe, and the OSCE were an important force moving the Hungarian transitional government to the status

---

[36] An alternative set of estimates yields slightly different results. Changing the *MajPowerIO* variable from a continuous to an indicator variable leads the estimate of *IOScore* to remain statistically significant, although the new *MajPowerIO* variable is also statistically significant. Thus, regional organizations in combination with major powers seem to play a role in these new estimates. The results of the Gasiorowski estimates do not change.

[37] It is useful to note that the frequency of democratic completions in the Polity98 data is nearly equal to those cases of full democratic transitions (analyzed in the next section). There are 27 cases of democratic completions in the Polity98 data and 25 cases of full transitions. Thus, democratic completion cases do not comprise the bulk of the general transition cases.

of a full-fledged democracy. Multilateral institutions played a key role in legitimizing Hungarian reforms domestically (Fitzmaurice 1998: 184; Kun 1993: 47). It is doubtful this process could have been accomplished solely by the major powers, since the legitimization arose from association with a multilateral "club," not from one or two particular states (Batt 1994: 176).

The four European cases account for the difference between the democratic completion estimates and the remainder of the estimates in this chapter where the major power variable is not statistically significant. It should also be noted, however, that the case studies of Turkey (Chapter 5) and Greece (Chapter 7) suggest that the US did attempt to play a unilateral role in the democratization process. As I discuss in each of those studies, however, the balance of the evidence suggests that the multilateral institutions also played an important role. Still, we are reminded that the major powers are important actors that we cannot fail to account for in explanations of outcomes involving international and regional institutions.

As a further check for omitted variable bias, I estimate a version of Model 4.3 including region-specific fixed effects. The results are shown formally in Table A4.3 in the appendix. When one accounts for region-specific effects, the influence of regional IO membership strengthens in the Polity98 data and remains minimal in the Gasiorowski estimates. The results appear to be robust against the inclusion of region-based influences unaccounted for in the model. As shown in the bottom of the table, however, the chi-square test of inclusion of the fixed effects shows that they can be safely excluded in the Polity98 model while their inclusion in the Gasiorowski model is questionable.

Finally, I examine the influence of non-regional organizations and IFIs on the democratic completion process. Recall from Chapter 3 that while these other organizations could influence democratization, they are likely to do so in ways that are not captured by the current measurement scheme. These estimates may be found in columns 3 and 4 of Table A4.3. In neither the Polity98 nor the Gasiorowski estimates is the new version of $IOScore_{it-1}$ statistically significant. Thus, although the addition of non-regional organizations did not influence the previous two models, the current model weakens significantly. I emphasize that these findings are not the final word on this issue, but rather indicate the robustness of the previous results to the inclusion of other international institutions. Clearly, alternate model specifications and additional case studies are necessary before one could assert any relationship with confidence.

Testing the argument: full transitions

The final type of transition to analyze is the movement from complete authoritarianism to full democracy, which I label full transitions. Although this type of transition is rarely treated as a separate process in the comparative politics literature, it is important to ensure that this particular political process does not lie outside the scope of the current theory. To determine the influence of regional organizations on full transitions, I estimate the following model:

$$
\begin{aligned}
(4.4) \quad \text{FullTrans}_{it} &= \alpha_0 + \beta_1 \text{IOScore}_{it-1} + \beta_2 \text{pcGDP}_{it} \\
&+ \beta_3 \Delta \text{pcGDP}_{it} + \beta_4 \text{Contagion}_{it} + \beta_5 \text{PastDemocracy}_{it} \\
&+ \beta_6 \text{RegConflict}_{it} + \beta_7 \text{InternalViolence}_{it-1} \\
&+ \beta_8 \text{MilitaryRegime}_{it} + \beta_9 \text{Independence}_{it} + \beta_{10} \text{MAR}_i + \mu_{it}
\end{aligned}
$$

All independent variables in Model 4.4 are identical to the previous models. The dependent variable measures transitions of states that begin as authoritarian regimes, and make a complete transition to a democratic regime. The theory predicts that membership in regional organizations should have a positive influence on the probability for a full transition to democracy.

Statistical results: full transitions

The estimates of Model 4.4 are presented in columns 1 and 2 of Table 4.7. In both the Polity98 and Gasiorowski estimates, the influence of regional IOs is positive and statistically significant. Table 4.8 presents the changes in predicted probability based on the estimates of Table 4.7. Note that the *IOScore* variable has a substantively strong effect on the probability of a full transition. Increasing the value of this variable by one standard deviation yields a 75 percent and 50 percent increase in the probability of transition for the Polity98 and Gasiorowski data respectively. A state lacking any memberships in regional IOs suffers a significant decline in the probability of transition – in both sets of estimates, a drop of over 50 percent. Clearly regional organizations play an important role in this final subset of transitions.

Turning to the control variables, many of the estimates are consistent with previous models. Consistent with the general transition results (Model 4.1), regional military conflicts as well as the presence of a military regime continue to decrease the probability of democratization, although these estimates are only statistically significant in the Polity98 estimates. Past experience with democracy also continues to greatly increase the

Table 4.7 *Estimates of the determinants of full democratic transitions, 1950–92*

	Polity98	Gasiorowski	Polity98	Gasiorowski
IOScore$_{it-1}$	0.112**	0.136*	0.132***	0.142*
	(2.53)	(1.90)	(2.98)	(1.80)
MajPowerIO$_{it-1}$	–.–	–.–	−0.439	−0.075
			(−1.17)	(−0.21)
pcGDP$_{it}$	1.77×10^{-5}	−0.0004	1.60×10^{-5}	−0.0004
	(1.38)	(−1.50)	(0.36)	(−1.43)
ΔpcGDP$_{it}$	−0.0003	0.002	−0.0003	0.002
	(−0.87)	(1.18)	(−0.91)	(1.16)
RegContagion$_{it}$	1.385**	−4.790	1.032	−4.806
	(2.09)	(−1.33)	(1.47)	(−1.36)
PastDemocracy$_{it}$	1.287	1.852**	1.160	1.874**
	(1.33)	(2.07)	(1.19)	(2.06)
RegConflict$_{it}$	−0.609*	−0.276	−0.684*	−0.269
	(−1.73)	(−0.81)	(−1.77)	(−0.82)
InternalViolence$_{it-1}$	3.683***	0.368	3.693***	0.390
	(3.77)	(0.44)	(3.77)	(0.44)
MilitaryRegime$_{it}$	−3.019**	−1.388	−3.014**	−1.402
	(−1.99)	(−1.23)	(−2.06)	(−1.25)
Independence$_{it}$	0.004	0.003	0.004	0.003
	(0.63)	(0.29)	(0.76)	(0.28)
MAR$_i$	−0.111	0.183**	−0.111	0.182**
	(−1.38)	(2.13)	(−1.24)	(2.13)
Constant	−8.241***	−6.791***	−8.177***	−6.814***
	(−8.00)	(−6.68)	(−8.09)	(−6.48)
N =	2432	2473	2432	2473
Log likelihood	−99.88	−53.78	−98.86	−53.77
Chi-square	69.24***	34.03***	71.45***	33.11***

Figures in parentheses are asymptotic z-statistics computed using Huber/White/sandwich standard errors.
*** − p <= .01; ** − p <= .05; * − p <= .10; two-tailed tests.

Table 4.8 *Probabilities of full transitions*

	Polity98 estimates	Gasiorowski estimates
Increase IOScore 1 standard deviation	+75%	+50%
State is a member of no regional IOs	−51%	−60%
Past experience with democracy	+150%*	+170%
Military regime	−95%	−43%*

* = estimate is not statistically significant.

chances of transitions, especially in the Gasiorowski estimates where this variable is statistically significant.

Interestingly, the economic-based variables show little influence in these estimates, suggesting that political, military and social factors are more important than economic forces. In all four sets of models in this chapter, economic factors are rarely statistically significant, suggesting a broad trend in the data. Namely, when one controls for a host of regional and domestic political factors, economic forces fade in significance. Taken together, these estimates are strong evidence in favor of the Przeworski and Limongi (1997) hypothesis that economic conditions do more to influence the prospects for democratic survival than democratic transition. I return to this issue in Chapter 6.

Additional tests on full transitions: omitted variables and robustness checks

As with the previous models, it is important to ensure that full transition results are robust with respect to omitted variables and other model specification checks. First, I include $MajPowerIO_{it-1}$ to control for the influence of democratic major powers in the most democratic regional institutions for each state i. As shown in the third and fourth columns of Table 4.7, the regional IO variables continue to achieve statistical significance. Moreover, the estimates of the major power variable are of the wrong sign – the presence of more democratic great power members depresses the probability that a state will make a full transition to democracy, although these estimates are not statistically significant. As discussed in the previous section, only in the completion of democracy model are democratic major powers correlated with democratization. We can be relatively confident that regional organizations have an independent influence on full transitions to democracy.

A check for omitted variable bias in the form of region-based fixed effects yields similar results. These estimates are shown in columns 1 and 2 of Table A4.4 in the appendix. Note that in the Gasiorowski estimates, the addition of the fixed effects does weaken the influence of $IOScore_{it-1}$, yet, the chi-square test for the appropriateness of the fixed effects allows us to confidently reject their inclusion. Thus, little evidence of omitted variable bias surfaces.

As a final check, I re-estimate Model 4.4 including all international organizations in the $IOScore_{it-1}$ variable. These results are presented in columns 3 and 4 of Table A4.4 in the appendix. Similar to the completion results, the addition of the non-regional organizations lowers the influence of the IO variable in the Polity98 estimates (although the estimate would be significant at the p < .1 level with a one-tailed test). The same pattern does not hold for the Gasiorowski estimates that remain robust to the inclusion of non-regional organizations. Altogether, in two cases out of eight the addition of non-regional organizations decreases the correlation between IOs and democratization. Although it is beyond the scope of this book, further theoretical and empirical work could be done to explore how and why these larger, non-regional organizations have varying influences on the different types and phases of democratic transitions.

One final note is in order regarding the statistical results of this chapter. One could argue that one statistical test for different causal mechanisms would be to distinguish between different issue-orientations within regional organizations (e.g. security versus economic). Unfortunately, the theoretical foundations of these causal mechanisms do not suggest that they will work exclusively through a particular type of organization, even though the empirical evidence may push towards this conclusion. For example, all examples of socialization discussed in Chapter 2 involved military organizations. Yet, there is no reason why the various causal processes cannot occur within different types of organizations.

As a robustness check, however, I re-estimate each model in this chapter using only particular types of organizations. For example, in one set of runs, I include only membership in economic organizations as the explanatory variable. Another set includes only military/security organizations. In each of these cases, there is no evidence that any particular type of organization encourages democracy more strongly than another. Rarely is one organization type statistically significant, and there is variation in the size and direction of this impact given the data set employed and the type of transition. Rather than draw inferences from these weak results, I simply conclude that issue area plays little role in determining whether regional organizations influence the prospects for democratization in member states.

Conclusion

These statistical results provide substantial support for much of the theory linking regional IOs to transitions presented in Chapter 2. Of course, as one may notice, examining the comparative probabilities of Tables 4.2, 4.4, 4.6, and 4.8, changes in the "democraticness" of a regional IO does not have the largest impact on the probability of a transition to democracy, liberalization, the completion of a transition, nor the prospects for a full transition to democracy. Indeed, my argument is not that external factors, including regional IOs, are *the* most important factor in determining the fate of an autocratic regime. Rather, I argue that one important influence on the dynamics of transition and liberalization is the degree of a state's involvement in regional organizations.

Factors such as previous experience with democracy, economic stability, and the nature of the previous regime may be more important than variables external to the state. The results in this chapter validate much of the existing democratization literature's emphasis on these internal variables. Still, these statistical tests have shown that the external dimension, especially regional organizations, cannot be ignored. The key issue is that these statistical analyses allow us to control for internal factors while estimating the influence of external processes. These sets of variables are not mutually exclusive – indeed my theory suggests that at times, internal and external factors may work in concordance with one another to encourage democratization, as in the case of regional institutions creating economic pressures on states to democratize (or redemocratize).

Numerous alternative explanations were also tested in this chapter and received little support. Nearly all of the results remain consistent when European cases are excluded from the analyses using the Gasiorowski data (the exception is the completion results in Table 4.6). This allows us to rule out the idea of European exceptionalism as the driving force in these findings. Moreover, controlling for the presence of democratic great powers (again, excepting one case) yields no evidence that it is American-led policies that are wholly accounting for the observed association between regional organizations and democracy. Finally, the inclusion of broader non-regional organizations and international financial institutions has a minor degrading influence on the results as predicted in Chapter 3.

Of course, these large-N tests cannot tell us which of the causal mechanisms function in any given case. The following chapter presents three case studies investigating which of these causal processes are at work.

Appendix

Table A4.1 *Estimates of the determinants of the transition to democracy,*
1950–92, with region-specific fixed effects and non-regional IOs

	Region fixed effects		Non-regional IOs[b]	
	Polity98	Gasiorowski	Polity98	Gasiorowski
IOScore$_{it-1}$	0.119***	0.1024***	0.104***	0.116***
	(2.81)	(2.84)	(2.72)	(3.19)
ΔIOScore$_{it-1}$	0.085*	0.034	−0.365	−0.158
	(1.87)	(0.65)	(−1.62)	(−1.45)
pcGDP$_{it}$	5.52×10^{-5}	-2.99×10^{-6}	2.60×10^{-5}	-3.39×10^{-5}
	(1.43)	(−0.06)	(0.81)	(−0.71)
ΔpcGDP$_{it}$	−0.0004*	0.0006	−0.0003	0.0007*
	(−1.71)	(1.62)	(−1.32)	(1.88)
RegContagion$_{it}$	0.598***	0.533	1.137**	0.730*
	(1.08)	(1.22)	(2.47)	(1.76)
PastDemocracy$_{it}$	1.588***	0.356	1.586***	0.637**
	(4.59)	(1.12)	(4.80)	(2.45)
RegConflict$_{it}$	−0.445***	−0.132	−0.469***	−0.167
	(−2.80)	(−1.20)	(−2.92)	(−1.45)
InternalViolence$_{it-1}$	2.306***	1.036***	2.285***	0.987***
	(4.04)	(2.89)	(4.08)	(2.84)
MilitaryRegime$_{it}$	−2.197***	−1.804***	−2.028***	−1.694***
	(−2.97)	(−3.29)	(−2.92)	(−3.19)
Independence$_{it}$	0.007	0.007	0.007**	0.006*
	(1.50)	(1.17)	(2.10)	(1.68)
EUROPE	−0.635	−.−[a]	−.−	−.−
	(−0.91)			
NORTHAMERICA	−0.878	−1.031	−.−	−.−
	(−0.85)	(−0.97)		
SOUTHAMERICA	−0.001	−0.184	−.−	−.−
	(−0.00)	(−0.39)		
AFRICA	0.269	0.296	−.−	−.−
	(0.50)	(0.71)		
MIDDLEEAST	−0.976	−0.947	−.−	−.−
	(−1.42)	(−1.51)		
Constant	−7.334***	−5.453***	−7.653***	−6.031***
	(−10.03)	(−9.50)	(−11.46)	(−10.72)
Inclusion Chi-square	6.39	7.04	−.−	−.−
p > Chi-square	0.270	0.134		
N =	3291	2722	3296	2733
Log likelihood	−204.47	−269.09	−209.54	−271.38
Chi-square	115.93***	68.35***	105.24***	75.87

Figures in parentheses are asymptotic z-statistics computed using Huber/White/sandwich standard errors.

*** − p <= .01; ** − p <= .05; * − p <= .10; two-tailed tests.

[a] -> Because Europe is not included in the Gasiorowski data set, the dummy for this region is excluded from the model.

[b] -> Includes non-regional organizations and IFIs.

Table A4.2 *Estimates of the determinants of liberalization, 1950–92, with region-specific fixed effects and non-regional IOs*

	Region fixed effects		Non-regional IOs[b]	
	Polity98	Gasiorowski	Polity98	Gasiorowski
IOScore$_{it-1}$	0.130***	0.107**	0.140***	0.114***
	(4.21)	(2.51)	(4.38)	(3.11)
pcGDP$_{it}$	2.30×10^{-5}	3.57×10^{-5}	-1.02×10^{-5}	-1.15×10^{-6}
	(0.73)	(0.80)	(−0.36)	(−0.03)
ΔpcGDP$_{it}$	-5.91×10^{-5}	0.0003	−0.0001	0.0003
	(−0.20)	(0.51)	(−0.39)	(0.58)
RegContagion$_{it}$	0.707	0.425	1.069***	0.822**
	(1.39)	(0.82)	(2.62)	(2.02)
PastDemocracy$_{it}$	0.895	0.606*	0.888	0.906***
	(1.52)	(1.75)	(1.56)	(2.88)
RegConflict$_{it}$	−0.264*	−0.210*	−0.325*	−0.243**
	(−1.70)	(−1.78)	(−1.87)	(−2.14)
InternalViolence$_{it-1}$	1.339***	0.464	1.349***	0.429
	(4.05)	(1.42)	(4.26)	(1.34)
MilitaryRegime$_{it}$	−0.966**	−0.323	−0.691*	−0.072
	(−2.11)	(−0.90)	(−1.68)	(−0.21)
Independence$_{it}$	0.003	0.007	0.002	0.007**
	(0.60)	(1.38)	(0.50)	(2.13)
EUROPE	−0.711	–.–[a]	–.–	–.–
	(−1.15)			
NORTHAMERICA	−1.025	−1.370	–.–	–.–
	(−1.40)	(−1.60)		
SOUTHAMERICA	0.096	0.279	–.–	–.–
	(0.16)	(0.51)		
AFRICA	0.332	0.195	–.–	–.–
	(0.77)	(0.40)		
MIDDLEEAST	−0.724	−1.158	–.–	–.–
	(−1.09)	(−1.54)		
Constant	−5.252***	−5.272***	−5.891***	−5.960***
	(−10.74)	(−9.03)	(−12.56)	(−10.97)
Inclusion Chi-square	9.82*	11.93**	–.–	–.–
p > Chi-square	0.08	0.02		
N =	2447	2399	2447	2406
Log likelihood	−298.59	−245.23	−306.53	−249.92
Chi-square	92.81***	98.57***	87.48***	73.75**

Figures in parentheses are asymptotic z-statistics computed using Huber/White/sandwich standard errors.

*** − p <= .01; ** − p <= .05; * − p <= .10; two-tailed tests.

[a] -> Because Europe is not included in the Gasiorowski data set, the dummy for this region is excluded from the model.

[b] -> Includes non-regional organizations and IFIs.

Table A4.3 *Estimates of the determinants of democratic completion, 1950–92, with region-specific fixed effects and non-regional IOs*

	Region fixed effects		Non-regional IOs[b]	
	Polity98	Gasiorowski	Polity98	Gasiorowski
$IOScore_{it-1}$	0.119***	0.101	0.076	0.004
	(2.86)	(1.48)	(1.38)	(0.05)
$pcGDP_{it}$	0.0001	−0.001*	0.0001	−0.0001*
	(1.57)	(−1.73)	(1.48)	(−1.70)
$\Delta pcGDP_{it}$	−0.002**	0.0001	−0.001*	0.0003
	(−2.25)	(0.09)	(−1.83)	(0.39)
$RegContagion_{it}$	0.439	0.826	0.621	0.606
	(0.52)	(0.87)	(0.84)	(0.79)
$PastDemocracy_{it}$	1.784	−0.775	1.968***	−0.697
	(3.10)	(−1.61)	(4.39)	(−1.49)
$RegConflict_{it}$	−0.388*	0.431*	−0.281	0.465**
	(−1.94)	(1.85)	(−1.58)	(2.31)
$InternalViolence_{it-1}$	1.187	0.762	1.170	0.716
	(1.45)	(1.25)	(1.59)	(1.32)
$MilitaryRegime_{it}$	−1.268	−1.344	−1.237	−1.508
	(−1.55)	(−1.32)	(−1.54)	(−1.62)
$Independence_{it}$	0.014**	0.015	0.008	0.006
	(2.01)	(1.26)	(1.61)	(0.80)
MAR_i	−0.088	−0.373	−0.074	−0.427*
	(−0.98)	(−1.41)	(−0.81)	(1.64)
EUROPE	−1.510	−.−[a]	−.−	−.−
	(−1.15)			
NORTHAMERICA	−2.136	−1.923	−.−	−.−
	(−1.28)	(−0.52)		
SOUTHAMERICA	−0.943	−1.424	−.−	−.−
	(−1.18)	(−1.26)		
AFRICA	−.−[b]	0.881	−.−	−.−
		(0.98)		
MIDDLEEAST	−1.435**	−2.688***	−.−	−.−
	(−1.99)	(−2.86)		
Constant	−6.316***	−3.283***	−6.505***	−1.953
	(−6.96)	(−2.70)	(−7.20)	(−1.62)
Inclusion Chi-square	4.68	8.96*	−.−	−.−
p > Chi-square	0.32	0.06		
N =	864	405	864	405
Log likelihood	−96.18	−88.87	−99.70	−93.82
Chi-square	86.17***	33.11***	77.71***	20.87**

Figures in parentheses are asymptotic z-statistics computed using Huber/White/sandwich standard errors.

*** − p <= .01; ** − p <= .05; * − p <= .10; two-tailed tests.

[a] -> Because Europe is not included in the Gasiorowski data set, the dummy for this region is excluded from the model.

[b] -> Includes non-regional organizations and IFIs.

Table A4.4 *Estimates of the determinants of full democratic transitions, 1950–92, with region-specific fixed effects and non-regional IOs*

	Region fixed effects		Non-regional IOs[b]	
	Polity98	Gasiorowski	Polity98	Gasiorowski
$IOScore_{it-1}$	0.132**	0.139	0.103	0.308***
	(2.08)	(1.57)	(1.59)	(3.22)
$pcGDP_{it}$	3.58×10^{-5}	−0.0004	1.76×10^{-5}	−0.0004*
	(0.47)	(−1.55)	(0.42)	(−1.87)
$\Delta pcGDP_{it}$	−0.0004	0.002	−0.0002	0.002
	(−0.81)	(1.13)	(−0.68)	(1.16)
$RegContagion_{it}$	1.376	−4.674	1.637**	−4.800
	(1.46)	(−1.35)	(2.36)	(−1.37)
$PastDemocracy_{it}$	1.599	1.950**	1.431	1.972**
	(1.26)	(2.08)	(1.51)	(2.29)
$RegConflict_{it}$	−0.453	−0.217	−0.580*	−0.254
	(−1.30)	(−0.57)	(−1.74)	(−0.75)
$InternalViolence_{it-1}$	3.747***	0.360	3.680***	0.418
	(3.89)	(0.44)	(3.75)	(0.51)
$MilitaryRegime_{it}$	−3.600*	−1.320	−3.147**	−1.321
	(−1.69)	(−1.21)	(−2.00)	(−1.19)
$Independence_{it}$	0.005	0.003	0.005	0.003
	(0.53)	(0.24)	(0.83)	(0.36)
MAR_i	−0.107	0.191*	−0.119	0.143*
	(−1.51)	(1.86)	(−1.59)	(1.65)
EUROPE	1.071	–.–[a]	–.–	–.–
	(0.80)			
NORTHAMERICA	0.563	0.770	–.–	–.–
	(0.33)	(0.96)		
SOUTHAMERICA	1.594	–.–[c]	–.–	–.–
	(1.37)			
AFRICA	2.194**	0.192	–.–	–.–
	(2.03)	(0.19)		
MIDDLEEAST	0.406	0.379	–.–	–.–
	(0.27)	(0.46)		
Constant	−9.918***	−7.056***	−8.597***	−9.373***
	(−6.83)	(−4.78)	(−7.69)	(−6.35)
Inclusion Chi-square	8.90	0.40	–.–	–.–
p > Chi-square	0.11	0.94		
N =	2432	2473	2432	2481
Log Likelihood	−95.43	−53.58	−102.03	−52.12
Chi-square	80.55***	41.46***	72.50***	44.93***

Figures in parentheses are asymptotic z-statistics computed using Huber/White/sandwich standard errors.

*** − p <= .01; ** − p <= .05; * − p <= .10; two-tailed tests.

[a] -> Because Europe is not included in the Gasiorowski data set, the dummy for this region is excluded from the model.

[b] -> In these models, $IOScore_{it-1}$ includes non-regional organizations and IFIs.

[c] -> The fixed effect for South America is omitted since there are no cases of democratic completion in South America during this period.

5 Regional organizations and the transition to democracy: evidence from cases

The following two chapters provide six illustrative case studies that examine the causal relationship between regional organizations and democratization. The statistical evidence presented in Chapter 4 provides substantial confirmation of the hypothesis that regional IOs are associated statistically with democratic transitions. Yet, the macro-oriented nature of those tests makes it difficult to identify the particular causal processes behind the correlations in the data. These case studies will help to tease out the exact nature of the link between regional IOs and democratic transitions.

Turning to the cases in this chapter, Hungary and Peru are categorized as a success and partial success as a result of their respective status democracies. Both provide evidence that regional institutions can play a role in both the initial movement to democracy (liberalization in Peru) and the completion of democratic transitions (Hungary). The third case study in this chapter, Turkey, illustrates the effectiveness of several European organizations at encouraging redemocratization, but also points to the failure of those organizations in assisting in the consolidation of democracy. Chapter 7 presents studies of how regional organizations have enhanced the prospects for democracy's survival in Greece, Paraguay, and Guatemala. Again, Turkey is a key case providing evidence against these propositions concerning consolidation, although I place Turkey with the transition studies.

Case selection

Before moving into the case studies, I discuss the criteria used to select cases. I have attempted to select cases to maximize variation on several factors in order to enhance the ability to draw valid inferences from the population at large. Each case is broken down temporally, which yields more observations from which to draw inferences (King, Keohane, and Verba 1994). For example, Turkey, Peru, and Paraguay contain multiple episodes allowing for multiple observations and examinations of causal mechanisms. The cases were chosen to introduce variation on the dependent variable, the wealth of the state, and geographic region. To test my hypothesis while controlling for the influence of other factors, I utilize process tracing as my method of inquiry (see George and McKeown 1985).

Including cases that vary in outcome is important since it allows one to highlight and explore empirical anomalies. Turkey and Peru are included for this reason. A member of several highly democratic international organizations, Turkey has suffered three breakdowns of democracy in the past forty years. It is important to discover what processes are at work that may provide countervailing evidence to my hypotheses. What makes Turkey an intriguing puzzle is that its membership in IOs *has* helped it to redemocratize, especially in the early 1980s, yet has not enhanced its democratic longevity. Peru, on the other hand, has made progress toward redemocratization with pressure from the Organization of American States (OAS). Yet, many observers of Latin American politics contend that it has yet to complete its transition to democracy (Hakim 2000). This study will investigate the OAS's role in this controversy and its current efforts to pressure Peru to advance liberalization.

Variation among the cases in terms of wealth is also important, given the democratization literature's emphasis on development as a factor in transitions and consolidation. Although none of the six states is enormously wealthy, there is variation among them in terms of national income. Guatemala (I\$1480 per capita GDP), Paraguay (I\$2663 pcGDP) and Peru (I\$3422 pcGDP) can be labeled "poor" states, while Turkey (I\$4525 pcGDP) and Hungary (I\$5290 pcGDP) belong to a class of "semi-periphery" states that are neither fully developed nor hopelessly underdeveloped.[1] Finally, Greece (I\$9436 pcGDP) represents a developed state, although by Western European standards, Greece barely crosses this threshold. Given the importance of economic pressures and incentives to both the transition and consolidation argument, it is important to introduce variance on this variable to ensure there is no systematic bias in the influence of the causal mechanisms in relation to the income level of the state.

Regional variation is essential if one is to make inferences concerning regional organizations and democracy. These cases provide examples from Europe (Southern and Eastern) and Latin America. This variation allows one to investigate the possibility that the causal mechanisms at work in Peru, Paraguay, and Guatemala also influence Eastern European

---

[1] Figures are from 1996 expressed in 1987 constant international dollars, based on a purchasing-power parity index. Data taken from World Bank 1998.

democratization. It also guards against the possibility that only certain regional organizations (e.g. the EEC/EU) are helpful in the democratization process.

One criticism of the cases selected is that there are no "hard" instances of transition or consolidation, given that I have chosen Europe and Latin America as my regions for inquiry. I argue that these concerns are misplaced. The purpose of these case studies is not to test a broad hypothesis connecting regional IOs to democratization. The statistical tests of Chapters 4 and 6 are appropriate for that task. Rather, I seek to explain why these correlations exist in the aggregate data in order to test for the presence of the various causal mechanisms. The danger is that selecting easy cases will undermine the inferences drawn from these cases, since it is possible that common background influences give rise to the correlation. This omitted variable bias would mean that *none* of the causal mechanisms specified by my theory was at play, but rather a set of unspecified conditions driving the behavior of the actors. In each case, however, I identify evidence that regional IOs had an independent influence on the outcome and that my findings are not the result of omitted variable bias. I discuss a number of background conditions while highlighting the presence and/or effectiveness (or ineffectiveness) of my hypothesized causal mechanisms.

I would also disagree with the characterization of these regions, especially Latin America, as "easy." The cases demonstrate that there were *real* threats to democracy in each state. If underlying conditions were as propitious for democracy as some observers claim, why would these threats have arisen in the first place? Moreover, while these underlying conditions might have meant that the threats would fade in the absence of the regional organization, these cases demonstrate that in each instance the regional institution itself is a key actor. Each case highlights other influences and pieces together the causal story in the context of each country's background conditions. In addition, not all of these cases provide complete support for my conclusions, suggesting that these were not all "easy" cases for my theory.

Second, these case studies demonstrate that an important element of the "underlying conditions" is the regional organizations themselves. I would argue that one of the major factors that creates the perception of Europe as a stable environment for democracy is regional organizations such as the EEC/EU and the Council of Europe which reinforce regional norms of democracy (Gunther, Puhle, and Diamandouros 1995: 409–10). Regional organizations are a strong *reason* these cases appear to be easy. In other words, I have identified a key underlying condition – the absence of which would decrease the probability for democratic success.

In hindsight, we consider the cases "easy" partially because of the IOs themselves.

Third, to label Latin America an "easy" region for democracy because of underlying conditions or because of US involvement in the region is to forget the history of democracy in that region. Current observers of Latin American politics continually express fear that some states of the region are still fragile democracies (Hakim 2003). Moreover, as I discuss in the conclusion of this book, the recent case of Venezuela reminds us that not only is democracy still fragile in Latin America, but that it is not clear that the US will always stand in support of democratic processes. Finally, within the Latin American case studies I attempt to parse out the effects of regional organizations as opposed to US foreign policy to ensure that it is not the US making these cases "easy," but regional organizations behaving as my theory suggests.

Ideally, one would like even more regional variation than Europe and Latin America (although Turkey is arguably a state in the Middle East). Unfortunately, so few transitions have occurred in the Middle East that it is difficult to find well-documented cases in that region. In addition, fewer regional IOs operate in Asia, while African states are members of fewer organizations than states in other regions (Pevehouse, Nordstrom, and Warnke 2004). While it is true that my argument should apply if only one regional organization can perform the functions hypothesized in Chapter 2, with few democracies and few regional organizations, there will be little opportunity for democratically dense IOs to exist.

This last point is important for my argument. If democratically dense regional organizations are necessary for the functioning of the causal mechanisms, those regions with few democracies and few democratically dense organizations will not be particularly good tests for my theory. It is not surprising that there are few cases where regional organizations assist in democratization in Africa, the Middle East or Asia – this is exactly what the theory suggests. What does this mean in terms of the generalizability of the theory, especially for nascent democratic regimes in regions with few democracies and where underlying conditions appear to be absent for democracy? I return to this issue in the final chapter where I discuss how three different sets of new democracies have dealt with this issue.

Reviewing the causal mechanisms: transitions to democracy

Each case will be examined for evidence of the hypothesized causal mechanisms linking involvement in regional IOs and democratic transitions. Table 5.1 briefly outlines these mechanisms as discussed in Chapter 2.

Table 5.1 *Hypothesized causal mechanisms
linking IOs to transitions*

Transition mechanisms (Chapters 2 and 4)
Pressure by regional IO members
Acquiescence effect
– Preference lock-in
– Socialization
Legitimization of interim regime

In addition, any additional "international" causal factors that are present will be highlighted. While the discovery of other causal processes linking IOs to democratic transitions or consolidation would not necessarily undermine my general argument, it would falsify my hypotheses concerning the actual causal processes behind the statistical correlations. Thus, it is important to make sure that the dynamics that lead to the statistical findings in Chapter 4 are fully uncovered and explored.

Each case study will begin with a brief historical introduction including background information concerning the development of democracy. For each study, I will review each causal mechanism, discussing whether there is evidence of IO influence by these mechanisms. Finally, for each study I will discuss countervailing evidence concerning the impact of regional IOs on the democratization process.

Hungary: completing the transition to democracy

As one of the "velvet revolutions" of 1989 in Eastern Europe, Hungary began its most recent experience of democracy with high hopes. Hungary's escape from the tutelage of the Soviet Union and its establishment of multiparty democracy in a peaceful fashion led to high expectations concerning its economic and political transformations. Unlike some of its neighbors, Hungary has fared relatively well on its journey towards democracy. Still, its transition to a pluralist democracy and a market economy is by no means a foregone conclusion. While Hungary has experienced bumps on the road to political and economic reform, it has continued to move towards democracy and a free-market system.

This case study will show how Hungary's links to several regional organizations has assisted in this journey towards democracy in the years after 1989. This case provides insight into the causal mechanisms at work linking IOs to the *completion* of the transition to democracy – moving from an interim government to a full-fledged democracy. Specifically, the three mechanisms which assisted Hungary in its completion of democracy were: (1) the acquiescence effect of membership in NATO and the Conference on Security and Cooperation in Europe (CSCE) programs helping to reassure the military elite of their continued importance in Hungarian policymaking; (2) the psychological benefit of association with these Western organizations; and (3) direct economic and technical assistance provided by these organizations. I discuss this third mechanism in some depth, given that it was not hypothesized in Chapter 2 as a force for the completion of democracy. I also conclude that over the long term, regional IOs will help to consolidate Hungarian democracy.

Background

Hungary's past includes several experiences with democracy and partial liberalization.[2] Prior to 1989, its most recent attempt at liberalization occurred in 1956, when Imre Nagy attempted to liberalize the single-party system by allowing the formation of political parties, unions, intellectual organizations. This liberalization was short-lived, however, as Soviet leaders squelched Nagy's reform attempts, intervening in a "counter-revolutionary" action in December 1956 (Lomax 1991: 155–6). Nagy was arrested and, along with many reformers in his government, executed.

Janos Kadar replaced Nagy and ruled until 1988. During his tenure, Hungary took steps to chart a more independent foreign policy from Moscow, especially after Gorbachev's rise to power in 1985 (Lomax 1991). Independent civic organizations began to form in 1986 and as early as June 1987, public calls for political liberalization became quite common (Kis 1989: 143–52). The string of events leading to the fall of Kadar, however, centered around the 1956 revolution. Beginning in 1988, a movement began calling for the exhumation and proper burial of Imre Nagy's body. With the help of several reformers within the ruling party, the government passed a resolution allowing this action in January 1989. Shortly thereafter, several prominent reformers within the government stopped referring to the 1956 uprising as a "counter-revolution," and called it instead "a popular uprising against an oligarchic form of rule that had humiliated the nation" (Lomax 1991: 163). These statements touched off four months of an "uncontrolled explosion in independent political activity" (Lomax 1991: 164). By November of 1989, the renamed Communist Party (now the Hungarian Socialist Workers'

---

[2] Unless otherwise noted, many of the historical details from this section are drawn from Lomax 1991 and Korosenyi 1992.

Party – HSWP) lost its hold on power when 95 percent of Hungarians voted to strip it of its properties and offices (Lomax 1991: 168). Finally, in the spring of 1990, free and open parliamentary elections were held in Hungary. With these elections, Hungary had once again embarked on the path of multiparty democracy.

As part of the effort to strike a more independent foreign policy, Hungary began to expand its membership in international and regional organizations. Initially, Hungary was the first Eastern European state to sign an agreement with the EC, doing so before the initial transition of 1989 (Pinder 1991: 32–3). In addition, it signed an association agreement promoting the establishment of a free-trade area with EC members in industrial goods, while liberalizing trade in many other economic sectors (see below; also Gower 1993: 290–3).[3] It was a leader among Eastern European states in attempting to join NATO and eagerly joined the Partnership for Peace (PFP), an "ante-chamber" for NATO aspirants (Hyde-Price 1996: 243). Finally, it was the first Eastern European member admitted to the Council of Europe (Hyde-Price 1996: 191). Hungary also played a leading role in creating and perpetuating indigenous regional organizations, including some arising out of the ashes of the Council on Mutual Economic Assistance (CMEA) and the Warsaw Treaty Organization (WTO).

Encouraging the completion of democracy: causal mechanisms

These regional organizations have played a role in encouraging the completion of democracy in Hungary. Rather than encouraging the initial liberalization by applying overt pressure on the HSWP to relinquish power in Hungary, organizations such as NATO, the EC/EU, and the Council of Europe provided incentives and assistance to legitimize the transition to democracy so the emerging institutions and practices would be truly democratic. Membership in and association with several regional IOs helped to push Hungary to become a full-fledged democracy, rather than becoming caught in an "anocratic" status. Thus, there is little evidence of direct pressure by IO members to push liberalization, yet the acquiescence effect and the legitimization influence of these organizations is apparent. Moreover, one additional mechanism not included in Chapter 2, the provision of direct financial and technical assistance, is found in the Hungarian case. Each of these causal processes will be discussed in turn.

---

[3] This agreement, one of the three signed by the EU along with Czechoslovakia and Poland, became known as the "Europe Agreements" (Pinder 1991).

Pressure from the IO and its members

There is little evidence of direct pressure on Hungary to liberalize its political system on the part of IOs. Most of Hungary's IO affiliations prior to the 1988–9 period (e.g. the CMEA and the Warsaw Pact) were with organizations guided by the Soviet Union. Even after the initial transition of 1989, direct pressure in the form of threats or sanctions was absent. Because Hungary was a willing "convert" to Western-style political and economic systems, no pressure from Western democracies was necessary.

One IO deserving mention in this context is the CSCE, which observers claim did play an "enabling" role in the Eastern European transitions of 1989. During the first period of détente in the 1970s, the Soviets and their Warsaw Pact allies agreed to the Helsinki Final Act in 1975. One part of the Helsinki Act was to guarantee respect for "human rights and the free contact of peoples" (Pinder 1994: 122). While the US paid little attention to this aspect of the Helsinki Act, opposition groups within Eastern Europe used this treaty as an opportunity to expand their activities and independent political organizations (e.g. Charter 77 in Czechoslovakia and Solidarity in Poland; see Thomas 2001). According to one observer, "without the Final Act . . . opposition in Eastern Europe would have been weaker, less coherent, [and] easier to suppress" as full-fledged movements towards democracy began in the late 1980s (Richard Davy quoted in Whitehead 1994: 51). Thus, while there may have been some pressure by IOs during the period of Communist rule, it was much more passive than the type of pressure discussed in Chapter 2.

The acquiescence effect: civil–military relations in transition

One of the causal mechanisms outlined in Chapter 2 linking regional IOs to political liberalization and/or the completion of a democratic transition is the acquiescence effect. The idea is that international institutions can either lock in policies which protect actors' interests or socialize actors to change their behavior through interactions with these elites. In the case of Hungary, both parts of this causal mechanism are at work. The issue area in which we find this process concerns civil–military relations through the influence of NATO (especially the Partnership for Peace – PFP) and the CSCE.

The external guarantee of policy preferences arises from military spending requirements dictated by the PFP and NATO, which softened parliamentary attacks on the military's budget and allowed the military to pursue modernization. Besides these externally mandated requirements, financial assistance from the PFP and NATO has helped the Hungarian military to modernize using external resources. Thus, the military has not had to become heavily involved in politics to protect its institutional interests. The socialization aspect arises from integration into broader security arrangements (CSCE, the PFP, and now, NATO) with other democracies. This has helped to socialize military commanders to accept civilian supremacy, a hallmark of liberal democracy.

Integration into the CSCE, the PFP, and later, NATO, has provided large amounts of assistance for the Hungarian military, especially in the form of modern weapons and material. This came at a critical time when the Hungarian military was suffering from massive budget cuts and extremely low soldier morale (Agocs 1997: 86–8; Bebler 1997: 130). For example, between 1989 and 1991, the military budget dropped nearly 35 percent while over 40 percent of Hungarian tanks were being recycled for scrap metal (Agocs 1997: 87). In addition, crime and sui-cides among the Hungarian military reached an all-time high in 1990 (Agocs 1997: 91).

Involvement in PFP and NATO has helped to stabilize Hungary's defense forces from a financial standpoint. First, because it is a mem-ber of a multilateral defense pact, its armed forces feel less pressure to demand funds to protect itself from external threats (Gyarmati 1999: 114). Second, NATO now requires increases in defense spending (one-tenth of a percent per year) to keep Hungary's forces within NATO stan-dards (Wright 1998: 3). Finally, Hungary has received large amounts of assistance to modernize and update its military forces (Wright 1998: 3). Without NATO and PFP assistance, this commitment to modernization would probably not have occurred, especially given pre-NATO defense spending patterns (Barany and Deak 1999: 47; Gyarmati 1999: 114). By improving the lot of the Hungarian military and guaranteeing some access to resources, these regional security organizations have encouraged the military not to become involved in politics.

The second process at work involved the physical integration of Hungarian officers into security-related IOs such as the PFP and the CSCE.[4] Training and interaction with officers trained in Western-oriented styles of civil–military relations helped to "reorient" Hungarian officers towards their new role in a democratic society (Inotai and Notzold 1995: 96; Valki 1998: 99–100). This was especially important given their previous role as both an internal and external security force. Through the retraining of military leaders in Hungary, both the PFP and the CSCE encourage this reorientation process (Nye 1996: 154–5; Vetschera 1997: 19).

---

[4] This is also true to a much smaller extent of the EU. See Pridham 1999: 65.

In addition, specific PFP and NATO requirements including transparency of the military budgeting process and national defense planning can help to promote civilian control over the military (Keiswetter 1997: 5). Hungary's military command structure has undergone a drastic overhaul designed to promote civilian control in order to "reflect NATO principles" (Freeman 1997: A7). These measures can prevent "any national armed force from achieving too much independence of influence in a [NATO] member state" (Valki 1998:103). In the words of one observer, "integration into Western [security] institutions will help democratization by refocusing on the armed forces of Eastern Europe away from politics" (Herring 1994: 109).

All of these factors have helped to complete the transition process in Hungary. Many observers see the subjugation of the military to civilian rule as an essential part of the transition process (Aguero 1995) and liberal democracy itself (Foster 1996; Keiswetter 1997: 3). While it is difficult to say whether Hungary's military would have moved against any democratic regime without involvement in these IOs, the NATO/PFP requirements for civilian-supremacy of the military provided a strong incentive to deter the military elite from doing so (Braun 1999: 19).

It should also be mentioned that an indirect link between NATO and the transition to democracy is through military security itself. The idea that democracies are difficult to create and continue with a significant external threat directly links the provision of security (or at least the perception of security) to the promotion and maintenance of democracy. Thus, given Hungary's concerns over its own security from its neighbors and from Russia, it is plausible that membership in these security organizations helped the process of democratization, especially in light of Hungarian concerns over nationals in neighboring states (Nelson 1999: 311, see also Barany 1999: 78–9).

In the end, however, there is not overwhelming secondary evidence that feelings of insecurity threatened the transition in Hungary.[5] The Antall regime did fear a reemergence of Soviet expansionism (especially in light of the August 1991 coup attempt) and often justified Hungary's interest in NATO in these terms. There were also concerns about Romania's treatment of its minority Hungarian population, as evidenced by large redeployments of Hungarian troops near the Romanian border (Bugajski 1992: 167). Still, there is no evidence that anti-democratic measures were undertaken or seriously considered in response to perceived threats

---

[5] In addition, recall from Chapter 3 that the presence of regional military disputes has no impact on the probability of a transition to democracy in the statistical analyses. While this is only a general pattern in the data and not for Hungary in particular, it does suggest that such influences on democratization are rare in the aggregate.

from neighbors or the former Soviet Union. Hungarian Foreign Minister Laszlo Kovacs expressed this argument quite succinctly:

Hungary wants to join NATO not because it perceives an external threat, nor because it seeks protection from its neighbors, but because it regards integration into the European community, that is, membership in NATO, the European Union, and Western European Union, an indispensable condition of its security, stability, and economic development. (Quoted in Valki 1998: 96)

The symbolic effects of IOs

One of the most important effects of involvement in IOs for Hungary has been the psychological legitimization that membership has granted the leadership and the emerging democratic system. Membership in (and to a lesser extent application to) several Western and European organizations provided an immediate signal of foreign policy reorientation for the post-Communist regime. This signal of a pro-Western stance helped to legitimize that country's transitional democratic institutions for both internal and external actors.

For internal actors, membership in the Council of Europe, NATO, as well as the "Europe Agreements" signed with the EC/EU helped provide credibility to domestic political elites, furthering the process of democratization. Popular sentiment overwhelmingly favors these memberships and even before the rise of multiparty democracy, political elites were given credit for creating ties to the West (Batt 1994: 178). The issue of Hungary's "orientation" goes back hundreds of years and has always been a salient issue for citizens and political parties alike (Gedeon 1997: 101; Kolozsi 1995: 108). Many Hungarians pin their hopes of successful political and economic reform on their ability to link themselves to the West (Goldman 1997: 212). According to one scholar of the Eastern European transitions, joining (as well as the potential to join) Western international institutions "played a very important role in the [new regime's] legitimation by providing some kind of seal of approval or guarantee of their credibility vis-à-vis their own societies" (Batt 1994: 176).

Particularly important in this regard are both the Council of Europe and the EC/EU. Hungary was the first Eastern European state to join the Council in November of 1990 (Klebes 1999: 10; Tuohy 1991: 2). For Hungarians, membership was an early "seal of approval" from the West for their early democratization efforts (Fitzmaurice 1998: 184; Kun 1993: 47). In addition to the psychological benefit, the Council encouraged the continuation of the transition by monitoring reform progress agreed upon at Hungary's accession, thus providing "security for democracy" (van Brabant 1994: 455; see also Fitzmaurice 1998: 185). In the words of one observer, the Council "provides a valuable safeguard against subsequent backsliding on human rights and democratic practices. It also has a powerful symbolic value which should not be underestimated" (Hyde-Price 1996: 193). The EC/EU played a similar role in helping to signal to internal observers the regime's, commitment to "move West" (Kun 1993: 61). In fact, one of the first policy initiatives by the newly elected Antall government was "the establishment of direct diplomatic ties between Hungary and the [European] Community" (Kun 1993: 72; see also Batt 1994: 177).

External actors also perceived this signal as a sure sign that Hungary was committed to a policy of political and economic reform. While this may have had a positive effect on the Hungarian psyche (external validation of the reform process feeding the legitimization process), it also provided a much more direct benefit: private investment.[6] One observer has argued that even NATO membership provides a spur to such economic activity: "As of 1997, when Hungary started gradually joining [NATO], its international prestige and importance grew as well . . . Although precise calculations are not available at the moment, NATO member-states enjoy much more favorable financial and business ratings due to decreased political risks" (Gyarmati 1999: 114; see also Valki 1998: 103).

In addition to providing a psychological stabilization for Hungary's emerging institutions, this "external" source of legitimization for the political elite did prove to defuse a potentially dangerous situation that could have undermined Hungary's transition. A major issue of importance between Hungary's parties, its citizens, and its neighbors is the government's policy towards ethnic Hungarians living abroad (Goldman 1997: 213; Kozhemiakin 1998: 80–1).

As broader research on the issue of democratization and war has shown, transitional regimes can and do make overt attempts to spur nationalist sentiment regarding certain issues such as ethnic identity (Mansfield and Snyder 1995, 2002; Snyder and Ballentine 1996). Thus, the transitional Antall (or the Nemeth) regime could have easily tried to legitimate itself by arousing nationalist sentiment in Hungary over the Magyar population of its neighbors. In fact, Antall himself made an early statement that he desired to be the "Prime Minister of 15 million Hungarians" (there are only 10 million Hungarians in Hungary; see Goldman 1997: 213). His statement was interpreted by Hungary's neighbors as "a revival of traditional Hungarian revisionist nationalism"

---

[6] The next section discusses investment and assistance from the international organizations themselves.

(Kozhemiakin 1998: 81).[7] Thus, Hungarian democracy could be under-mined by a combination of appeals to extremist nationalism or through the insecurity created by perceptions of such nationalism abroad (Gower 1993: 286).[8]

As Alexander Kozhemiakin (1998) has argued, however, Hungarian parties and other political elites (with a few exceptions) have not attempted to base their legitimacy and popularity on nationalist issues. Rather, "when other sources of political legitimacy are not too difficult to find, nationalist sentiments in Hungary can be contained" (Kozhemiakin 1998: 82). External legitimization derived from IO membership serves as a substitute for appeals to nationalism. Kozhemiakin (1998: 83) contends "Hungarians value their internationally recognized democratic status too much to allow their unqualified desire to protect Magyar minorities to hurt it and, by implication, impede Hungary's efforts to integrate itself fully into the West."

Finally, Hungary's own belief that membership in regional organiza-tions serves as a signal of intentions has been so strong that it has led the way to creating new regional organizations among its neighbors. Central among these has been the Central European Initiative (CEI) and the Cen-tral European Free Trade Association (CEFTA).[9] While it is difficult to say that these indigenous regional organizations had a direct effect in com-pleting the transition to democracy in Hungary, these organizations did serve an important purpose for Hungary during the transition. Specif-ically, CEI and CEFTA showed a willingness among the new Central European democracies to cooperate with one another and signaled their interest in political liberalization, market reforms, and economic integra-tion (Felkay 1997: 103; Inotai and Notzold 1995: 97). Although impor-tant ends themselves, for Hungary, these organizations were meant to signal these interests to both NATO and the EC/EU (Barany 1999: 84).[10]

---

[7] According to Batt (1994: 183), the question is not "whether nationalism will play a role in Hungarian politics, but whether it will be nationalism of a more moderate variety which can coexist and support the transition to democracy."

[8] This argument holds that by arousing nationalist sentiment and creating disputes amongst its neighbors, Hungary would be unable to concentrate on finishing the demo-cratic transition. Rather, as is discussed in the arguments concerning peace and democ-racy (see Chapters 4 and 6), the expansion of the state security system could undermine the transition.

[9] The CEI has undergone several iterations. Originally known as the Adria–Danube agree-ment, it became known as the Hexagonale in 1990 with the accession of Czechoslovakia. After Poland's accession in 1991, it became the Pentagonale. Finally, with invitations to the former Yugoslav republics of Slovenia and Croatia, it became known as the CEI. See Banks and Mueller (1998: 1078).

[10] In fact, the EU had explicitly noted that Central Europeans' ability to "cooperate with one another" was a central issue in their accession to the Union. See Bunce (1997: 251).

These new regional organizations played a facilitating role in the democratization process by signaling the intent of the Hungarian regime to pursue more comprehensive political and economic liberalization (Bunce
1997: 244).

Direct economic benefits

A final causal process linking IOs to Hungary's completion of democracy
are direct economic and technical benefits that flowed from the organizations. Note that this was not a causal mechanism considered in Chapter 2.
In the case of Hungary, the EC/EU and the Council of Europe provided
both monetary and technical assistance facilitating the completion of the
transition to democracy.[11]

This assistance was targeted to support a broad array of economic
reforms, yet the failure of this economic reform could have spilled over to
the political process. The fear is that a poor economy will give rise to anti-
democratic (especially nationalist) elements within Hungary, reversing
the trend towards greater political and economic reform. As one observer
of the Eastern European transitions has argued, "The main threat to liberal democracy in Eastern Europe apart from the former Yugoslavia is
economic insecurity" (Herring 1994: 111; see also Pinder 1991: 51).
Economic crises can give rise to extremist groups or undermine public confidence in reform efforts. To counter these possibilities, several
regional IOs have attempted to help Hungary undertake economic and
political reform.

The EU was the first IO to institute a large aid program to Eastern
Europe. The program, known as the Poland–Hungary Assistance for
Economic Reconstruction (PHARE), was undertaken before Poland or
Hungary had signed their association agreement with the Community.
Nonetheless, PHARE did step up its activities after the "Europe Agree-
ments" were signed.[12] The purpose of PHARE was to help cushion the
problems associated with the transition to a market economy in Hungary
(Hyde-Price 1996: 199; Kovrig 1999: 258–9). Grants included assistance
in the process of privatization, small enterprise development, debt for-
giveness, increasing job-training programs, and assisting reform of the

---

[11] The second section discussed the economic benefits of NATO membership, which could
be considered more of a direct form of bribery (of the military elite). The economic
assistance discussed in this section was quite diffuse in that it was not targeted to any
social group in particular. Thus, I hesitate to label this assistance "bribery."

[12] In addition, assistance was later extended to other Eastern European states and the
Baltics. See van Brabant 1994: 534. Hungary's portion of PHARE assistance did decline
after the expansion of the program. By 1994, Hungary received only 8.6 percent of
PHARE's outlays. See Kovrig 1999: 258.

financial sector (Gedeon 1997: 131; Mayhew 1998: 14–16; Pinder 1991: 89–90).

In addition to direct economic assistance, other forms of aid have been provided as well. The Council of Europe has concentrated on providing technical assistance to Hungary and the other new Central European democracies (Klebes 1999: 41). In 1990, the Council created the Demosthenes Program to provide "expertise and experience acquired by the Council of Europe and its member states in all aspects of the organization and functioning of participatory democracy" (Kritz 1993: 25). This program has explicitly attempted to "strengthen the reform movement towards genuine democracy" (Hyde-Price 1996: 192). In fact, in response to requests from the Council, Hungary has reformed its entire legal system, especially criminal codes, to meet standards set by the European Convention on Human Rights (Hyde-Price 1996: 193).

Finally, through the "Europe Agreements," the EU member states have opened their markets to Hungarian goods. The agreement also sets a timetable for tariff reductions on other goods excluded from the initial agreement (e.g. industrial and agricultural goods) (Koop 1997: 316). The purpose of this agreement with Hungary is to help support economic and political reforms by contributing to export-led growth while ensuring against "massive protection" of Western European goods "once the initial liberalization euphoria has passed" (Mayhew 1998: 23).[13] Moreover, the EU states have attempted to stabilize the Hungarian economy by spurring exports. This is important given the downturn in Hungary's economy during the initial reform period. Although there is some evidence that this agreement has helped, most observers have criticized the EU for not liberalizing trade enough with Central Europe, concentrating instead on protecting their own domestic industries (see Brown et al. 1997: 25–6; Gower 1993: 289–90; Messerlin 1992).

These monetary, trade, and technical assistance programs provided by IOs continue to encourage the reform process. Whether through economic assistance, export opportunities, or technical assistance, these IOs have provided both a cushion to difficult economic adjustments and information on the best way to undertake these adjustments. Moreover, the explicit conditions attached to this assistance provide a deterrent to those who would derail the reform process (Bugajski 1992: 212; Gower 1993: 290–1). This continued support from a variety of IOs is important given the long-term nature of the transition process (Pridham 1999: 61). According to *The Economist*, "The continuation of the region's [reform]

---

[13] On the importance of export-led growth to all the Visegrad states, see Hyde-Price 1996: 201–2.

policies depends on the EC, which provides markets to help the countries grow over time and also provides disincentives to extremism. Central Europe might remain stable outside the EC. But its chances of doing so would be smaller, and would shrink over time."[14]

Hungary: discussion and conclusion

Three issues arise when reflecting on this case. First, one could argue that regional IOs were epiphenomenal in this case. That is, Hungary was committed to democracy early and there was never a danger that it would not complete the transition, with or without assistance from regional organizations. As pointed out numerous times throughout the study, however, there were several threats to Hungarian democracy that could have easily emerged after initial political and economic liberalization. Appeals to nationalism could have played a part in the unraveling of reform in Hungary. In combination with poor economic performance, these trends could have presented a major roadblock for the completion of the transition to democracy.[15] Without security enhancements from NATO/PFP membership, fears of nationalism from *neighbors* could have also led to military conflicts, potentially undermining the transition process. As one observer noted in 1993, "the future [of democracy] is by no means secure" (Kun 1993: 126). Regional IOs can be extremely valuable in spurring the democratization process to completion. According to Adrian Hyde-Price (1996: 212): "Western governments and multilateral organizations can provide positive economic and financial incentives for democratic reform in the East. By raising the costs of political recidivism, a significant disincentive can be created which might help deter East European elites from reverting to pre-war patterns of authoritarian populism."

Second, some could argue that Hungary's case shows that the relationship between IOs and democracy works in the opposite direction – transition to democracy increases involvement in IOs, not the other way around. For example, it is not difficult to find a plethora of statements from EU officials claiming that only when Hungary is a full democracy will it be allowed to enter the Union (Palmer 1995: 9). Although states may join comparatively *more* IOs after they complete the transition to democracy, Hungary demonstrates that many organizations are joined before the completion. For example, the association agreement with the

---

[14] "SURVEY: Eastern Europe," *The Economist*, March 13, 1993, S20.
[15] For more details concerning these problems and others for the post-transition period in Hungary, see Goldman 1997: 197–211.

EC/EU, CEFTA, entry into the PFP, and accession to the Council of Europe all occurred within a very short time after initial moves to political liberalization. Although, based on this case, one may conclude that *liberalization* may influence joining IOs, this does not imply that these IOs may not assist in the *completion* of democracy. Indeed, given the potential start-and-stop nature of the reform process, John Pinder contends "stable democracy is not a *fait accompli*. Economic failure or the rise of destructive nationalism could reverse the [reform] process" (Pinder 1991: 41; see also Bartlett 1997: 259).

Finally, this case highlights an important element missing from the causal mechanisms discussed in Chapter 2: direct economic and technical benefits provided by IOs. It should be noted that some of the financial assistance provided by the EC/EU occurred before Hungary had joined this organization as an associate member. Still, this illustrates another powerful mechanism through which IOs can encourage the completion of the democratic transition. By providing monetary and technical assistance to ease the transition process, IOs can increase the probability of this process coming to fruition.

In conclusion, Hungary demonstrates the power of multiple IOs in assisting the completion of democracy. By providing financial incentives, conditional assistance, external validation and legitimacy, and socialization of military elites, these multilateral organizations can "give practical encouragement to liberal and reforming coalitions in the East, and . . . impede the emergence of autarkic, repressive and nationalist policies in these fragile polities" (Hyde-Price 1996: 212; see also Snyder 1990).

Peru: a partial success

Peru provides evidence that IOs can help to pressure authoritarians to redemocratization. Through the exertion of diplomatic pressure, the threat of economic sanctions, and the use of the institution as a forum for discussing democracy-related issues, the Organization of American States (OAS) has assisted in the redemocratization of Peru. I label this case a "partial" success since the OAS has been given credit and criticism by observers of Latin American politics on this account (see Hakim 2000; McClintock 2001). The OAS has twice become involved in Peruvian politics in the last decade: after the *autogolpe* of Alberto Fujimori in 1992, and after tainted presidential elections in the spring and summer of 2000. Although Peru may not yet be a consolidated democracy, I argue that without the pressure of regional organizations, in particular the OAS, Peru would have strayed from the path of democracy long ago.

Round 1: Peruvian democracy and the autogolpe

Peru's transition to democracy in 1980 took place under extremely difficult circumstances. High poverty, a well-armed and active anti-government insurgency, a weak political party system, and the highest ethnic heterogeneity in Latin America all contributed to the difficulty in building a solid democracy in Peru. These obstacles led one Latin American scholar to suggest that Peru was the "least likely case" for democratic consolidation (McClintock 1989). Unfortunately, these words would turn out to be quite prophetic.

Peru's first two democratic regimes, led by Fernando Belaunde and Alan Garcia, attempted to confront widespread poverty as well as rising civil violence especially in the Peruvian countryside. Neither president experienced much success. By the end of the Garcia administration (1990), inflation had risen to a staggering 7,650 percent and growth fell by 32 percent through the 1980s (Palmer 2000). Garcia suspended all debt-servicing payments to international lenders, further eroding international confidence in the Peruvian economy.

Perhaps the greatest threat to democratic stability in Peru, however, has come from the threat of armed rebellion. Two major guerilla groups seeking to topple the Peruvian government have emerged in the past twenty years. The most widely known group, the *Sendero Luminoso*, or Shining Path, is a Maoist insurgency known for its extreme violence in both rural and major metropolitan areas (Degregori 1997). From 1980 to 1987, *Sendero* violence claimed over 11,000 lives (McClintock 1989) and in 1990 alone, over 3,800 deaths were a result of their terrorist attacks (Palmer 2000). The lesser known of the guerilla groups, the Tupac Amaru (MTRA) movement, is less violent, yet still active against the Peruvian government (Durand 1997: 166). Neither Belaunde nor Garcia were able to make significant progress in fighting these rebel groups during their administrations, yet both came under heavy criticism for allowing the military a free hand in dealing with these groups. Critics contend that this action allowed massive human rights violations by the military, which were then reciprocated by the rebels (McClintock 1993: 113).

Peru's party system is highly fragmented and few of the parties are highly institutionalized. The four major parties in Peru remain independent from one another, yet none is able to establish a coherent base of support. Fighting among the parties is increasingly viewed with disdain, which has led to the alienation of Peruvians from the current party system (McClintock 1989: 130–2).

Finally, Peru's ethnic heterogeneity provides an additional challenge to democracy. Indian, Spanish, and Asian cultures provide a number of religious and ethnic cleavages exacerbated by income inequalities that follow similar dividing lines. These cleavages are also reinforced by a rural–urban division. Thus, rural dwellers tend to be of Indian descent and poor, while urban dwellers are either of Spanish or Asian descent, well educated, and relatively wealthy. These divisions are exploited by both the rebel movements and the political parties of Peru, intensifying an already difficult situation.

In 1990, however, a political underdog with no party affiliation rose to power. Alberto Fujimori captured the presidency with an overwhelming majority in that year's elections. Fujimori was a newcomer to politics and represented a protest vote against the existing party system (Costa 1993: 29).[16] Upon taking office, he moved quickly to consolidate presidential power and improve his relations with the military. While both Belaunde and Garcia had been "somewhat constrained" by their political parties, because of the independent nature of Fujimori's campaign, he had few constraints when making presidential policy (Costa 1993: 30; McClintock 1993: 114). He used this autonomy to make major changes in Peru, including increasing counterinsurgency efforts, reestablishing relations with the international financial community, deepening efforts at neoliberal market reform, and entering an agreement with the United States to begin a massive anti-drug program (McClintock 1993: 114).

By the end of 1991, however, the courts and legislature began to exert their ability to check Fujimori's power. On several occasions, the judiciary or the legislature (or both) attempted to overturn Fujimori's executive orders. In addition, charges of corruption against the Fujimori family were beginning to arise in the spring of 1992. After weeks of rising tensions between Fujimori, the judiciary, and the legislature, Fujimori announced the implementation of a Government Emergency and National Reconstruction, dissolving parliament and suspending the judiciary on April 5, 1992. Fujimori had instituted a coup against his own government – an *autogolpe*.

IOs and democratization: the pressure of the OAS

Fujimori's actions were quite popular within Peru. The population had become unhappy with the fragmented party system and the bickering amongst the more powerful parties over Fujimori's reform efforts. Polls taken immediately after the *autogolpe* found that an astounding 70 percent favored Fujimori's actions (Costa 1993: 33; Mauceri 1997). Most

---

[16] Fujimori's own party *Cambio 90* was formed only in the year of the election as a vehicle for his candidacy; see McClintock (1993: 113).

observers trace this support to Peruvians' disenchantment with "politics as usual" and the fact that Fujimori had implemented a series of successful economic reforms.

Fujimori anticipated his actions would be popular at home given the widespread discontent with the status quo (Cameron 1997: 62–4). What he drastically underestimated, however, was the response from abroad. None of the military officers supporting Fujimori was concerned with external reaction, since in the words of one officer, "the measures were not perceived as a *golpe* because there was to be no change in the president" (quoted in Cameron 1997: 64). Even the cabinet minister for external relations purportedly told Fujimori that the external situation was "under control" (quoted in Cameron 1997: 65). Yet Fujimori and his supporters were unprepared for the world response to come (Cameron 1997: 64–6).

In 1991, the OAS had approved the Santiago Declaration, which gave that group the right to defend democracy in member states (Munoz 1993). The Declaration mandates that the OAS must begin immediate consultations if there is an interruption of democracy in any member state (Munoz 1998: 1). The Declaration does not require an immediate imposition of sanctions, but calls for a meeting of the OAS general assembly in these cases can make decisions regarding any punishment or pressure to be meted out against the offending state. This mechanism was first used in the case of Haiti in 1991. It was also invoked in the case of Peru.

The reaction of the OAS and most of its members was swift and clear: Fujimori's move was a blow to democracy and he was called upon to restore democracy immediately. The OAS, under the obligations of the Santiago Declaration, publicly condemned Fujimori's actions and called an emergency assembly meeting in the Bahamas. Before the meeting, Fujimori had refused to receive an OAS delegation investigating the status of human rights in Peru after the coup. There was little expectation that Fujimori would heed OAS calls to restore democracy. In the words of one observer, "it appeared as if the government had little interest in re-establishing democratic institutions" (Mauceri 1997). Fujimori had ruled out an elected assembly to draft a new constitution and promised to undertake sweeping judicial and congressional reforms (Coad 1992: 10).

Fujimori would make an about-face over the next month. International pressure, especially from the OAS and its members, played a key role in this process. First, the OAS, under the Santiago Declaration, called the emergency meeting in Nassau, Bahamas, for mid-May. After a series of coordinated visits from OAS ambassadors, Fujimori decided to attend and address the Bahamas Conference. Specifically, some observers have argued that the efforts of Hector Gross, an Ecuadorian foreign minister with the OAS, convinced Fujimori to address the OAS assembly concerning his actions (Coad 1992: 10). Without the institutional backing of the OAS, however, it is doubtful that Ambassador Gross would have had this influence on Fujimori.

Second, the OAS planned to consider placing sanctions on Peru in the wake of Fujimori's actions. Although there is mixed evidence on whether such sanctions would have been enacted (see Costa 1993: 37; McClintock 1993: 115), the possibility of such action clearly worried Fujimori (Cameron 1997: 66). Carlos Bolona, Fujimori's minister of the economy and a close political ally, had threatened to resign after the *autogolpe* in fear of sanctions from the OAS and the suspension of assistance from the international financial community (Cameron 1997: 66).

During his visit to the OAS conference, Fujimori committed to a new schedule for elections in Peru for a Constituent Assembly that would draft a new constitution. This schedule promised elections more quickly than Fujimori had previously indicated, moving them forward several months to November of 1992 (Palmer 1996: 72).[17] He also agreed to suspend his plans for a plebiscite to legitimize his *autogolpe*. With these announcements and the signing of the Bahamas Resolution, the OAS and its members eased their restrictions on aid and credit to Peru (Costa 1993: 37; Kay 1996: 63). In addition, Fujimori's concessions forestalled any move towards placing sanctions on Peru by the OAS.

It is clear that Fujimori and his supporters had not counted on any international outcry in response to the *autogolpe*. Thus, the swift and clear reaction of the OAS and its members surprised and "agitated" Fujimori (Cameron 1997: 66), which certainly contributed to its influence in persuading Fujimori to restore democracy more quickly than he planned. Many Latin American observers have credited the OAS efforts with helping to restore some semblance of democracy in Peru through its pressure on Fujimori (Hakim 1993a: 42; Muñoz 1993: 12).

Did the OAS make a difference? Political will and the realist hypothesis

This conclusion that the OAS made a difference is not universal. Some observers have questioned the general OAS commitment to democracy, and, more importantly, their efficacy in the case of Peru. The first argument is mainly that the OAS does not possess the political will to

---

[17] Fujimori had initially promised a plebiscite on the acceptability of the coup in "18 months to 2 years" (Cameron 1994: 155). Thus, the movement of *full legislative elections* to November of 1992 was a significant concession.

effectively defend democracy in Latin America. Specifically, the Santiago Declaration does not require anything other than a meeting concerning the suspension of democracy (Hakim 1993a: 40). Moreover, in the case of Peru, some have even argued that the lack of a solid defense of democracy in both Panama and Haiti encouraged Fujimori to undertake the *autogolpe* without fear of reprisals from the OAS (Smith 1994: 40).

Despite these criticisms of the OAS, the organization did play a role in convincing Fujimori to back down and even its critics admit it acted quickly in the Peruvian case (Hakim 1993a). Although it is correct that the OAS is under no legal obligation to impose sanctions to restore democracy, in this case the pressure exerted through the OAS, short of sanctions, was enough to bring concessions from Fujimori. At a minimum, the OAS serves as a forum to facilitate international pressure on regimes whose commitment to democracy wavers. Historian Richard Millett (1994: 20) has emphasized that "the support of the international community in general, and the OAS member states in particular, for efforts to advance, consolidate, and support democratic regimes in the Americas has gained steadily in importance over the last decade."

An extremely important counterargument also arises from the realist camp. Some observers have argued that the United States alone played the important role in convincing Fujimori to back down, relegating the OAS to a bystander in this case. In fact, the US did play an important role in this crisis (Youngers 1994). The US immediately suspended aid to Peru and pressured several aid organizations, including the IMF, to withhold over $2 billion in financial assistance (Palmer 1996: 71). Some argue it was this US response, not the OAS actions, that drove Fujimori to make concessions towards democracy.[18]

While it is true that US opposition was an important element to the wave of pressure placed on Fujimori, even US officials admit that the OAS facilitated their opposition to his coup. The US coordinated its suspension of aid and diplomatic pressure with the OAS (Roberts and Peceny 1997: 217). This helped to bolster both the US and the OAS response. During this time period, the US was focused on the OAS as a key actor in both the Peruvian and Haitian crises occurring simultaneously. The American ambassador to the OAS stressed the need for a "multilateral framework" in dealing with Haiti and Peru since Latin American states were hesitant to be seen as caving in to US wishes (Madison 1992: 1408). The US and the OAS served to mutually reinforce one another in this case, since the

---

[18] "Peru; Bending, Maybe," *The Economist*, May 23, 1992, 44. See also Hakim 1993a.

OAS was able to serve as a mechanism by which all interested parties could coordinate their responses to the crisis.[19]

Highlighting the US role in the crisis does not, however, undermine the broader argument made in this book. The realist argument that major power preferences, rather than institutions, drive outcomes is not supported in this case. Recall that the key prediction of the realist position is that since outcomes reflect major power preferences, the counterfactual outcome with no regional IO involvement would be no different than the actual outcome. State interests, not influenced by institutions, drive results. Yet to say that because the preferences of a major power are identical to those of the institution means that the institution is epiphenomenal is misleading. It is possible that the preferences of both actors are identical in a particular case. What the realist must be able to show (or what the institutionalist must be able to disprove) is that *absent the institution*, the outcome would be the same. Only then can one say whether institutions matter. Evidence that preferences between major power actors and the institutions coincide is not *prima facie* evidence either way.

In the case of Peru, there is a clear counterfactual scenario to test the realist position – the US decides to act unilaterally in opposition to Fujimori with the same results. Would this pressure alone have been effective? US policymakers, including the US ambassador, did not believe so (Madison 1992). The prospect of cries of "imperialism," especially from the nationalist Fujimori, could have spelled trouble for all Latin American states since this could have given the embattled president an issue around which to rally at a crucial juncture. Did the OAS facilitate US opposition to the coup? Yes. Does this mean this was the only role the OAS played? No. Most importantly, would the outcome have been the same with only unilateral US pressure on Peru? No. The OAS served its purpose as a regional forum to discuss issues and take action. Latin American nations were able to coordinate a unified front against Fujimori and pressure him to take actions that he would not have taken otherwise (Cameron 1998b: 225). Fujimori would not have scheduled constituent elections had not the position of the OAS and other regional organizations been so clear (Cameron 1997). Non-US actors and regional institutions were essential to this outcome as "the coup clearly precipitated international isolation" (Mauceri 1998: 29). Mauceri (1998: 29) continues: "Peru's participation in critical regional associations like the Rio Group and the Andean Pact was suspended, and several countries curtailed diplomatic ties, including Venezuela, Spain, and Panama." As one scholar of Latin America noted

---

[19] On the coordination efforts of the US in the OAS during the Peruvian crisis, see Cameron 1994: 155. On coordination efforts in other cases, see Vaky 1993: 29.

in 1994: "Though the country is far from being a model democracy, absent the international pressure the situation might have remained, or become, even worse" (Millett 1994: 15; see also Mauceri 1998: 31).

IOs and democratization: other causal mechanisms?

In this first round of the Peruvian case only the pressure mechanism appears to be present. Neither the acquiescence effect nor psychological benefits from IO membership are evident. While business interests were surprised by the OAS response, it is not the case that these groups changed their views on democracy because of guarantees offered by the OAS, nor because of a socialization process within the organization. Moreover, because the *autogolpe* was initially quite popular within Peruvian society (see Balbi and Palmer 2001: 65), it is difficult to make an argument for the symbolic benefits of membership. In the second round of OAS involvement, however, both the pressure from the organization (although of a more subtle nature) and the acquiescence effect played a role in returning Peru to the democratic path.

Round 2: tainted elections and the OAS

After the *autogolpe* and the partial reestablishment of multiparty rule, Peruvian politics returned to a state close to "normalcy." Fujimori continued to hold a tight grip on power and refused to submit most of his (and the military's) actions to judicial or legislative review (Palmer 2000). He won resounding reelection in 1995 and, while his popularity waned steadily since the coup, he retained fairly significant support in Peru at least until 1999. His popularity was no doubt due to his successful counterinsurgency and economic policies that increased safety and prosperity in Peru (Hakim 2000). Fujimori's policies of privatization, for example, spurred tremendous growth in the Peruvian economy. By 1994, Peru was experiencing 12 percent growth and was the "darling of the international financial community" (Kay 1996: 64). *Sendero Luminoso's* leader, Abdel Guzman, and several of his aides were captured by Peruvian secret police in September of 1992 and deaths from domestic terrorism fell to under 150 a year in 1998 (Palmer 2000: 60).

Critics argued that United States and OAS opposition to Fujimori was relatively short lived, allowing Fujimori more latitude to remake a system that was less democratic than before (Cameron and Mauceri 1997: 241; Hakim 1992: M2; 1993a: 42). Although the US did withhold financial assistance, after Fujimori's commitment to the OAS to hold new elections, the US released $400 in World Bank loans in June 1992 (Monshipouri 1995: 121). Furthermore, the OAS resumed normal relations with Peru, although it has been active in monitoring elections over the past eight years.[20]

Fujimori's stable grip began to unravel, however, in 1999 and the seemingly benign election monitoring by the OAS served as an important source of pressure on his administration. In December 1999, Fujimori changed the Peruvian constitution (which he had written) to allow himself a third term as president. This move was met with widespread disapproval in Peru and support for Fujimori plummeted (Balbi and Palmer 2001). To guard against opposition forces gaining ground in the forthcoming election, Fujimori turned to harassment of these groups – an effort led by the National Intelligence Service (SIN) and its leader, Vladimiro Montesinos. Opposition-group activities were stunted and only one candidate, Alejandro Toledo, became a serious contender (largely because of his late emergence and a lack of time for Fujimori to undermine his candidacy).[21]

The OAS, along with the EU and private non-governmental organizations, monitored the April 2000 elections that saw Fujimori defeat Toledo, but not gain the required majority for victory. During that election, there were many reports of voting irregularities and it appeared as though Fujimori would "manufacture" a victory until a combination of domestic and international pressure pushed him to call a runoff between himself and Toledo to be held in May (Balbi and Palmer 2001: 67). At this point, the OAS was willing to give Fujimori yet another chance and the organization's Election Observer Mission began to prepare programs in Peru to increase the transparency in the runoff election.

Fujimori allowed many of these efforts to come to fruition, but he drew the line at the installation of new vote-counting software that could be independently verified by external observers. Thus, on May 17, eleven days before the runoff election, the OAS mission left Lima announcing the upcoming vote would be flawed. In response, Toledo withdrew his candidacy for the presidency. Fujimori stood alone in the runoff election and (not surprisingly) won the May 28 contest. Fujimori's actions touched off protests domestically and internationally. Mass protests greeted the electoral outcome, with opposition parties and other segments of civil society calling for opposition groups to unite against Fujimori.[22]

At the OAS, it appeared that while Peru had suffered international public humiliation, it would pay few costs. In June 2000, Peru was able to kill the invocation of the Santiago Declaration with the help of Mexico and

---

[20] Some observers have criticized the OAS role in the Constituent Council Elections, noting that by legitimizing those elections, the OAS has de facto legitimated Fujimori's actions. For criticisms of the OAS generally, See McClintock 2001.

[21] For a review of the events leading to the "fall" of Fujimori in 2000, see Basombrio 2001.

[22] These details are taken from a variety of sources including Balbi and Palmer 2001; Cooper and Legler 2001; McClintock 2001.

Brazil. Rather, Peru accepted an OAS mission to Peru under the adoption of Resolution 1753 which authorized a high-level team of ministers to travel to Peru to "strengthen democracy" (Cooper and Legler 2001: 128). Thus, it appeared that the OAS might allow a second power-grab by Fujimori to stand.

The OAS and the fall of Fujimori

What Fujimori did not anticipate, however, was the continued pressure that would be placed on him by the observer mission from the OAS. The mission created a roundtable (*mesa de dialogo*) which brought together government representatives, opposition parties, and prominent members of civil society to discuss how to improve democracy, ranging from issues of civil–military relations to judicial reform (Cooper and Legler 2001). The roundtable created a forum for opposition groups and although it did not serve as a pressure point from the OAS to Fujimori, it did "provide an important mechanism for democratic reforms" (Cooper and Legler 2001: 123). As of September 2000, however, the OAS mission would take on an increasingly important role.

Fujimori's downfall can be tied to the release of a videotape on September 14, 2000 which showed SIN leader Montesinos bribing an opposition member of Congress to join Fujimori's coalition. This set off a wave of mass protest within Peru and calls for Fujimori to dismiss Montesinos. Several tense weeks followed, including allegations of gun-running by Montesinos, the acceptance of campaign funds from drug lords by Fujimori, many rumors of military coups and the disappearance (twice) and reappearance of Montesinos.[23] In the end, Fujimori faxed his resignation to Congress from Japan in November of 2000, ending a ten-year reign as Peru's president.

The OAS assisted in the democratization process in two ways: through pressure and the acquiescence effect. Although there was little direct pressure from the OAS on Fujimori to hold new elections after the controversial May 2000 runoff, the OAS-sponsored roundtable was "to signal that the international community was watching political events in the country and would not tolerate blatant dictatorship" (McClintock 2001: 139). After the September 2000 revelations of corruption within Fujimori's regime, the roundtable played an especially critical role as an institution with "de facto decision-making power" (Cooper and Legler 2001: 132). It served as an institutional forum through which domestic and international forces could pressure Fujimori during the crisis. This pressure bore

[23] For details, see Balbi and Palmer 2001.

fruit during the showdown with Montesinos as Fujimori began instituting a set of reforms designed to restore domestic and international confidence in Peruvian democracy. Although these reforms were too little, too late for Fujimori, they set a course for the return of a more liberal democracy after Fujimori's resignation and served as an internationally supported "buffer against the threat of military disruption" (Cooper and Legler 2001: 132).

Although weaker, there are signs of the acquiescence effect at work as well. During the chaos of the Fujimori–Montesinos chess match, it was unclear how the coalitions loosely aligned with Fujimori would proceed. While they could continue to have their lot cast with the failing leader, they could also support a Montesinos-led military coup or they could simply stay on the sidelines. Under the auspices of the OAS-sponsored roundtable, these pseudo-proponents of Fujimori decided to stick with the reform process and take their chances in a democratic system. According to two observers of the Peruvian crisis, "[the roundtable] provided an attractive route for the forces loosely coalesced around Fujimori to reinvent and relegitimate themselves" (Cooper and Leger 2001: 135).[24]

Conclusion: Peruvian democracy and the OAS

The case of Peru highlights the importance of international pressure and, to a lesser extent, the acquiescence effect in assisting the redemocratization process. Stepping back, it is clear that the OAS itself has learned throughout multiple crises in the 1990s. As many observers have noted, the OAS's hands-off approach after pressing Fujimori to call elections in 1992 could have encouraged his bold behavior in the 1999–2000 period. In that sense, the recent challenge was seen by the OAS as a test of the credibility of its democracy guarantee. Thus, it highlights the importance of the discussion of enforcement – because domestic elites' calculations are based on potential behavior by regional organizations, reputation for enforcing conditionality is important. Although there was certainly criticism of aspects of the OAS actions in the 2000 crisis, it also represents the dynamics discussed in Chapter 2: "International diplomacy mixed with domestic policy making" (Cooper and Legler 2001: 125). This produced an outcome which would have been *much* more difficult absent the pressure of the OAS. Domestic agents were important, but they operated in a context shaped by regional organizations.

---

[24] It should be noted that as in the 1992 case, US pressure was also an important factor in Fujimori's calculations. Again, however, much of the US pressure was directed *through* the OAS. See Balbi and Palmer 2001: 69.

Turkey: successful liberalization or failed consolidation?

Turkey's history provides several examples of the breakdown of and transition to democracy. Turkey's military has intervened in Turkish politics in 1960, 1971, and 1980, to unseat civilian-led governments. What makes these breakdown and redemocratization episodes especially important to this work is that in all three instances Turkey was a member of several IOs that were highly democratic. Thus, Turkey appears to provide three cases falsifying the general theory proposed in Chapter 2 – that IOs effectively assist in the consolidation process.

Although regional organizations have failed to assist in democratic consolidation in Turkey, I find significant evidence in support of several of the propositions concerning these organizations and transitions to democracy. Specifically, I find that IOs encouraged the liberalization process after the 1980 intervention by the military. This study will begin with a very brief history of the development of Turkish democracy. I then examine the failure of IOs to assist in consolidating democracy in Turkey, focusing on the 1980 case.[25] Next, I turn to the question of regional IO influence in pressuring Turkey to redemocratize after the 1980 coup. I conclude with an examination of the current state of EU, NATO, and Turkish affairs.

The cycles of Turkish democracy

After the First World War, Turkey began its first affair with democracy with the rise of Atatürk and the establishment of the secular state in Turkey in 1923. Atatürk began the liberalization process and continually made steps towards democracy (creating an independent judiciary, increasing parliamentary responsibility, etc.) until his death in 1938 (Henze 1991; also Sunar and Sayari 1986). His chosen successor, Ismet Inonu, continued the liberalization process until it reached its fruition in 1946 with the "self-transformation of an authoritarian, one-party system into a democratic, competitive party system" (Huntington 1981: 250). Although the political party founded by Attaturk and Inonu (the Republican People's Party or RPP) maintained control after this initial election, opposition parties began to grow in strength and numbers throughout the 1950s (Henze 1991: 92–3).

Eventually, opposition leader Adnan Menderes' Democrat Party (DP) came to power in May 1950 (Ozbudun 1995: 230). While continuing the

[25] I limit my study to 1980 for two reasons. First, there are far more detailed secondary accounts of the events surrounding this episode. Second, several IOs were especially active throughout this episode which makes it an even bigger anomaly for my theory.

general direction of Attaturk's reform including an anti-Communist, pro-Western foreign policy, the Menderes government began to face increasing opposition from left- and right-wing opposition groups. Finally, in the face of a mounting economic crisis, the military ousted the regime in 1960, arresting and executing Menderes and his associates (Henze 1991: 94). Within a year, the military government had cleared the way for new elections and a revised constitution (Sunar and Sayari 1986).

During this next phase of democracy (1961–71), new opposition parties again gained ground on the RPP. The RPP's major competition was the Justice Party (JP), headed by Suleyman Demirel. Demirel was avowedly pro-Western and pro-capitalist, but upon his assumption of the premiership of Turkey in 1965, anti-American feelings were on the rise (Henze 1991: 95–7). In addition, the Kurdish minority of Turkey began a coordinated effort to strike economic and military targets, causing outbreaks of civil violence across the country. In this milieu of civil unrest, on March 12, 1971, several leading Turkish generals asked Demirel to step aside. He agreed and the second interruption in Turkish democracy began.

While in power, the military attempted to squash various terrorist organizations while suspending elections (Dodd 1990: 15–17). Scholars of this coup have labeled it the "coup-by-pronouncement," given its peaceful and highly planned nature (Heper 1987: 57). The military attempted to serve as a neutral "caretaker" with respect to political parties by appointing a non-partisan prime minister, Nihat Erim, who would form three coalition governments before the reintroduction of free elections (Henze 1991: 98).

By 1973, the third phase of democracy in Turkey began with the holding of parliamentary elections. Unlike their first experience in the 1960s, the Turkish military made few actual changes to political institutions during this second interruption (1971–3) (Sunar and Sayari 1986; Heper 1987: 57). Unfortunately, the same factions that contributed to the civil violence of the 1960s returned to this behavior as the 1970s progressed. Turkey once again suffered massive civil unrest in its largest cities, involving left- and right-wing extremists. Kurdish rebel groups added fuel to the fire in rural areas, where bombings and shootings became ubiquitous (Henze 1991: 103–5).

On September 12, 1980, the military began its third reign over the political institutions in Turkey, unseating Demirel for the second time (Dagi 1996). The crackdown on "rogue elements" was much tougher during this interregnum. The military established a National Security Council (NSC) to oversee its law-and-order campaign, and in the first eighteen months, confiscated over 800,000 weapons from "liberated areas"

(Henze 1991: 105). This began the military's longest and most involved tenure in Turkish politics. Under General Kenan Evren, the military banned all political parties and arrested the leaders of the four largest parties. Between the coup of September 1980 and February 1983, over 60,000 people were arrested (Dagi 1996). Mass trials were held and many civil organizations, including labor unions, were declared illegal. This military intervention was far-reaching and, according to one observer, "dramatically changed the domestic political scene" (Dagi 1996: 125).

In 1982, the military leadership of the NSC drafted a new constitution for Turkey. A nationwide referendum approved the constitution by over 90 percent. Parties became legal in 1983, yet any politicians active before the 1980 coup were banned from participating in politics (Henze 1991: 107). With the election of Turgut Ozal's Motherland party (the successor to the RPP) in 1983, Turkey returned to the status of a multiparty electoral system.

IOs and democratic backsliding: failed causal mechanisms?

Why were regional organizations unable to hinder the breakdown of democracy in Turkey? Were the causal mechanisms not present in this case or did other conditions mitigate their impact? This section will explore these questions by reviewing which (if any) of the causal mechanisms *could* have assisted in the consolidation of Turkish democracy before the 1980 coup. Recall from Chapter 2 that I hypothesize four causal mechanisms that will link regional organizations with consolidation: binding winners and binding losers through credible commitments, bribery of societal groups, and legitimization of nascent democratic regimes.

The answer to this puzzle cannot be found in a lack of IO involvement on the part of Turkey. In its attempt to portray itself as a "Western" nation, it joined several Western European IOs in the late 1940s and early 1950s, namely, NATO, the OECD, and the Council of Europe (Muftuler-Bac 1998: 243). Turkey also signed an association agreement with the European Economic Community in 1963 (the Ankara Agreement). This agreement was expanded in 1970 with the signing of the Additional Protocol between the EC and Turkey (Muftuler-Bac 1998: 241). Not only was Turkey an active member of these groups, but each organization's membership was highly democratic – a sign that these organizations should have been able to play some role in preserving democracy in Turkey.

Which of the causal mechanisms could have operated to prevent democratic backsliding in Turkey? None of the regional organizations to which

Turkey belonged attempted to bribe any segment of society. The largest flow of aid to Turkey came from the US and NATO. The clear purpose of this military assistance was to support Turkey as a bulwark against potential Soviet aggression. Non-military assistance did attempt to engender domestic stability, but there were never conditions relating to the governmental system (Henze 1991). The EC did provide some financial assistance, but this was not targeted to any particular group (EC Bulletin 1981).

Other causal mechanisms, committing both winners and losers to democracy through both conditionality and legitimization, should have been important in this case. By 1980, Turkey continued to retain membership in several IOs that explicitly required a democratic form of government, including their association agreement with the EC. In addition, these organizations possessed the economic resources to create credible threats against Turkey: as of 1985, roughly 35 to 40 percent of its exports went to the EC, while over 25 percent of its imports originated from Community members (Barchard 1985: 68). Moreover, much of the Turkish population places a high value on membership in "Western" organizations that have helped to legitimize democracy.[26] These potential costs (both in real economic and symbolic terms) should have helped to deter the military from moving against the democratically elected government, yet they did not.

The European response to the 1980 coup was quite strong. The OECD suspended economic aid, the EC–Turkey association agreement was frozen (Pridham 1991c: 216), and Turkey was suspended from attending the Council of Europe (Karaosmanoglu 1991: 162; Yesilada 1999). These measures did impose direct economic costs on Turkey, which was already suffering from one of its worst economic crises in history.[27]

All of these efforts, however, came *after* the coup. Why did the Turkish military not anticipate this response of IOs to the breakdown of democracy? Was the conditionality of these organizations and their assistance of little importance to the generals or to opposition groups which had become increasingly violent before the coup? Although there is little secondary evidence relating to the generals' calculations, there is much speculation about the absence of concern over these issues.

First, the military probably expected little or no punishment from these organizations or their members since little action had been taken against it in the past. The military had barely received a slap on the wrist for its behavior in 1960 which set an early precedent that IOs would pay little

[26] I discuss this issue further in the next section.
[27] On the economic crisis, see Kuniholm (1985: 221).

attention to internal Turkish politics. Although few organizations had democracy requirements or conditions at that time, those that did took no action with regard to the 1960 coup. The Council of Europe was the major organization requiring democracy as a condition of membership, yet the Council made little mention of the coup in its public pronouncements. Moreover, because of the coup's acceptance domestically and its non-violent nature, the council chose to take no action against Turkey (Dodd 1990).

The 1971 coup, however, did result in punishment from several European organizations. Economic assistance was suspended by several European states and calls for a return to democracy soon echoed across Western Europe (see Yesilada 1999: 145). Turkey also had an additional IO tie at that point, the European Community. Nonetheless, no sanctions were placed on Turkey and other organizations such as NATO continued their strong support. Thus, if precedent was any guide to the coup con-spirators of 1980, they had no expectation that this transgression against democracy would bring any significant economic or political costs. After all, Turkey was a front-line state against the Soviet threat and held in high esteem by the United States as one of its strongest allies against Communism (Kuniholm 1985: 231).

It was thus a genuine surprise when Turkey's European counterparts severely criticized the military and the coup (Kuniholm 1985: 225). Some observers have even noted that the EC's *initial* reaction to the military takeover was, in fact, "rather mild" (Dagi 1996: 128). As the length of the military's stay in power grew longer, however, the EC response grew harsher, eventually including the suspension of aid (Dagi 1996: 129–30).

Second, even if the Turkish military did expect some hostility from Europe, it certainly expected unconditional support from the US. Again, this inference was probably based on past behavior. In the first two coups, the US had stood by its ally. Since the Truman Doctrine in 1947, Turkey had been a key ally to help protect both the southern flank of Europe and the Middle East. Its strategic importance for US grand strategy led to an interest in Turkey's overall stability, regardless of the type of regime in Ankara. The US embraced the Menderes government after the 1960 coup, even as it began to behave arbitrarily towards its citizenry (Henze 1991). The US did not use its leverage within NATO or the OECD to express concern over the internal situation in Turkey, nor did it encourage either organization to punish the perpetrators of the 1960 coup. Similarly, in the 1971 coup, the US did not react negatively and even pressured its NATO allies to treat the situation with a "business as usual" attitude.

While the generals were surprised by the European response to the coup, their anticipation of US behavior proved well founded. After the 1980 takeover, the US pressured the EC, the Council of Europe, and NATO *not* to punish General Evren's takeover (Dagi 1996: 127). NATO and the US continued to provide military assistance to the regime while helping to push an aid package through the IMF (Dagi 1996: 127; see also Whitehead 1996c: 12–17). In the end, the strategic importance of Turkish membership in NATO kept that organization from attempting to punish the Evren regime (Karaosmanoglu 1994: 130). Evren and his colleagues knew their strategic importance to NATO and the US, anticipating a non-response from that organization (Mackenzie 1984: 14). This does suggest the realist emphasis on great power preferences is apropos in this particular case. The US pushed NATO not to punish Turkey, supporting the contention that the institution itself was no more or less than its great power leader. Still, NATO is the only regional institution where this argument holds for Turkey.

The story of policy convergence brought about by a regional IO is found when exploring a third factor explaining why these international forces failed to initial secure Turkish democracy. During much of the postwar era, European states behaved very differently towards Turkey depending on whether the context of the interaction was bilateral or multilateral. This no doubt contributed to Turkish expectations that European IOs would not punish Turkey. For example, Steinbach (1994: 110) has argued that there is a preference among European states to "distinguish between EC relations with Turkey as a possible future member of the community and bilateral relations with Turkey." Although the Turkish military could have anticipated verbal condemnation from European IOs, it most likely felt Turkey's individual trade relations and economic assistance from the members of these organizations would be uninterrupted.

In 1980, however, this belief proved incorrect. Individual European states did reduce their economic and political ties with Turkey, largely as a part of multilateral efforts to coordinate a response to the coup. Evren and his colleagues expected the words of the regional organizations and the deeds of the member states to be quite different. Yet members of the EC and the Council of Europe matched their state positions to those of the organizations – Turkey's move from democracy was to be criticized and punished, even though several members of these organizations would have preferred milder responses to the coup (Steinbach 1994; see also Yilmaz 2002: 73). Thus, although the NATO story supports the realist view concerning state preferences and multilateralism, European states coordinated their positions through regional organizations to punish the Turkish military – a testament to the influence of the institutions.

Finally, the military could have made a simple cost–benefit calculation that any ill effects of condemnation and/or punishment through regional organizations were significantly less than the gains from restoring order to the Turkish government and society. In the two years preceding the coup, violence had reached an unprecedented level in Turkey. During the first eight months of 1980, 25,000 "terrorist incidents" were reported and almost 3,000 people were killed in civil violence in Turkey (Henze 1991: 104). By August of 1980, the pace of assassinations and politically motivated killings had reached twenty-eight a day (Kuniholm 1985: 221). Although martial law had been declared in most of Turkey's provinces, the Demirel government was unable to quell the violence. It was this condition of civil unrest that prompted the Turkish military to act (Henze 1991: 104–5). On top of this civil violence, Turkey was in the grip of an economic crisis with nearly 40 percent unemployment and inflation over 100 percent (Spain and Ludington 1983).

Given this unstable political and economic situation, could any threat by the EC, the Council of Europe or even NATO have convinced the Turkish military not to act? Although it is possible that concern over international responses influenced the timing of the intervention, the ultimate answer to this question is probably no. The Turkish military felt that the very fabric of its state was at risk (Couloumbis 1983: 161). As many observers have noted, the Turkish military leaders consider themselves the "saviors" of Turkish democracy (Heper 1987: 58–60). Their response to pressure would probably have been one of indignation, given the military's past moves to relinquish power to civilian governments. In fact, in 1978 Prime Minister Bulent Ecevit froze relations and negotiations with the EC, demonstrating the lack of concern over breaking off EC–Turkish relations (Barchard 1985: 63; Steinbach 1994: 109). Although this tension arose from issues unrelated to Turkish democracy, it was a clear demonstration that Turkey was willing to pay the price inflicted by poor EC–Turkish relations almost two years before the coup. Weighed against the prospect of allowing civil violence to continue, the benefit of Turkey–EC relations could well have been a cost General Evren and his associates were willing to pay.[28]

Despite this conclusion, it has also been hypothesized that concern over the potential EC response to the 1980 coup did, in fact, influence the timing of the action. Metin Heper (1987: 58–9) has argued that the military allowed the situation in Turkey to deteriorate (in the areas of civil violence and the economy) in order to solidify internal and external

---

[28] Although this example has concentrated on the events of September 1980, violence was very high during the 1971 intervention as well. A similar argument concerning the perceived costs and benefits of intervention could be made for that episode as well.

opinion on the need for a coup. Heper argues that the generals plotted to intervene much earlier, but, in part because of concerns of perceptions from abroad, waited to move against Demirel. Although this concern over international perceptions was not enough to prevent the action, this does show that international forces did play a small role in the process of the military takeover. In the end, however, the pressing civil and economic crisis of Turkey spurred the generals to take control in September 1980.

This case illustrates the importance of the enforcement issue in discussing the efficacy of regional organizations in supporting the consolidation of democracy. As discussed in both Chapters 2 and 3, enforcing conditions of membership set by IOs is an important aspect of creating an externally supported commitment to democracy as well as a deterrent to anti-democratic forces. Equally important is the *expectation* that conditions will be enforced. The lack of action on the part of the EC, Council of Europe, or NATO to punish Turkey in 1960 or 1971 created a dangerous precedent for the military's actions in 1980.[29] Since the generals did not expect punishment or expulsion from these organizations, it is difficult for conditionality (whether as a commitment or deterrent device) to be effective. While the EC and the Council of Europe were certainly guilty of this behavior, neither organization defected on its enforcement more than NATO. NATO made no attempt to pressure Turkey for democracy before or after any of the three autocratic interregnums, at times reinforcing its support of any regime in Ankara after coups, so long as it maintained its pro-Western stance.

This is a case where even with clear signals and a more favorable precedent, the Turkish military may have moved against democracy. IOs can influence the cost–benefit calculations of those who would overthrow a democratic system, but they can do so only to the extent that they can raise the costs of action higher than the perceived benefits. Obviously if the benefits of coups are perceived to be large, a regional IO's power to influence outcomes may be limited.

IOs and Turkey: the pressure for liberalization

Despite the fact that IOs had little influence in deterring non-democratic forces from toppling democracy in Turkey, these same IOs did play an important role in influencing the timing as well as the process of *liberalization* after the 1980 military coup. This is especially true of the EC,

---

[29] For example, Barchard (1985: 58) has argued that the Council of Europe often turned a "blind eye" to human rights and democracy violations in Turkey, especially before the 1980 coup.

the Council of Europe, and to a lesser extent, NATO. This section will examine how these three organizations assisted in encouraging the Evren regime to liberalize its authoritarian rule and push subsequent Turkish governments to complete the transition to democracy.

Initially, I do not claim that if not for these IOs, the Turkish military would have necessarily attempted to establish a permanent rule in Turkey. In each case, immediately after intervention, the military leaders declared that they had no intention to remain in power for an extended period of time (Ozbudun 1995: 237). It would be an overstatement to say that regional IOs played a *decisive* role in convincing the military to step down. Yet, the pressure from IOs did influence the timing and the process of liberalization.

The strongest causal mechanism found in this process is the pressure brought by IOs to push Turkey back towards democracy. Turkey's association agreement with the EC as well as its membership in the Council of Europe provided a potent source of pressure on the military regime which held power from 1980 until 1983. Not only did direct financial pressure arise from these organizations, but Turkey's desire to become a full member of the EU exerted an independent pressure to democratize as well (Heper 1992: 107). Turgut Ozal, the prime minister from 1983 to 1989, recognized the importance of democracy in Turkey for this purpose: "If Turkey wants to be in the European Community, there has to be democracy in Turkey" (quoted in Muftuler-Bac 1998: 246).

Financially, the EC began to turn the screws on the military regime almost one year after the takeover. Its first move was to *increase* financial assistance to Turkey in June 1981, then hold that aid, conditional upon improvements in human rights and democratization (Dodd 1990: 62). Simultaneously, Turkish leaders announced their desire to become a full member of the Community (no doubt spurred by Greece's 1981 accession). Observers have noted that this announcement "enabled the European Community to press more rigorously for the restoration of democracy as quickly as possible" (Dagi 1996: 129). Thus, demarches by the EC with respect to Turkey's domestic situation took on added importance given Turkey's push for full accession.

General Evren noted the importance of European behavior towards his regime in his own memoirs. Over twenty-five entries a year concern his perceptions of the European response to his policies, including expressing relief when the Council of Europe did not permanently expel Turkey (Dagi 1996: 137–8). This first-hand evidence of the military's concern over European actions demonstrates the potential leverage of the Community during this time. Thus, although General

Evren did not want to appear pressured, his "over-sensitivity is a sign that European pressure was there and influencing his decisions" (Dagi 1996: 138).

The psychological dimension of the European–Turkish relationship also provided an important source of leverage for European organizations. For Turkey, membership in the Council of Europe and its association agreement with the EC provided a psychological anchoring of Turkey to the West (Mackenzie 1984: 22–3; Tachau 1984: 199–200). The Council's major actions included sending multiple fact-finding missions to Turkey to investigate reports of human rights abuses and pressure the generals to set a timetable for new elections (Dagi 1996: 131–2). Although Turkish leaders continually expressed frustration at these efforts of the Council, they did prove effective on several occasions, including convincing Ankara to accept a 25-member delegation to monitor the return of parliamentary democracy to Turkey (Dagi 1996: 137). Rather than a financial pressure, the Council's weapon was mainly a psychological one: "The symbolic, even psychological, significance which Turkey attached to the Council of Europe was a means of influence for the Council . . ." (Dagi 1996: 131).

Both the Council and the EC were able to exert significant financial and psychological pressure on the military regime to move towards redemocratization. Although these efforts clearly strained Turkey's relations with many states of Western Europe, in the end, "pressures exerted by Europeans nevertheless did accelerate the process of democratization in Turkey" (Karaosmanoglu 1994: 129).

Evidence of the acquiescence effect is tenuous. The argument that NATO's contribution to the redemocratization of Turkey flowed from its socialization of officers in the Turkish military is fairly weak. As previously discussed, NATO exerted little direct pressure on the generals. In fact, NATO continued to support the Ankara regime with military assistance and, along with the US, preached a "pragmatic" approach to internal Turkish politics (Couloumbis 1983: 37; Karaosmanoglu 1994: 130; Tirman 1998: 60). Yet it can be argued that Turkey's involvement in NATO helped to ensure that the interventions by the military would be short lived. The military clearly held democracy as the "ultimate, if not [the] immediate, goal" (Heper 1987: 54). Some scholars of the Turkish military contend that this tradition of "returning to the barracks" has been inspired by military leaders' involvement in NATO. For example, Ali Karaosmanoglu (1993: 31) has argued that interactions between US and Western European NATO officers and their Turkish counterparts have contributed to their overall respect for democracy:

Most of Turkey's high-ranking officers have either visited or served in various NATO headquarters in Europe or in the United States. Such experiences abroad gave them an international outlook and contributed to their sense of professionalism . . . Its commitment to professionalism appears to be one of the reasons the Turkish military has disengaged itself from politics as quickly as possible following each intervention. (Karaosmanoglu 1994: 126)

Because of their continued involvement in politics, however, one must question how much influence NATO has on the "professionalization" of the Turkish military officers.

There were limits, however, to the influence of these IOs in the liberalization process. Although I have argued they were effective at pushing for the initial liberalization of the Turkish regime, they were unable to bring about a completion of the transition to democracy. Turkish democracy is still far from perfect, despite continued pressure from the EU (Yesilada 1999). Still, Europeans continue to push for the full democracy in Turkey. Even since 1983 and the return of elections in Turkey, "a step-by-step democratization has been carried out . . . Constant European pressure has even succeeded in drawing the attention of the Turkish leadership to the sensitive issues of human rights and in making the government publicly admit shortcomings and take measures to correct them" (Steinbach 1994: 115).

Epilogue: Turkish democracy into the twenty-first century

Throughout the late 1990s, the Turkish military nervously eyed the emergence of a powerful Islamist party that had risen largely because of an increasingly stagnant economy. The Welfare Party, led by Prime Minister Necmettin Erbakan, was a member of a coalition government with the True Path Party, led by Tansu Ciller. On February 28, 1997, the military leadership in Turkey presented the Erbakan government with a list of eighteen demands to be implemented, "including a clampdown on reactionary Islam" (Ozel 2003: 87). These measures proved to be popular and by the summer of 1997, Erbakan's government had fallen and the Welfare Party was banned by the Constitutional Court (Candar 1999).

It is interesting that the military chose not to directly overthrow the Erbakan government. Doing so would have no doubt brought tremendous pressure from Europe, as it did in 1980. The military kept the position of the EU in mind as it contemplated its moves in February 1997. Some observers noted the military clearly anticipated European reaction when it choose not to pursue an open coup (Doxey 1997). The banning of the Welfare Party was criticized in Europe and the United States, but the party was allowed to reform under new leadership.

As new elections were held in 2002, however, the Islamist party reemerged in Turkish politics. The Justice and Development Party (AKP) captured 363 of the 541 seats of the Grand National Assembly. In a fascinating turn of events, however, the AKP party became a strong proponent for Turkish membership into the European Union. The logic behind this embracing of Europe by an Islamist party is consistent with the argument made here. The AKP has promoted the idea of democracy and EU-membership to send credible signals to both domestic and international audiences that it is a moderate Islamic party that believes in Western-oriented market reforms (Onis and Keyman 2003: 99). Ironically, "the much-maligned EU and its norms became a key source of support for the persecuted Islamist parties" (Ozel 2003: 89). The EU has helped to socialize members of the AKP and convince its leadership of the need for more reform in Turkish politics (Onis 2001). By pushing EU accession, the AKP has established itself as a moderate force in Turkish politics. It is too early to tell if the AKP will be more successful than its predecessors at gaining EU concessions, but the AKP clearly realizes that it has an international audience and this guides its thinking on economic and political issues (Onis 2001; Ozel 2003: 106).

Conclusion

This final case study has demonstrated the presence and efficacy of several of the causal mechanisms concerning democratic transitions from Chapter 2. External pressure to liberalize (from the EC and the Council of Europe) in terms of both financial and psychological mechanisms played a role in the liberalization process in Turkey after the 1980 military intervention. Thus, it is an important case for the study of IOs' influence on the process of liberalization and redemocratization.

It is also an important case falsifying the theory presented in Chapter 2. These same IOs have had little success in influencing the consolidation process in Turkey. I have attempted to sketch an explanation for why the conditions and warnings of the IOs seem to have little effect on the military's decision to intervene in politics: given the history of democratic interregnums and the *lack* of response by regional organizations, Turkish generals felt little fear of punishment. The conditions were themselves conditional. Much to their surprise, Europe did respond in a way that both surprised the military administration and led to a *faster* return to civilian rule than would have occurred otherwise. If General Evren could have anticipated this response, would the Turkish military have moved against the civilian government anyway? I would answer yes – civil violence had reached a point that the military felt it needed to intervene and only *very* high costs imposed by regional organizations could have avoided this outcome.

Of course, the fact that Turkey does not fit the model as outlined here may not be entirely surprising. In the words of one student of Turkish politics and history, "Model-makers among political scientists have difficulty fitting Turkey into their categories. In the words of Attaturk, it resembles no one so much as itself" (Mango 1997: 4).

Conclusion: assessing the transition cases

Table 5.2 presents the findings on the three cases of a transition to democracy. Several conclusions can be drawn from these findings. First, the acquiescence effect, although certainly supported by theoretical material on democratic transitions and international institutions, is only moderately supported in these studies. Moreover, only one part of this mechanism seems to be relevant – the effect of military-oriented IOs on civil–military relations. In Hungary, and to a lesser extent Turkey, membership in highly democratic military IOs seemed to improve the prospects for stable civil–military relations through a socialization process. The involvement of Hungarian and Turkish officers with other (in both cases NATO) officers, helped to socialize them into accepting civilian supremacy and their proper role in guaranteeing *only* the external security of the state.[30]

Unfortunately, there was little evidence of the acquiescence effect in the interaction of regional organizations and their interaction with domestic economic elites. Recall that one hypothesis was that membership in certain economic-oriented IOs would calm elite fears of threats to their property rights and other policies supported by non-democratic governments since the IO represented an external guarantee of these rights and preferences. I found no strong evidence of these dynamics in the cases presented here. Chapter 2 did provide anecdotal evidence of this causal mechanism involving Southern Europe, but outside of those transitions I find little evidence for this argument in any of my cases.

There are three potential explanations for this finding. First, the acquiescence effect may play a larger role in the consolidation of democracy, rather than the transition (see Whitehead 1989: 84–5). While this is certainly plausible, one must question the timing of entry into the organization. That is, if elite fears have led them to support authoritarianism in the past, why would they first acquiesce to democracy, *then* attempt to join

---

[30] For Turkey, I argue that that the speed with which the military leaders left power (and the fact that they did at all) is partially explained by this socialization process. Still, because they directly intervened in Turkish politics in the first place, this finding is weak at best.

these regional organizations? It would seem that these assurances would be required before the transition occurs. Still, it is possible that these assurances are important after the initial transition, as the implications of new political institutions become apparent.

A second possibility is that internal guarantees are utilized to assure powerful elites that they will be protected in the democratization process. Power-sharing arrangements, the exclusion of particular opposition groups, or reserve domains could be used to make sure that key elite actors feel protected during the transition period, even though the credibility of such guarantees can certainly be questioned. Third, it is possible that in most transitions, most of the powerful elites have an innate desire for democracy. If democracy truly is "an equilibrium outcome," then elites may feel that they can do just as well under an open competition system without having to pay the costs of repression (Przeworski 1991). In addition, they can benefit from the added legitimacy of a democratic system (Mainwaring 1992). There would be little need for elite assurances under these conditions, whether internal or external.

The second conclusion drawn from these case studies is that membership in IOs is most effective in assisting the completion of democratization (moving from an anocracy to a democracy) and in the process of *redemocratization*. I could find little evidence that the IOs included in these studies pushed states to begin the liberalization process *unless* they had recently undergone a change from democracy to autocracy. The cases of Peru and Turkey are typical in this respect. In both of these cases a significant movement from authoritarianism to anocracy or democracy occurred, but in both instances, it was very soon after a slide towards autocracy. I found little evidence in these or any other cases that membership in highly democratic regional organizations can pressure or facilitate an authoritarian state's move to democracy when the regime has been in power for many years.

There could be several explanations for this pattern. One is that the transition literature on the determinants of liberalization is correct that external factors play a miniscule role in determining when a state *begins* the process of democratization. External forces may play little or no role in the process of "splitting" the ruling coalition – a factor much of the transitions literature argues is a prerequisite to liberalization (cf. Przeworski 1991; O'Donnell and Schmitter 1986). Second, autocratic states may stay out of IOs which consist mostly of democracies due to fear that membership could push them to liberalize. If they foresee the influence of these regional IOs, they may opt to stay away from them even if they offer other significant political or economic benefits. These are clearly testable propositions which, if properly investigated through large-N and/or further case studies, could help clarify this seeming lack of relationship between regional IO membership and the initial liberalization process.

A third finding in this chapter was the discovery of an additional causal mechanism: the transfer of resources from the IO to the member state (here, Hungary). Considering Hungary was a case of democratic completion rather than liberalization or redemocratization, one hypothesis would be that this transfer of resources is essential for the later stages of democratization. To overcome the short-term challenges of shifting from an interim government to an open political system, especially when this is accompanied by a transition to a more liberal economy, IOs can provide valuable economic assistance (whether in the form of direct aid, loans, or increased trade). These short-term challenges to the transition are highest when a dual (economic and political) transition is underway.[31] States must face the difficulties associated with a political transition (e.g. creating new political institutions, reforming political parties) along with the economic costs of a neoliberal economic transition (e.g. shifting to free markets, privatization of state-owned industries, trade liberalization). These resources from IOs can help to legitimize interim regimes to ensure they do not succumb to pressure arising from poor economic conditions.

The pressure mechanism was found in two of the three cases examined. Based on these cases, it would appear that pressure is commonly found in instances of redemocratization. Organization members who suffer a breakdown of democracy are susceptible to pressure through the institution. This is consistent with the arguments of institutionalist theory in international relations. Institutions increase information exchange, assist in the construction of focal points, and lower transaction costs, all of which make it easier to coordinate pressure on a new authoritarian regime.

In fairness, some evidence surfaced concerning the realist hypothesis regarding regimes – that major power preferences play the key role and that the institutions themselves are not essential to shaping outcomes. The US pressure on NATO not to punish Turkey after the suspension of democracy there is evidence that large preferences can dictate the behavior of institutions. The European institutions in the Turkish case provide a counterexample, however, to the NATO case. Although European states were expected to pay lip service to democracy through multilateral institutions, while privately supporting the new military regime, their individual policies came to mirror those of the institutions. This is strong evidence of what institutional theorists label "convergence" (see Botcheva and Martin

---

[31] On the challenges of dual transitions see Armijo, Biersteker, and Lowenthal 1995; Bartlett and Hunter 1997.

Table 5.2 *Transition cases and evidence of causal mechanisms*

Case/Mechanism	Peru	Turkey	Hungary
Acquiescence effect	–	Weak	Moderate
Legitimization/psychological	–	Weak	Strong
Pressure	Strong	Moderate	–
Financial assistance[*]	–	–	Strong

*–not included in Chapter 2 causal mechanisms.

2001). In the context of placing pressure on states to redemocratize, multilateral pressure is often more effective than unilateral efforts (Whitehead 1989). Institutions may not *always* bring democracy, but this does not make them epiphenomenal.

Finally, these cases illustrate the importance of the legitimization or psychological impact of membership in IOs in only one case. The case of Hungary suggests that this influence is strongest when the state has a long history of non-democracy. In other words, the more of an authoritarian past a new democratic regime must overcome, the more important is membership in highly democratic regional organizations. This is intuitive since it will be states that have a distant history or no history with democracy that may have a more difficult time signaling their intention (to international and domestic observers) to become a full-fledged democracy.

These cases also highlight the importance of the enforcement issue. In both Peru and Turkey, questions arose concerning how rigorously membership conditions would be enforced. Particularly in the Turkish case, the US was clear that it did not believe that NATO should pursue any punishment of Turkey in the wake of the 1980 coup. The Turkish case highlighted the importance of domestic elites perceiving that conditions will be enforced. If elites believe they will be allowed to escape any consequences for their actions, the role of regional institutions in encouraging democracy or preserving democracy will be limited at least.

Nonetheless, there is substantial evidence that regional organizations can be associated with the transition to democracy, whether in the case of redemocratization or the completion of the transition. Chapter 3 provided statistical support for this proposition, while these case studies have allowed the examination of particular causal mechanisms, adding depth to the statistical findings. The next two chapters turn to the question of the survival of democracy.

6　Regional organizations and democratic consolidation

The question of the survival of democracy has received less theoretical and empirical attention than transitions to democracy. This imbalance has begun to change, however, in reaction to the "third wave" of democratization. As these transitions reached their completion, both scholars and policymakers turned their attention to the next task: guaranteeing democracy's survival (Huntington 1991). In many cases, this would be a daunting task, including (re)building institutions grounded in democratic practices and (re)legitimizing democracy to the elites and the general public within the state. Most importantly, it means overcoming short-term opposition to new institutions by groups that could halt the reform process, or even return the state to authoritarian rule.

As with the literature on transitions, the empirical literature on democratic survivability has largely ignored the international context. Quantitative and qualitative investigations of regime consolidation routinely ignore international factors that could influence the longevity of democracy.[1] Rather, these studies focus on issues of economic development (Haggard and Kaufman 1995b; Huntington 1991), economic performance (Gasiorowski and Power 1998; Przeworski and Limongi 1997), and institutional variations including political parties (Power and Gasiorowski 1997; Sartori 1976; Shugart and Carey 1992). Rather than supplanting these domestic factors, I contend that international variables such as regional organizations serve as a structural factor which can be used by domestic agents to cope with the challenges of cementing nascent democratic institutions.

This chapter tests the hypothesis that regional organizations can be used by domestic actors to increase democratic longevity. Specifically, membership in regional organizations helps create credible commitments to democracy on the part of new regimes. This commitment helps to

---

[1] There are two small sets of exceptions: some studies consider regional context (in the form of contagion – see Gasiorowski 1995), while debates on NATO expansion occasionally broach this issue (see Reiter 2001b).

convince key elite groups as well as the masses to abide by these new institutions. The commitment arises out of the conditionality often associated with membership in these organizations, which serves to increase the costs of anti-regime action on the part of domestic groups. Thus, membership in democratic regional organizations serves to bind both winners and losers in the democratization process. In this chapter, I conduct a statistical test of this proposition while controlling for other factors that have been linked to democratic durability. I also test a number of competing hypotheses concerning the theory of regional organizations' influence on democratic survival.

Testing the argument

If the theory presented in Chapter 2 is correct, democratic regional organizations should increase the chances for the survival of democracy. To test this argument, this section will build and estimate several models using the measures of democracy and IO involvement discussed in Chapter 3. The expectation is that membership in regional institutions with a high "democratic density" will be positively associated with the endurance of democracy. Moreover, the association between *joining* a highly democratic organization and the consolidation of democracy is likely to be especially strong. Recall that much of the value of regional organizations for nascent democracies comes from their signaling value in terms of credible commitments to domestic and international actors. Thus, it is possible that joining a highly democratic IO would have an independent effect from a continuing membership.

The dependent variable in the following models is the length of time a regime persists as a democracy, labeled $DTIME_{it}$. This measures the number of years since a transition to democracy until a democratic breakdown (both defined in Chapter 3). Thus, if a transition occurs in state i in 1973, while a breakdown occurs in 1977, $DTIME_{it}$ would take a value of 1 in 1973, 2 in 1974, and so on until 1977 when it would be coded as 5. This counter would stop and the variable would be missing from 1978 until another democratic transition occurs.

$DTIME_{it}$ also measures democratic persistence if the state begins its time in the sample as a democracy. $DTIME_{it}$ begins at 1 for all democratic states entering the sample in 1950 or upon their independence if this occurs after 1950.[2] The variable is incremented by 1 each year the state

---

[2] The results of the analysis do not change significantly if the counter is started at a previous point in time. Of course, there will always be left-censoring in our measures of democratic endurance since we have little data on regime characteristics before 1800. Thus, any starting date for the counter may be considered arbitrary.

remains a democracy. Only a democratic breakdown stops the counter. If a breakdown does not occur for the remainder of the observation period, the counter runs until 1992 and the observation is right-censored. As discussed in the next section, event history or duration models are excellent statistical techniques to deal with this issue of right-censoring (Box-Steffensmeier and Jones 1997).

The two data sets discussed in Chapter 3 are used to measure democracy and transitions. Recall that because Gasiorowski does not code a host of developed states, the number of observations in the Gasiorowski models is lower than the Polity98 models. It should be noted that for the Gasiorowski data, the $DTIME_{it}$ counter reverts to missing if a transition from democracy to autocracy occurs, but if a transition from democracy to semi-democracy occurs, the counter stops, but is immediately restarted at 1 since, according to the Gasiorowski criteria, these regimes still contain many democratic traits.[3] For all event history models, I use time-varying covariates.

Modeling regime duration

To test whether democratic IOs are associated with consolidation, I estimate the following model:

$$
\begin{aligned}
(6.1) \quad DTIME_{it} = {} & \alpha_0 + \beta_1 IOScore_{it-1} + \beta_2 \Delta IOScore_{it-1} \\
& + \beta_3 pcGDP_{it} + \beta_4 \Delta pcGDP_{it} + \beta_5 RegContagion_{it} \\
& + \beta_6 PastBreakDown_{it} + \beta_7 RegConflict_{it} \\
& + \beta_8 InternalViolence_{it-1} + \beta_9 Presidential_{it} \\
& + \beta_{10} StableDemocracy_{it} + \beta_{11} Independence_{it} + \mu_{it}
\end{aligned}
$$

The model is estimated using event history analysis. These duration or hazard models are an appropriate methodology for testing the timing of events.[4] Each model shows the effect of each independent variable (covariate) on the probability (hazard rate) that state i will fail at time t. "Failure" here is synonymous with democratic breakdown. Recall that the model will be estimated using two different dependent variables based on the two data sets of regime transition. Before discussing the methodology of event history analysis, I provide a brief theoretical justification for each

---

[3] Recall from Chapter 2 that several "partial" transitions to democracy were included in the Gasiorowski coding. Moreover, the results are nearly identical if the counter is not restarted and continues until these states suffer a complete breakdown of democracy.

[4] These models have become ubiquitous in political science in the past five years. For a general overview, see Box-Steffensmeier and Jones 1997.

independent variable of the model, discussing coding issues only for those variables not discussed in Chapter 4.[5]

The first independent variable, $IOScore_{it-1}$, is the measure of the democratic density of the most democratic IO of which state i is a member in year t. The coding of this variable is discussed in Chapter 2. The next independent variable, $\Delta IOScore_{it-1}$, is computed to isolate the effects of joining a democratic international organization. It is the simple one-year difference of $IOScore_{it-1}$. As previously discussed, the signaling value of joining a highly democratic IO is important to domestic and international economic, as well as domestic political interests.

The next two independent variables tap the economic context of the regime. The first variable, $pcGDP_{it}$, measures the per capita GDP levels of each state in year t. Since one of the most recent contributions to this debate holds that higher income can *preserve* a transition to democracy (Londregan and Poole 1996; Przeworski et al. 1996), per capita GDP is included to control for this possibility. The second economic variable, $\Delta pcGDP_{it}$, controls for growth rates, which can influence the likelihood of anti-regime activities (Londregan and Poole 1990).

$RegContagion_{it}$ controls for diffusion effects from other established democracies. If a state is surrounded by democracies and if the democratic countries are more pacific towards one another, then we would expect a more hospitable environment for democracy to survive. In addition, because a state's *own* experience may influence its propensity to remain a democracy, I include $PastBreakDown_{it}$ in the model. Recall that while some scholars argue that past experience with democracy may bode well for new democracies (Linz and Stepan 1996), others scholars note that prior experience with democracy implies prior breakdowns that can decrease the probability of consolidation (Przeworski et al. 1996).

As in Chapter 4, two variables are coded to measure the effect of external and internal conflict. $RegConflict_{it}$ measures the presence of the threats or uses of force involving state i's region at time t. Whitehead (1996c), among others, has argued that involvement in military conflict is often associated with regime breakdown since the losers in these conflicts are often forced to take new governments by the victors (e.g. Second World War). Recall, however, Thompson's (1996) argument that a stable military environment is important to guard against the centralization of power within states. Internal violence may also harm the prospects for democratic endurance. To control for the effects of internal violence, I include the variable $InternalViolence_{it-1}$ in the model. Consolidating a

---

[5] For information on data sources and coding issues, see Chapter 4 for most of the variables in this model.

regime change will be especially difficult for new regimes which face massive domestic violence, as military and economic elites will have little tolerance for widespread anti-regime activity (see Linz and Stepan 1996).

The next independent variable is $Presidential_{it}$, which equals 1 if a state has a presidential or mixed democracy, and 0 otherwise.[6] Beginning with the work of Juan Linz (1990), a common argument in comparative politics is that parliamentary democracies tend to be more stable than those with presidential systems. The contention is that presidential systems tend to produce all-or-nothing outcomes that can cause instability among elites in young democracies (Linz 1990). In addition, proponents of this theory contend that immobilism is more likely under young presidential systems since presidents are likely to square off against legislatures, even if both are controlled by the same party (Przeworski et al. 1996).

Recall that democracies that existed at the beginning of the observation period (1950) and recently democratized states are included in the sample for this model. There is reason to believe, however, that states entering the observation period as stable democracies (e.g. the United States, Canada, Great Britain) are influenced less by regional organizations. In states which have been democracies for many years, there is little likelihood that membership in a democratic IO will influence the duration of that polity. In order to control for the factors that may differentiate established democracies from newly democratic polities, I code a dummy variable, $StableDemocracy_{it}$, which equals 1 if the state began its tenure in the analysis as a democracy, and 0 otherwise.[7]

The last control variable is $Independence_{it}$ which counts the number of years since state i's political independence, since very young states may have little opportunity to develop stable institutions of any kind, especially since their first government is usually heavily influenced by their colonizer. Finally, μ_{it} is a stochastic error term.

Statistical results

Because the dependent variable measures the duration of an event (how long a state remains a democracy), event history or duration analysis

---

[6] Data is taken from Alvarez et al. (1996) and updated from the CIA Factbook (1999), Gasiorowski (1993), and Gurr (1990) to include new democracies formed after 1990 (the end of Alvarez et al.'s coding period).

[7] This also includes a handful of newly independent states that began as democracies. Although these states may be different from the "stable" democracies that this variable is designed to control for, the next independent variable should adequately account for these states.

provides an excellent means for estimating this model. Event history models are used to estimate the probability that an event ends between time t and time $t + \Delta$, where Δ is any positive length of time (in this case, a year). This technique examines the dependent variable and estimates a baseline hazard rate, or the rate at which the "modal" event will end. These models then estimate the influence of a set of independent variables on that baseline hazard function. One decision to be made in using this technique is whether to specify the functional form of the hazard rate in advance. The Cox proportional hazard model allows model estimation without specifying the functional form of this hazard rate *a priori*. Given the flexibility of the Cox model, I estimate Model 6.1 using this technique.[8]

It is important to note that the interpretation of event history models is slightly different than traditional regression models. The most important difference is in the interpretation of the effects of individual coefficients on the dependent variable. A negatively signed coefficient estimate means that the hazard rate of experiencing an event (here democratic breakdown) is proportionally lower. In essence, this means a regime lasts longer. Conversely, a positive coefficient signifies an increase in the hazard rate and a shorter duration for the polity.

Columns 1 and 2 of Table 6.1 present the Cox estimates of Model 6.1, based on the Polity98 and Gasiorowski data, respectively. The first variable of interest, $IOScore_{it-1}$, is negative but not statistically significant in either model. Membership in an IO with higher levels of democracy does not appear to be associated with longer-lasting democratic regimes. Table 6.2 shows the percent change in the probability of a democratic breakdown given variations in the values of the independent variables. Given two democracies, each of which belonged to a different set of international organizations, the state which belonged to a more homogenously democratic organization would be 9 or 10 percent less likely to suffer breakdown than one whose IO membership was less homogenously democratic, depending on the data set. This substantively small change is not surprising given the variable's statistical insignificance.

The effect of joining a highly democratic IO is assessed by turning to the second independent variable, $\Delta IOScore_{it-1}$. In both models, this estimate is negative and statistically significant. This indicates that the

---

[8] I also estimate all models discussed in this chapter using a Weibull parameterization. I chose this distribution based on an examination of the Kaplan-Meier survival functions. The results, especially with regard to the independent variables of interest, are nearly identical to the Cox estimates. Because of the equivalence of results, I choose to present the estimates of the model with the least number of assumptions concerning functional form.

Table 6.1 *Cox estimates of the determinants of the duration of democracy, 1950–92*

	Polity98	Gasiorowski	Polity98	Gasiorowski
$IOScore_{it-1}$	−0.023	−0.023	−0.029	−0.007
	(−0.57)	(−0.54)	(−0.60)	(−0.17)
$\Delta IOScore_{it-1}$	−0.700***	−0.377***	−0.689**	−0.408***
	(−2.64)	(−3.06)	(−2.54)	(−3.05)
$MajPowerIO_{it-1}$	−.−	−.−	0.093	−0.225
			(0.31)	(0.96)
$pcGDP_{it}$	−0.0005***	−0.0003*	−0.0005***	−0.0003*
	(−3.35)	(−1.88)	(−3.40)	(−1.84)
$\Delta pcGDP_{it}$	−0.002***	−0.004	−0.002***	−0.0003
	(−2.84)	(−0.61)	(−2.93)	(−0.50)
$Contagion_{it}$	−0.765	−0.262	−0.755	−0.382
	(−0.77)	(−0.35)	(−0.75)	(−0.54)
$PastBreakDown_{it}$	0.024	−0.102	0.047	−0.183
	(0.09)	(−0.34)	(0.18)	(−0.59)
$RegConflict_{it}$	−0.259	−0.076	−0.267	−0.066
	(−0.98)	(−0.47)	(−0.98)	(−0.41)
$InternalViolence_{it-1}$	0.435	−0.118	0.410	−0.079
	(0.96)	(−0.37)	(0.89)	(−0.25)
$Presidential_{it}$	−0.641	0.197	−0.614	0.228
	(−1.24)	(0.49)	(−1.15)	(0.57)
$StableDemocracy_{it}$	−0.413	−0.482	−0.407	−0.480
	(−0.74)	(−1.48)	(−0.74)	(−1.48)
$Independence_{it}$	0.008	0.001	0.008	0.001
	(1.33)	(0.22)	(1.35)	(0.18)
N =	1575	866	1575	866
Log likelihood	−94.69	−212.58	−94.65	−212.10
Chi-square	43.76***	31.19***	46.70***	30.21***

Figures in parentheses are asymptotic z-statistics computed using Huber/White/sandwich standard errors. *** = p < .01; ** = p < .05; * = p < .10; two-tailed tests. Cox Models do not include a constant. It is absorbed into the baseline hazard.

risk of democratic breakdown decreases for a state joining a regional organization with a more homogenous democratic membership than any previous organization of which it is a member. Table 6.2 presents the percent change in the baseline rate if the value of $\Delta IOScore_{it-1}$ is increased by one standard deviation. This increase results in an over 60 percent drop in the hazard rate in the Polity98 estimates and a corresponding drop in the Gasiorowski data of over 50 percent. This is a substantial impact

Table 6.2 *Percentage changes in probability of democratic breakdown*

	Polity98 estimates	Gasiorowski estimates
Increase in IOScore$_{it-1}$ 1 standard deviation	−9%*	−10%*
Increase in ΔIOScore$_{it-1}$ 1 standard deviation	−65%	−51%
Increase in pcGDP$_{it}$ 1 standard deviation	−95%	−61%
Increase in ΔpcGDP$_{it}$ 1 standard deviation	−53%	−68%*

* = estimate not statistically significant.

that shows the importance of *joining* certain regional organizations. This is strong confirmation of the theory suggesting that democratic regional IOs can play a role in lengthening the tenure of democracy.

The estimates of the economy-related control variables, $pcGDP_{it}$ and $\Delta pcGDP_{it}$, are both statistically significant and in the expected direction in three of four cases. Consistent with the political development literature previously discussed, higher levels of per capita GDP are related with longer-lasting democracies. Along with the results of the previous chapter, this result is yet another piece of evidence in support of Londregan and Poole (1996) and Przeworski et al.'s (1996) argument that higher income levels stabilize existing democracies, rather than create new democracies. The other economy-related independent variable, $\Delta pcGDP_{it}$, is consistently negative across the two data sets, but does not achieve statistical significance in the Gasiorowski data. These results partially accord with prior literature on growth and the survival of democracy. Regimes that increase growth face a higher chance of survival, while those which suffer economic downturn are vulnerable to democratic breakdown.

Table 6.2 shows the percentage changes in the baseline hazard rate given variation in per capita GDP and changes in per capita GDP. An increase of one standard deviation from the mean of per capita GDP yields an over 90 percent decrease in the hazard rate for the Polity98 estimates. Likewise, an increase of one standard deviation from the mean $\Delta pcGDP_{it}$ results in an over 50 percent decrease in the hazard rate faced by democracies for the Polity98 estimates. Economic factors thus play a key role in the survivability of democratic institutions.

Interestingly, none of the remaining control variables achieves statistical significance regardless of the data set examined. Many of the estimates are not of the expected sign. For example, the estimates of $RegConflict_{it}$ are negative in both models indicating that more hostile regional neighborhoods actually increase the durability of democracy. This result is inconsistent with the theory of Thompson (1996), who argues that democracies need a peaceful environment to survive, but is consistent with previous statistical studies on the effects of war on democracy (see Reiter 2001a). Still, given the statistical insignificance of these findings, little confidence can be placed in these interpretations.

Many of the estimates vary in sign across data sets. For example, $InternalViolence_{it-1}$, $Presidential_{it}$, and $PastBreakDown_{it}$ show differing influences on democratic duration depending on the data set analyzed. Both the inconsistent sign and lack of statistical significance of the $Presidential_{it}$ variable undermine Linz's (1990) logic that presidential democracies face a higher risk of failure than parliamentary systems. Although in the Gasiorowski data the estimate of this variable is of the sign predicted by Linz, the estimate is not statistically significant. The Polity98 estimate (again, not statistically significant) suggests that presidential systems are more likely to survive than their parliamentary alternatives.

Surprisingly, the length of time a country has been independent does not augur well for its survival as a democracy. For both the Polity98 and Gasiorowski estimates, $Independence_{it}$ is positive, indicating that the longer a state has been politically independent, the more likely that state will suffer the breakdown of democracy. This result is contrary to the theoretical expectation that older states will have developed more stable and active civil societies that could assist in the consolidation effort. It is possible that Latin American states drive this particular result since these are states which have been politically independent for many years, yet still suffered numerous breakdowns of democracy during the period of observation. Moreover, both data sets include Latin American states, which lead to the consistent sign of these estimates.

In sum, the results indicate two main influences on the prospects for democratic survival: regional organizations and state-level economic forces. While existing membership in regional IOs does not appear to systematically influence the prospects for democracy, accession to highly democratic regional IOs does lead to increased democratic durability. The strongest influences on regime duration, however, are found in the influence of economic development and growth rates – both of which have positive effects on the survival of democracy. Still, it is important to ensure that these results are not explained away by alternative hypotheses or generated in the presence of omitted variable bias (a concern given the statistical insignificance of many control variables).

Assessing alternative hypotheses and omitted variable bias

As discussed in Chapters 3 and 4, the realist counter to this study is that regional IOs will only pursue state interests, especially those of the major powers. Thus, we might expect that when democratic major powers are present in regional IOs, these organizations are more likely to be associated with the duration of democracy. To test for this possibility, I utilize the same variable used in Chapter 4 – $MajPowerIO_{it-1}$. Adding this variable to Model 6.1 should test for the presence of the impact of major powers since the variable counts the number of democratic great powers in the most democratic regional organization of which state i is a member.

The third and fourth columns of Table 6.1 show the estimates of this expanded model. Initially, note that this new variable does not achieve statistical significance in either data set. The presence of large, democratic powers does not have a systematic influence on the survival of democracy. More importantly, the estimates of $\Delta IOScore_{it-1}$ remain nearly identical to those without this additional variable. The clear conclusion drawn from this test of the realist hypothesis is that institutions do assert an independent influence apart from simply the presence of democratic major powers.

As in Chapter 4, I check the robustness of these findings by including region-based fixed-effects (cf. Feng and Zak 1999). Because some regions may be more or less vulnerable to democratic breakdown for reasons such as culture, history, or geographic context, the introduction of these variables is important to check for potential omitted variable bias. Although I have attempted to control for some of these regional factors by including the variable for regional democracy contagion effects ($RegContagion_{it}$), it is possible that other factors associated with various geographic regions are not captured by the contagion variable. To this end, I add a series of regional dummy variables as defined in Chapter 4. Although crude, these dummy variables should pick up any residual effect that region-based influences will have on democratic consolidation.

The statistical output concerning these models may be found in the appendix to this chapter (Table A6.1). The original estimates are quite stable in spite of the addition of the region-based variables. For both the Polity98 and Gasiorowski data, $\Delta IOScore_{it-1}$ remains negative and highly statistically significant. This is especially important since the chi-square statistic testing for the inclusion of the region-based fixed effects suggests that these additional terms add significant information to the model. The implication is that the dummy variables are picking up additional variation in the model and should remain. Even with the inclusion of the region-based dummy variables, however, the test for the importance of regional IOs receives support.

Note that in these new models, more of the control variables are statistically significant. In the Polity98 estimates, $PastBreakDown_{it}$, $RegConflict_{it}$, and $StableDemocracy_{it}$ now all attain statistical significance. Each of these variables is negative, suggesting that past failures of democracy and regional militarized disputes increase the duration of democracy. Moreover democracies created before 1950 also are more likely to survive. This later result holds for the Gasiorowski estimates as well. These findings suggest that there are important region-based factors to be included in models of democratic duration. When including these regional influences, many of the variables thought to influence the duration of democracy become statistically significant.[9]

As in the Chapter 4 robustness checks, Model 6.1 is reestimated with recoded regional IO variables including non-regional memberships in organizations. As discussed in Chapter 4, $IOScore_{it-1}$ and $\Delta IOScore_{it-1}$ are recomputed to include regional organizations, several non-large regional organizations (such as the UN) as well as international and regional financial institutions. Recall that the expectation is that the addition of these organizations should weaken the relationship between regional IOs and consolidation, since the theory outlined in Chapters 2 predicts that regional organizations can more effectively carry out the causal processes discussed. As shown in the appendix, when replicating Model 6.1, the estimate of $\Delta IOScore_{it-1}$ becomes statistically insignificant (at the $p < .05$ level) in both cases. Joining more democratic international organizations *in general* does not seem to predict longer regime duration – only regional IOs seem to influence the consolidation process. This is important support for the hypothesis that regional organizations are unique in their ability to protect democracy.

This support is not universal, however. The $IOScore_{it-1}$ term is statistically significant across both data sets, indicating that IO membership (versus joining) in universal organizations has a positive influence on regime duration. While this result is certainly consistent with the overall hypothesis that more highly democratic IOs can assist in the consolidation of democracy, it implies that even non-regional organizations can

---

[9] The model is also reestimated including "unweighted" variables for involvement in international organizations. I thus code two variables, labeled NIO_{it-1} and ΔNIO_{it-1}. The first is the number of IOs state i belongs to in year $t - 1$. Likewise, ΔNIO_{it-1} measures the change in the number of IOs of which state i is a member, from $t - 2$ to $t - 1$. I include this variable to see if the democratic density argument is robust. In neither case are these new variables significant in either data set. This provides empirical support for the idea that it is the nature of the membership of regional organizations, rather than simply membership, that is an important factor in the consolidation of democracy.

play some role in this process. Because the nature of this statistical relationship changes (the importance of joining versus membership), there is strong reason to believe that there are differing causal processes at work. Global institutions and IFIs may influence regime duration, but they apparently do so in different ways that emphasize continuing membership in these organizations. I do not explore this result further, but these limited tests of a broader IO–democracy relationship should not be taken as the final word on this subject. Clearly theorizing about the mechanisms associated with non-regional organizations and IFIs is required as is further statistical testing.[10] As discussed in Chapter 3, these tests would have to be carefully designed to control for the nature of IFI activity in order to correctly parse out their influence independent from economic trends. In the final analysis, these results show that the addition of these non-regional organizations does not influence the presence of an IO–democratization link, only its causal pathway.

Finally, as in Chapter 4, I code regional organizations by their issue area to investigate the possibility that certain types of organizations (e.g. economic versus military) have disparate impacts on democratic endurance. As in Chapter 4, there is no strong evidence that economic or military organizations play a stronger role in the consolidation process.

Selection effects?

One concern with the preceding theory and findings is that there could be a selection process at work. This selection process would be consistent with the "shallow cooperation" hypothesis. Namely, it is possible that only democracies likely to survive are admitted to the regional organizations. This hearkens to the argument of Downs, Rocke, and Barsoom (1996) that nations only sign agreements that are easy to enforce. Here the endogeneity arises when existing members only admit democracies that will be successful, making the regional organizations' influence on the process epiphenomenal. There are several problems, however, with this argument.

First, this argument supposes that organizations or their members will have clairvoyance concerning the probability of a state consolidating its democracy. If this was so, we should see almost no cases where members of democratic regional organizations suffer a breakdown or near breakdown of democracy. In fact, there are numerous cases of this, including Greece and Turkey. Because the breakdown of democracy can occur at

---

[10] For an example an attempt at theory relating to all international organizations, see Russett and Oneal 2001.

any time, no state is completely secure and it would be extremely difficult to judge the likelihood of this breakdown *ex ante*.

Second, in statistical terms, the effects of regional IOs in this model have been lagged. The probability that a state suffers a breakdown of democracy is influenced by its IO membership from the previous year and changes in its IO membership from $t - 2$ to $t - 1$. If a state's hazard rate drops dramatically between its second and third year (due to changes in other independent variables or the baseline hazard rate) and the state is then admitted to an IO, this change in $IOScore_{it}$ will be reflected the following year. The change in the hazard rate would statistically precede accession to a democratic regional organization.

Finally, the most powerful evidence against this type of endogeneity comes from an auxiliary regression. If the selection argument is correct, one observable implication is that a statistical relationship should exist between democratic stability and regional IO memberships. If states must show democratic stability before becoming members of IOs (association agreements notwithstanding), then one should find that the length of time a state remains a democracy should positively predict increases in $\Delta IOScore_{it-1}$. This, however, is not the case. Using Model 6.1 as a starting point, I move the dependent variable to the right-hand side of the model. If one makes the independent variable of interest, the dependent variable (including all other variables except $IOScore_{it-1}$), $DTIME_{it}$, is not significantly related (at the $p < .05$ level) to $\Delta IOScore_{it-1}$. This is true for both data sets, using OLS estimates with panel-corrected standard errors (Beck and Katz 1995). In fact, the estimates of $DTIME_{it}$ for both data sets are *negative*, indicating that the longer a state remains a democracy, the less likely it is to join highly democratic regional IOs. Although the selection argument is important, it does not appear to be accounting for these statistical results.

Conclusion

This chapter has tested the theory linking regional organizations to the successful consolidation of democracy. These tests were largely supportive of the theory. Accession to regional organizations that are more solidly democratic leads to a decline in the rate of the breakdown of democracies. This relationship holds even while controlling for the number of democratic major powers in the organization as well as the inclusion of region-based fixed effects. Although the statistical tests do not discriminate between the various possible mechanisms (e.g. bribing versus binding), the following chapter undertakes this task in a series of case studies.

Regional IOs are no guarantee of success for new democracies, but this chapter has shown that *joining* an IO with many democratic members can assist in lengthening the longevity of democratic regimes. Although there are several factors that are important for the consolidation of democracy, this chapter has shown that the external dimension of international politics should not be given short shrift. While domestic factors may still hold a privileged position in theories of democracy, regional factors can be equally important.

As in the statistical models of regime transitions, internal factors are clearly important. Again, these do not work at odds with regional organizations. Economic success can influence the underlying desire of potential regime opponents to act, while accession to regional organizations can influence their calculations of cost and benefits should those desires become stronger. The important finding here is that the influence of regional organizations persists even when controlling for economic successes and failures. Similarly, the association between regional IOs and democratic longevity holds when accounting for the possibility of neighborhood effects, domestic violence, ethnic heterogeneity, and other factors championed by past work on democratic consolidation.

Regarding competing external explanations, there is little evidence that the European experience single-handedly drives these results. The Europe-less results using the Gasiorowski data are consistent with the full sample statistical estimates using the Polity data set. Likewise, controlling for the presence of major powers within highly democratic regional organizations has no influence on the prospects for democratic longevity. Finally, the inclusion of IFIs and other non-regional international organizations does alter the basic findings of this chapter. Namely, the importance of joining IOs fades while the importance of continued membership in IOs increases. While this is consistent with the overall argument of the book, it highlights the different causal mechanisms linking IFIs and universal organizations.

These statistical results, however, are silent regarding which causal process occurs to link the joining of regional organizations to the endurance of democracy. The following chapter contains several case studies which attempt to elucidate these links in a systematic fashion.

Appendix

Table A6.1 *Cox estimates of the determinants of the duration of democracy,*
1950–92, with region-specific fixed effects and non-regional IOs

	Region fixed effects		Non-regional IOs	
	Polity98	Gasiorowski	Polity98	Gasiorowski
IOScore$_{it-1}$	−0.0002	−0.004	−0.155**	−0.138**
	(−0.00)	(−0.09)	(−1.98)	(−2.38)
ΔIOScore$_{it-1}$	−0.743***	−0.428***	−0.166	0.002
	(−2.56)	(−3.00)	(−1.43)	(0.02)
pcGDP$_{it}$	−0.0004***	−0.0003*	−0.0005***	−0.0003*
	(−2.67)	(−1.67)	(−3.33)	(−1.89)
ΔpcGDP$_{it}$	−0.002**	−0.0002	−0.002***	−0.0003
	(−2.54)	(−0.29)	(−2.64)	(−0.43)
Contagion$_{it}$	0.235	0.386	−0.315	−0.048
	(0.27)	(0.53)	(−0.29)	(−0.06)
PastBreakDown$_{it}$	−0.704**	−0.287	−0.136	0.008
	(−2.11)	(−0.84)	(−0.45)	(0.03)
RegConflict$_{it}$	−0.516**	−0.116	−0.206	−0.027
	(−2.02)	(−0.72)	(−0.79)	(−0.17)
InternalViolence$_{it-1}$	0.635	0.088	0.523	−0.094
	(1.41)	(0.29)	(1.23)	(−0.31)
Presidential$_{it}$	−0.533	0.581	−0.992*	−0.059
	(−0.71)	(1.55)	(−1.91)	(−0.14)
Independence$_{it}$	0.007	0.008	0.009	0.002
	(1.24)	(1.33)	(1.13)	(0.28)
StableDemocracy$_{it}$	−1.444**	−0.530*	−0.296	−0.339
	(−1.96)	(−1.70)	(−0.48)	(−1.00)
EUROPE	−0.769	−.–[a]	−.–	−.–
	(−0.55)			
NORTHAMERICA	0.109	0.348	−.–	−.–
	(0.15)	(0.46)		
SOUTHAMERICA	−1.604	−1.203	−.–	−.–
	(−1.48)	(−1.39)		
AFRICA	0.780	0.952*	−.–	−.–
	(0.84)	(1.85)		
MIDDLEEAST	2.114**	0.677	−.–	−.–
	(2.50)	(0.91)		
Inclusion Chi-square	12.96**	16.11***	−.–	−.–
p > Chi-square	0.02	0.00		
N =	1575	866	1578	866
Log likelihood	−88.21	−204.52	−95.79	−213.67
Chi-square	103.76***	65.98***	45.29***	19.87**

Figures in parentheses are asymptotic z-statistics computed using Huber/White/sandwich standard errors. *** = p < .01; ** = p < .05; * = p < .10; two-tailed tests.
[a] Gasiorowski does not include Europe in his data set.

7 Regional organizations and the consolidation of democracy: evidence from cases

IOs and consolidation: causal mechanisms

The purpose of this chapter is to evaluate three case studies to determine whether the causal mechanisms outlined in Chapter 2 are behind the statistical associations between regional organizations and democratic consolidation found in Chapter 6. The countries examined include Greece, Paraguay, and Guatemala. Table 7.1 presents a list of the causal mechanisms to be examined in each case study. In addition, the case of Turkey in Chapter 6 included a test for the mechanisms associated with consolidation since that case contains dynamics of both democratic breakdown and redemocratization within a relatively short time frame.

As in Chapter 5, each case begins with a brief historical introduction of the country. I then review the causal mechanisms, discussing whether there is evidence of IO influence via these processes. Finally, for each study I discuss any countervailing evidence mitigating the impact of IOs on the consolidation process.

Greece: European institutions and consolidation

Perhaps more than any other group in history, the Greek people have experienced an ebb and flow of democracy. From the origins of the concept of democracy in ancient Athens to the movement for independence in the early nineteenth century to the Greek civil war, the Greek populace has experienced monarchy, autocracy, democracy, and most systems in-between.

The twentieth century was no better for the Greek populace in terms of this vacillating experience with democracy. In recent times, the most significant and highly visible period of change came between 1967 and 1974, when Greek democracy was ended by a military coup and then reinstated. Today, most observers would consider the current Greek regime a consolidated democracy as well as "the most openly democratic regime in modern Greek history" (Diamandouros 1986: 140). But what role, if any,

Table 7.1 *Hypothesized causal mechanisms linking IOs to consolidation*

Consolidation mechanisms (Chapters 2 and 5)
Binding: deters losers
– Conditions on membership
Binding: deters winners
– Conditions on membership
Psychological legitimization and audience costs
Bribery of societal groups

did regional organizations play in helping Greece reach this status? This case study will give a brief historical background of the 1967–74 period followed by an analysis of the influence of several European organizations on the consolidation of Greek democracy.

Greece: background

The mid-1960s were a time of upheaval for the political system of Greece. From 1955 to 1963, Constantine Karamanlis was the premier of Greece as well as the head of the National Radical Union (ERE).[1] Under Karamanlis' watch, Greece successfully rebuilt its political and economic systems after its devastating civil war (1946–9). During this period, liberalization began by lifting many repressive laws enacted during the civil war. After Karamanlis' party was defeated by the liberal (but anti-Communist) Centre Union in 1963, Karamanlis went into self-imposed exile. The Centre Union was headed by George Papandreou, a "veteran liberal politician," who within two years was at loggerheads with King Constantine II over control of the military (Clogg 1979a: 110).

The dispute brought a rupture within the Centre Union which splintered into two opposing factions. July 1965 brought a political crisis between the ERE and both factions of the Centre Union. Unable to stabilize leadership positions in the government, Papandreou and the new ERE, chief, Panayiotis Kanellopoulos, agreed in late 1966 to hold elections the following May. These elections were cancelled, however, when on April 21, 1967, a small group of military officers (who became known as "the Colonels") overthrew the civilian government.

The motivation of the colonels is not entirely clear (Clogg 1979a), but a major factor was the possibility of a Centre Union victory in the following month's elections. Papandreou had threatened to put the armed forces under complete civilian control, undermining their autonomy. The

---

[1] These historical details are recounted from Clogg 1979a, 1979b.

coup marked the beginning of seven years of authoritarianism for this Southern European state. During this time, the colonels attempted to legitimize their regime by adopting a new constitution, abolishing the monarchy, and holding presidential elections (in which only one candidate was allowed to compete) (Clogg 1979a: 111–12).

The initial reaction of Greek citizens was mostly one of "apathy" (Clogg 1979a: 111). Popular sentiment did eventually turn against the colonels' regime, however, reaching its zenith during the brutal repression of the November 1973 Athens Polytechnic uprising. The reaction of Europe, however, was not apathetic. In the words of one observer: "In the face of such a general external acceptance of the abolition of democracy in Greece, Western Europe was a particularly eloquent exception" (Siotis 1983: 59). The Council of Europe expelled the colonels' regime from that community of nations (Pridham 1991c: 215).[2] Equally, if not more important, the European Community "froze" its association agreement with Greece (Coufoudakis 1977; Ioakimidis 1994: 141; Tovias 1984: 161).

The EC–Greek association agreement was signed in 1961. It conferred some of the membership benefits of the EC to Greece immediately and set a timetable for Greece's full entry into the Community by 1974 (Yannopoulos 1975).[3] Some scholars of the Greek transition have argued that the freezing of the association agreement had little effect on the colonels' regime (Clogg 1979a: 119; also Yannopoulos 1975). Despite this claim, the balance of scholarly research on the subject agrees with Verney and Couloumbis (1991: 109): "Greece suffered immediate financial consequences from the freezing of the Greece–EC Financial Protocol and the agricultural harmonisation talks. But the possible long-term consequences were far more serious." Greece became quite isolated politically and economically from its European neighbors. Whether these events support the hypotheses outlined in Chapter 2 – that is, whether the EC or other IOs assisted in the *transition* to democracy – will be dealt with in the final section of this study.

Soon after the Athens Polytechnic incident, the Turkish invasion of Cyprus brought a swift end to the colonels' regime. They proved to be completely unable to mobilize for the war in Cyprus, which proved disastrous for the Greek military's campaign against the Turks. In the analysis of one observer, preparation for the Cyprus conflict was "a shambles" (Clogg 1979a: 112). This external military crisis brought an internal

---

[2] Technically, the colonels quit the organization on the eve of the resolution to suspend their membership. See Verney and Couloumbis 1991: 109.

[3] Because much of the activity between the Community and Greece took place before the EC became the European Union, I will refer to this organization as the EC throughout this case.

political crisis as well. Several powerful Greek military leaders called for a return to civilian leadership and, within weeks, the colonels had stepped down in favor of a new civilian government, led by Constantine Karamanlis.

The new Greek democracy

The Karamanlis government faced many challenges in its quest to become a stable, consolidated democracy, including coping with a legacy of military repression, reestablishing ties with European allies, and pursuing economic stabilization in light of the 1970s oil shocks. A central part of Karamanlis' strategy to stabilize his fledgling regime was to push for membership in the European Community. Little more than a year after the fall of the colonels' regime (July 1975), the Karamanlis government applied for full membership (Siotis 1983: 59).

While the Community offered many economic benefits to Greece, many observers have stressed the political over the economic goals of membership (Ioakimidis 1994: 139; Wallace 1994: 18). Upon submitting the application to the European Commission, Karamanlis himself stated: "I would like to emphasize that Greece does not seek integration solely for economic reasons; it is primarily on political grounds that our application rests, reasons related to the consolidation of democracy and the destiny of our nation" (quoted in Pridham 1991c: 226). The Commission acted quickly on Greece's application and, in 1979, the Greek–EC Accession Treaty was signed. In 1981, Greece became a full member of the European Community.

Even at the time, despite the widely cited association between Greece's accession to the EC and the consolidation of democracy, few observers articulated the functional mechanisms behind this effect. If a major purpose of the EC was to consolidate democracy, almost no one seemed to elucidate how this would take place. Given the current state of Greek democracy, we may now ask whether the EC played a significant role in the consolidation process. My answer to this question is an unequivocal yes. The next section will elucidate the three causal mechanisms that underlie this answer.

IO membership and democratic consolidation: the causal mechanisms

Although some observers treat economic issues as secondary in the discussion of Greece's accession to EC membership, a major issue in the *consolidation* process was economics. The economic benefits (and potential economic benefits) which flowed from EC membership provided a mechanism to simultaneously bind some societal actors through the conditionality of EC membership, while bribing other domestic groups. In addition, the psychological benefits of reacceptance by the European Community as well as the Council of Europe increased the legitimacy of the new democratic regime, while creating potential audience costs for those who would move against democracy. Finally, changes in Greek political institutions required by EC membership further consolidated Greek democracy by increasing these institutions' openness and transparency – a mechanism not discussed in Chapter 2.

Perhaps the most powerful mechanism constructed by the Community to consolidate democracy and prevent breakdowns of democracy is clear membership conditionality. As previously discussed, after the 1967 coup, Greek political and economic relations with Western Europe became quite contentious. Clearly another slide away from democracy would bring similar sanctions from the Community and its members. EC membership thus offered tremendous economic gains to economic elites, all of which were contingent upon meeting the EC's conditions of membership. These conditions include adherence to EC-mandated economic policies, but also the maintenance of liberal democracy as well. This conditionality was (and is) a credible and costly deterrent mechanism for Greek elites for two reasons: (1) the significant (and growing) dependence of Greece on European trade, and (2) the large flow of financial aid from the Community.

Trade between EC member states was (and continues to be) extremely important to Greece. As of 1973, EC states accounted for 44 percent of Greek imports and 48 percent of Greek exports (Coufoudakis 1977: 124).[4] More importantly, given Greece's location (bordered to the north by Communist states) along with their external relations (bordered to the east by their traditional enemy Turkey), there was little possibility for substitution of these goods or markets, creating a situation of high dependence with respect to Western Europe (Verney and Couloumbis 1991: 109). Although the geopolitical situation of the region has changed, Greece is still highly dependent on EU member states for trade and markets. The high dependence of Greece makes violations of the EC/EU conditions extremely costly to Greek society. This link was explicitly drawn by Greek Foreign Minister Mitsotakis in the months before Greece's accession:

---

[4] In addition, the colonels' hands were tied concerning bargaining over trade and tariffs with Brussels. As of 1971, Greece's trade deficit with the EC states was larger than its total value of all exports (Verney and Tsakaloyannis 1986).

Naturally, we do not expect our nine partners in the Community to become the guardians of Greek democracy. By joining a broader group of like-minded Western democracies, however, our own democratic institutions will be reinforced, through constant contact and interchange, but mainly because from now on Greece will share the destiny of its Community partners . . . They [prospective dictators] are bound to know that the abolition of democracy entails immediate ostracism from the Community. This could have grave internal and external consequences. So, in this respect, the EC is a safe haven. (Quoted in Pridham 1991c: 226; brackets in original)

The second reason these conditions are quite credible and costly arises from the direct financial aid of the Community. According to the OECD, almost 5 percent of the Greek GDP in 1989 came from net financial transfers from EC member states (OECD 1990: 68). Given this tremendous flow of resources, "the cost of a successful overthrow of parliamentarism . . . has become forbiddingly high" (Verney and Couloumbis 1991: 119). As with trade, financial transfers from the EC/EU to Greece create a powerful economic binding mechanism.

Finally, the psychological impact of EC membership was quite important for the consolidation of democracy. As discussed in Chapter 2, a symbolic reorientation of a new democratic regime can be an important step in distancing itself from its authoritarian predecessor and establishing its own legitimacy. Given the Greeks' international isolation under the colonels, there were strong incentives to quickly establish Greece as a major regional and international force (Coufoudakis 1977). Membership in the Community as well as reentry to the Council of Europe allowed an easy avenue to achieve this goal.

Like other Southern European states, Greece had long struggled with its identity as an ally of the US, an aspirant to join the EC, and a bridge to the Middle East. Membership in the Community has served an important purpose in "anchor[ing] Greece securely to the West" (Macridis 1979: 147). Membership was a signal of legitimacy for the new regime and a signal of their desire to become part of "the West." By attempting to establish a Western identity, Karamanlis attempted to relay a picture of stability and democracy to both internal and external observers, attempting to strengthen the regime (Pridham 1991c: 226, 1995: 174–5; Verney and Couloumbis 1991: 115). Since Western European states did not suffer through coups or the breakdown of democracy, neither would Greece.

Any would-be coup conspirators would pay enormous audience costs (both internal and external) for moving against democracy. Coup leaders would certainly not be able to establish legitimacy in the eyes of external observers, eroding their support at home. As a pariah state in Western Europe, Greece would struggle in the political realm as it did in the

1967–74 period. Assuming the Greek public also cared about its status in the world community, a coup would bring domestic audience costs as well. These costs would entail a lack of legitimization for the new regime, making it difficult for the non-democratic regime to govern effectively. This is especially true since, although pockets of anti-EC/EU sentiment continue to exist in Greece, overall public support for membership is still very strong (Ioakimidis 1994: 151).[5]

Bribery: buying the success of democracy

Not only did economic incentives provide a powerful mechanism for groups such as the military and economic elites to stay out of the "coup business," economic assistance granted by the Community to Greece served as a powerful tool to buy the allegiance of certain actors in Greek society. As Basilios Tsingos has noted, rural Greece had been a traditional stronghold of anti-democratic forces, especially given rural interests' "susceptibility of authoritarian bribes" (Tsingos 1996: 341). EC membership brought monetary aid targeted to these rural areas, which had supported the colonel's authoritarian regime.

This assistance enhanced rural acceptance of democracy and cushioned the financial costs of the transition to democracy for these actors. According to Tsingos (1996: 341) this financial assistance "positively enhanced the prospects for democracy to the extent that they helped establish a clear, causal connection between democracy, EC membership, and the prosperity for the now heavily subsidized countryside." Thus, bribery became an effective mechanism to buy acceptance of democratic politics in rural Greece (Pridham 1995: 184).

The EC and institutional change

Institutional mechanisms provided another buttressing effect of the EC for Greek democracy. Rather than referring to the conditionality of membership benefits, I refer here to the changes in domestic institutions arising from specific requirements of the EC. Joining a regional trade bloc or other regional institutions often entails changes to domestic institutions. In the case of Greece, administrative reform was required upon its accession to the EC (Pridham 1995: 192). As one observer has noted,

---

[5] Anecdotal evidence in support of this proposition is that despite their opposition to Greece's entry into the EC, neither the Socialist Party of Greece (PASOK) nor the Greek Communist Party (KKE) have instituted policy changes towards the Community upon their respective election to office (Verney and Couloumbis 1991: 118).

"membership provides an ideal opportunity to bring about the modernisation of the Greek state and bureaucracy, which is long overdue" (Tsoukalis 1981: 110; see also Featherstone 1994). This reform and modernization enhanced the responsiveness and performance of the Greek government, which improved public perceptions of the regime (Pridham 1995: 193).

In addition to "reform from above", domestic institutions may change through interaction with their counterparts from other member states. In the case of Greece and the EC, membership expanded many social institutions and civic organizations. One of the best examples is that of workers' groups. Unions supported Community membership and, in fact, benefited from increased contact with the European Trade Union Confederation (ETUC) (Tsoukalis 1981: 113). In addition, other organizations, such as interest groups, began to flourish in Greece as they "acquired new habits of consultation, dialogue, and information to a degree not practiced in their home countries" (Pridham 1995: 182; see also Sidjanski 1991). While one cannot conclusively say that the development of a professional bureaucracy or of independent civic organizations contributes to democratic consolidation, these developments do contribute to a healthy overall civil society that can be important for the future of democracy (see Kamrava and Mora 1998). This openness of the bureaucracy and civil society, according to observers of Greek politics, "is an extremely important development for broadening the democratic process and diffusing political power" (Ioakimidis 1994: 145; Katseli 1990; Verney 1994).

It should be noted that these particular causal mechanisms were not discussed in Chapter 2. The expansion of civil society and the "opening" of government bureaucracy can have an important impact on democratic consolidation. Through both mandated directives and "osmosis," the interaction of individuals and governments can influence behavior and the nature of domestic institutions (Tsoukalis 1981: 110).

Critiques of the argument

Of course, the preceding story of EC membership and democratic consolidation is not without problems. First, the EC was not the only major regional institution of which Greece was a member. NATO also had the potential to be a powerful influence on domestic politics in Greece, at the time of the transition to democracy in 1974, Karamanlis had promised to remove Greece from the organization. The question may rightly be raised, given the highly democratic nature of NATO membership, why did this institution not play a role in the consolidation process? Second, if involvement in European institutions serves as a powerful factor preventing democratic backsliding, why did the presence of the EC–Greece association agreement and the Council of Europe not serve this role in 1967? I will address each of these questions in turn.

The response of NATO and its member states to the 1967 coup was muted at best (Garfinkle 1991: 73–4). Arguably the mildest response came from the US itself. The US "expressed with varying degrees of conviction, sadness at the turn of events."[6] In the end, NATO took no real action against the colonels and continued to support the regime with military assistance. Given the US concern with the "southern flank" of Europe and instability in both Greek and Turkish domestic politics, there was a low likelihood of action against the Greek regime. As discussed in Chapter 2, the will to enforce political conditionality is as important as setting the conditions. Although NATO had the potential to be an effective pressure point for the colonels, it chose not to pursue these goals. For better or worse, NATO placed its security interests over its interest in the domestic politics of its members.

In addition, during the war in Cyprus in the summer of 1974, NATO became regarded in many circles as "pro-Turkish." This, along with NATO's implicit support of the junta, led to a public outcry against the alliance. The result was that Karamanlis withdrew Greece from the military arm of NATO in 1975, hours after Turkey's second invasion of Cyprus (Papacosma 1985: 196). This foreclosed the option of NATO assisting with the consolidation process.[7] In the end, although both the EC and NATO had potential to pressure the colonels' regime, only the EC choose to do so. Indeed, this is one instance where realist expectations concerning the role of major powers in guiding an institution receives empirical support, at least in the case of NATO. Because the US wanted to preserve the NATO alliance, it refused to interfere in Greek politics (Garfinkle 1991). I return to this issue in Chapter 8.

If, in the post-1974 era, the prospect and the realization of Community membership exerted a strong influence on consolidation, why did the EC–Greece association agreement not serve this same purpose in 1967? Although there is little speculation in the literature as to how the colonels perceived any potential external response to their coup, there is reason to believe they assumed they would be supported by Greece's main ally, the United States. Because of the military's staunch anti-communism and support of NATO, they probably assumed (correctly, in hindsight) that

---

[6] "The Sweet and Sour Pill," *The Economist*, September 20, 1975, S4.

[7] Although, ironically, the act of withdrawing from NATO was an early popularity boost for the new government, cutting across party and ideological lines to receive broad support throughout Greece.

the US would be unconcerned with internal Greek politics.[8] Given the support of their "key" ally, the colonels probably paid no attention to the potential European response.

A second factor bolstering this conclusion is that there was little precedent for anti-coup stances on the part of European governments. In 1960, Europe turned a blind eye to the military-led coup in Turkey (which had a nearly identical association agreement with the EC). The colonels quite likely reasoned that the response to their move would be no different. This would also help explain why the Greeks seemed extremely indignant at attempts to expel them from the Council of Europe (they withdrew in protest before they could be ejected). Given this lack of precedent and the lack of salience to the colonels of Greece's relations with Europe (relative to the US), the EC association agreement could not serve as a deterrent mechanism to prevent the breakdown of democracy in 1967.

The EC as a determinant of the transition?

As Chapter 2 argues, IOs can play an important role in encouraging the *transition* to democracy as well as consolidation. Although this process functions through different causal processes, this chapter has pointed to evidence that the EC played an important role in the *redemocratization* of Greece. This case does provide support for some of the mechanisms linking IOs to transitions discussed in Chapter 2. The EC did exert significant pressure on the colonels through the "freezing" of the association agreement. Some scholars have gone so far as to credit this action by the Community as a key pressure undermining the regime (Coufoudakis 1977: 130–1). Moreover, this external pressure assisted internal opposition groups in their efforts to unseat the junta (Verney and Tsakaloyannis 1986).

Although this is certainly an important instance of the external pressure mechanism discussed in Chapter 2, the impact of the EC and Greece's membership is strongest when discussing the consolidation of Greek democracy. Although the EC did bring its economic strength to bear on the colonels, their efforts were not "decisive" in bringing the end of the regime (Tsingos 1996: 326; see also Yannopoulos 1975). Rather, the EC played a larger role in the consolidation of democracy by allowing Greece's entry into the Community during a critical time (Whitehead 1996d: 258). Membership provided economic, psychological, as well as institutional benefits that helped democracy to endure.

---

[8] On the strong US ties to the Greek military, including probable CIA involvement in the country, see Garfinkle 1991: 68–70.

Conclusion: the Greek experience

Several of the mechanisms at work in the Greek case directly support the hypotheses outlined in Chapter 2. The idea that the conditionality of IO membership binds domestic actors (both winners and losers) to democratic principles is supported quite strongly in this case. In addition, the idea that regional IOs may assist fledgling democracies by providing direct economic assistance to bribe domestic actors is also supported. Finally, the psychological impact of IO membership in providing incentives for officials to obey the conditions of those institutions also receives important confirmation.

It would be difficult to judge which of these causal mechanisms was the strongest in the case of Greece. My own reading of the secondary record, however, points to economics as a key driving force. Trade interdependence between the extant members and Greece created strong incentives for the continuation of democracy as did the substantial aid flows from the Community. The clear conditionality of these benefits was a strong message to would-be conspirators that the benefits of membership would be suspended if democracy ended. Basilios Tsingos (1996: 338) adequately summarizes this picture in his own take of EC–Greek relations:

The provision of resources contingent on the presence of democracy – backed by strong, legally binding material commitments based on international treaties and European law, as embodied in a framework of authoritative institutions – helped to convince domestic groups and actors representing large sections of society that threats to democratic values and procedures were tantamount to threats to material interests, thus raising the costs of repression in a manner significantly conducive to the Greek republic's stability, endurance, and political resilience.

Paraguay: MERCOSUR and fragile consolidation

As the third wave of democratization swept Latin America throughout the 1980s, Paraguay remained a holdout for authoritarianism. General Alfred Stroessner clung to power for most of the decade, supported by a powerful cadre of military elites and the Colorado Party, a political machine known for its corruption and intimidation tactics. When Stroessner was finally overthrown in 1989, Paraguay's new leader, Andres Rodríguez, decided to follow the rest of Latin America on the path of democracy. Unfortunately, that path has been riddled with potholes and detours. This case study will examine two major events since Paraguay's democratization, both of which severely threatened the continuation of democracy in this small, poverty-stricken state.

I argue that without the assistance of the Southern Cone Common Market (MERCOSUR), Paraguay would probably have turned off the path of democracy in both of these instances. Although it would be an overstatement to call Paraguay's democracy consolidated, this case demonstrates the efficacy of regional organizations instilling a credible commitment to democracy to halt democratic breakdown. Specifically, this case shows how IO conditionality can be effective in deterring anti-regime forces from moving against a fragile democracy. After outlining a brief history of Paraguayan democracy, the following two sections will discuss two recent events in Paraguay and show how MERCOSUR was indispensable to preserving democracy in both instances.

Paraguay: the last banana republic?

For thirty-four years General Alfredo Stroessner ruled Paraguay with an iron grip by creating a powerful one-party state and building a tight alliance with the military. Taking power in 1954, Stroessner ended half a decade of political instability in this small South American state (Writer 1996). Staunchly anti-Communist, Stroessner was supported by the United States during the Cold War and behaved no differently than many of the other authoritarian rulers of the 1960s and 1970s in Latin America (Mora 1998). As the single-party and military-led regimes of the region began their transitions to democracy in the 1980s, however, Paraguay remained the exception. Stroessner continued to have a tight hold on power and began supporting smuggling and pirating operations into his two larger neighbors, Brazil and Argentina.[9] Reports of widespread corruption and abuses of power by the military earned Paraguay the title of the "last banana republic."[10]

In early 1989, Stroessner's health took a turn for the worse, prompting a crisis of succession among his family members and inner circle of advisors. Finally, on February 3, 1989, General Andres Rodríguez led the army in a coup against his mentor and exiled him to Brazil (Powers 1992). Most observers assumed Rodríguez would follow the programs of Stroessner, including his tight grip on power and the suppression of all civil rights.[11] To everyone's surprise, Rodríguez began a program of political and economic liberalization, while attempting to put an end to much of the "criminal economy" which had developed under his predecessor.

---

[9] "Andres Rodríguez," *The Economist*, May 3, 1997, 79.

[10] This title is still often used today, even after the transition to democracy, largely because of the difficulty in ending the widespread corruption within the Paraguayan bureaucracy. See Faiola 1998.

[11] "Andres Rodríguez," *The Economist*, May 3, 1997, 79.

Rodríguez appointed himself president, yet presided over the drafting of a new constitution that called for the free election of the president (Wiarda 1995).

One of Rodríguez's major foreign policy initiatives was to join MERCOSUR. This organization originated from a free-trade agreement between Brazil and Argentina in 1987. Later, Uruguay was included while Paraguay was asked to join the trade agreement in 1989 (Abente 1989: 88). In 1991, all four states signed the MERCOSUR agreement, expanding their previous trade arrangement by promising to lower trade barriers as well as establish a common external tariff (Pena 1995). Trade among MERCOSUR states has grown at a rapid pace. In the early to mid-1990s, MERCOSUR was the fastest-growing trade bloc in the world, with trade increasing 400 percent from 1990 to 1997 (Dominguez 1998). In addition, foreign investment is on the rise and more than $20 billion in shared investment projects are slated between the member states (Pena 1995).

In 1993, Rodríguez fulfilled his promise to step down from the presidency and Juan Carlos Wasmosy, a civil engineer, became the first freely elected president of Paraguay. Still, the Paraguayan economy remained dismal and the transformation to a democracy was not supported by all of society, especially segments of the military. In addition, the legacy of the one-party system stunted early democratization efforts since the party of Stroessner (the Colorado Party) still possessed most of the financial resources in the new multiparty system. The institutional ties shared by the military and the Colorado Party (many of the party elite are military officers) only exacerbated the situation by giving the military a legitimate vehicle to be directly involved in civilian politics. Needless to say, these factors made the young democracy extremely fragile.

Two incidents in particular have brought Paraguayan democracy to the precipice: one involving an intransigent military general, the other involving the same general and the leadership of the Colorado Party. The next two sections will discuss these events in detail and the role of MERCOSUR in defusing these two threats to democracy.

The "almost" coup

On April 22, 1996, three years after assuming the presidency, Juan Carlos Wasmosy summoned General Lino Oviedo of the Army 1st Corps to the presidential palace to inform him that he was being replaced and relieved of his duties.[12] Throughout Wasmosy's tenure as president, General

---

[12] The factual details of this account are taken from Valenzuela 1997 and Writer 1996 unless otherwise noted.

Oviedo had pressured him on many issues of policy, including legislation, foreign affairs, even Supreme Court appointees. Oviedo was also a major player in the Colorado Party and had several times intervened in its internal election process. In the words of one observer, "Oviedo's involvement in governmental decisions and party politics constituted a direct challenge to the president's authority and a serious threat to Paraguay's fragile democratic transition" (Valenzuela 1997: 47).

Wasmosy's meeting with Oviedo, however, did not go smoothly. Oviedo refused to resign and returned to his barracks. In response to a second, but this time public, demand for his resignation, Oviedo warned that he would forcibly remove Wasmosy to maintain his position. He threatened to unleash "rivers of blood" on the capital if Wasmosy did not rescind the pubic demand for his resignation.

By the early morning of April 23, the crisis had reached breaking point. Oviedo had now demanded Wasmosy's resignation and Wasmosy had offered to take a "leave of absence" from the presidency. By noon on the 23rd, two events changed the tide against General Oviedo. First, support for Wasmosy poured in from around the world. President Clinton, almost every OAS member state, many EU members, the secretary-general of the OAS, and each foreign minister of MERCOSUR had contacted Wasmosy to encourage him to stand strong. In the meantime, however, Wasmosy had publicly offered a bargain to Oviedo: step down as army general and accept a post as the defense minister. This bargain, however, proved *extremely* unpopular, with mass demonstrations against Oviedo turning to demonstrations against both Oviedo *and* Wasmosy.

Oviedo's underestimation of public sentiment proved untimely for his attempted power grab. Oviedo offered his resignation late on April 23, assuming he would soon be reappointed in a new position. The following day, Oviedo listened to Wasmosy address the people of Paraguay, expecting to hear himself announced as the new defense minister. Rather, Wasmosy, citing the "will of the people," announced that Oviedo would have no official post in the government. Oviedo did not press the issue and disappeared from public view.

What can account for Wasmosy's sudden dose of courage and Oviedo's reluctance to push the president after April 24? By most accounts, a major factor was the support of international actors, especially MERCOSUR. Arturo Valenzuela (1997) has argued that while MERCOSUR was an important factor, internal dynamics such as public support and competition among service branches led Oviedo to back down. While it may be difficult to tell which factor contributed most strongly to the resolution of the crisis, most observers agree that MERCOSUR did play a key role in defusing the crisis (see Dominguez 1998).

MERCOSUR demands that all members remain a democracy or face expulsion from the organization. At the height of the crisis, President Carlos Menem of Argentina publicly stated that Paraguay would be expelled from the organization if Oviedo took control (Writer 1996). Foreign ministers from the three other MERCOSUR states visited Wasmosy during the crisis to express their solidarity and support for the embattled president (Perry and May 1996). Although the support of the public and other branches of the military were clearly additional factors, "it was probably the unhesitant support of Paraguay's allies in North and South America which persuaded General Oviedo not to attempt a coup" (Writer 1996).[13] I return to this issue in the final section to discuss the causal mechanisms at work.

A second presidential crisis

After the 1996 threat to democracy, Paraguay's institutions remained fragile. This point was underscored in early 1999 when a second major presidential crisis erupted. Not surprisingly, General Lino Oviedo was responsible for this crisis as well.

In early 1998, the Colorado Party underwent a bitter struggle to nominate a candidate for presidential elections. Surprisingly, General Oviedo defeated Wasmosy's political ally Luis Argana in the party primary. Wasmosy then threatened to annul the primary results since Oviedo's past actions had been a threat to democracy. Instead, Wasmosy had Oviedo arrested (on the charge of "insulting the president") and used this fact to disqualify him from running for office. The Colorado Party then chose Raúl Cubas, General Oviedo's vice-presidential running-mate, as their candidate for president. In an odd twist,the man who become Cubas' running-mate was his Colorado Party rival Luis Argana, whom Oviedo and Cubas had defeated in the party primary.

In 1998, Cubas was elected president with Argana as his vice-president. The two men continued their rivalry and differed over many policies, especially those concerning General Oviedo. Immediately after his election, Cubas pardoned Oviedo. Although opposed by the Supreme Court, the legislature, and Argana himself, Oviedo secured his initial release.

---

[13] There is some evidence that the OAS also played a role in the 1996 Paraguay crisis by sending high-level delegations in the hours after the attempted coup (Secretary-General Gaviria himself traveled to support Wasmosy; see Hakim 1996). The balance of the evidence suggests, however, that MERCOSUR played a much stronger role than the OAS. It is worth recalling the Chapter 2 quote from *The Economist*: "But for MERCOSUR, Paraguay would this year almost certainly have gone back to military rule" ("Survey: MERCOSUR," *The Economist*, October 12, 1996, S6).

Tragically, on March 23, 1999, Argana was assassinated on the streets of the capital by masked men dressed in army fatigues. Although they denied responsibility, both Cubas and Oviedo were linked to the assassination. On March 25, the legislature voted to impeach Cubas.

This set off a firestorm of public demonstrations against President Cubas, who eventually was forced to resign from office. In the end, however, the transition to the new president, Luis Macchi, was relatively smooth and peaceful. Cubas and Oviedo had threatened to ignore both the supreme court and the parliament, taking power by decree. Yet, Oviedo eventually fled to Argentina and Cubas stepped down as president, taking exile in Brazil. What accounted for the relatively smooth end to this potentially devastating crisis?

Again, MERCOSUR played a key role in diffusing this crisis. Negotiations for Cubas' resignation were directed by the MERCOSUR ministers. Both President Carlos Menem of Argentina and Brazilian President Henrique Cardoso publicly threatened Paraguay with expulsion throughout the crisis.[14] In the words of Paraguayan political analyst Carlos Martini, "[Paraguay's] democracy is so weak institutionally that its continuance is entirely dependent on outside pressures."[15]

IOs and consolidation: mechanisms at work in Paraguay

Why has MERCOSUR twice been effective at helping to preserve Paraguay's fragile democracy? One of the mechanisms discussed in Chapter 2 is notably absent: bribery on the part of the IO. At no point has MERCOSUR or any other regional organization given resources to Paraguay for the purpose of increasing support for democracy. The binding mechanism, especially deterring "losers" from moving against the regime, is clearly at work in this case. The conditionality of MERCOSUR membership and the resulting threat of expulsion greatly increased the costs of a coup to the point that coup planners backed down in the face of warnings from MERCOSUR states as well as other international actors.

Paraguay has always been extremely dependent on its two larger neighbors, Brazil and Argentina (Abente 1989). This has grown within the context of MERCOSUR. According to Richard Feinberg (1996: A13), "Paraguay's business and professional classes are now reliant upon external markets and supplies. Over one-third of Paraguay's trade flows involve its pact partners." It is this dependence along with the conditionality of MERCOSUR membership which provided a strong deterrent to

---

14 "Misplaced Loyalty Ends Cubas' Rule," *Financial Times*, March 30, 1999, 6.
15 "Misplaced Loyalty Ends Cubas' Rule," *Financial Times*, March 30, 1999, 6.

anti-democratic forces such as General Oviedo. In both crises, MERCOSUR ministers immediately threatened Paraguay with expulsion from the common market. In the words of Feinberg (1996: A13), "This credible threat heartened Paraguay's democrats, sent shivers through the country's commercial classes, and helped convince Oviedo's fellow officers that he could not prevail." Although Valenzuela's account of the 1996 crisis downplays the role of MERCOSUR, he also argues that conditions "will increase the cost of unconstitutional actions in the future" (Valenzuela 1997: 52).

The MERCOSUR conditionality mechanism was created to function in exactly this manner (van Klaveren 1993: 119). By linking the future of economic benefits of the organization to continued adherence to democratic principles, membership of MERCOSUR creates a situation for Paraguay in which "the costs of repression are now far higher than the costs of toleration, making military intervention a more risky venture" (Lambert 1997: 211).

The other side of the commitment hypothesis is that leaders may attempt to tie their own hands by joining regional organizations. While this aspect of MERCOSUR membership did not seem to play a role in these crises, there is evidence that part of the impetus for Rodríguez to join MERCOSUR was related to refocusing Paraguayan foreign policy by furthering Paraguay's integration into the international community.[16] One observer of Paraguayan politics has argued that economics played only a small role in the decision to join MERCOSUR, rather "the decision was a essentially a political one, which Rodríguez used to launch his policy of presidentalist diplomacy and to promote a new international image for the country" (Masi 1997: 178–9). For Rodríguez, joining MERCOSUR was a very open, public way to commit to political and economic reform. In doing so, he simultaneously created incentives for both winners and losers in the democratization process to comply with democratic institutions.

There is some evidence that the psychological mechanism was influential in these crises. Although this mechanism was outlined as being regime specific (IO membership serves as a signal to the population of regime intentions which encourages its support for democracy), here it operated in a more diffuse fashion. In both crises, it is clear that public outcry against Oviedo in support of democracy was important – citizens were "invested" in democracy, even if the military was not. Part of this "investment" is a result of international factors. Even Arturo Valenzuela, who previously has downplayed the role of MERCOSUR in ending the

---

[16] "Andres Rodríguez," *The Economist*, May 3, 1997, 79. See also Powers 1992: 13.

regime crises, discusses this as an important causal force. He argues that involvement by the international community, including MERCOSUR, the OAS, the EU, "signaled to the Paraguayan public the strong commitment of the international community to a new order of constitutional democracy. This commitment encouraged the population to come to the defense of the democratic institutions" (Valenzuela 1999). The population supported democratic reform as a result of the clear commitment provided by regional organizations and other international actors. This led to their vibrant defense of democracy in both 1996 and 1999.

Conclusions

In the end, MERCOSUR is not an iron-clad guarantee of democracy in Paraguay. Given the absence of a strong civil society, the institutional advantages of the Colorado Party, and the strength of the armed forces, Paraguay's democracy is still fragile. Nonetheless, membership in MERCOSUR has provided a significant deterrent to those who would act against the regime. It has also reinforced reforms by signaling to domestic and international observers that Paraguay is committed to reform.

Paraguay thus sheds light on how the relationships laid out in Chapter 2 work in practice. MERCOSUR has performed with flying colors in holding up its part of the conditionality bargain. Given the importance of the supply-side of these guarantees, this case proves that clear and swift action on the part of IOs can be effective in consolidating democracy. If MERCOSUR continues to remain a vigilant organization, prospects for democracy in Paraguay can only improve (Powers 1992: 15–16).

Guatemala: a foiled *autogolpe* and the OAS

The final case study is Guatemala. Despite Guatemala's lack of prior experience with democracy, it successfully completed a transition to democracy in the 1982–3 period. Although its institutions are not without problems, such as corruption and reserve domains governed by the military, Guatemala is considered by most observers to be a democracy. Its biggest challenge to that status came in 1993 when its freely elected president attempted to disband Congress and the Supreme Court in a power grab. In this section, I briefly review the development of democracy in Guatemala, discuss the 1993 *autogolpe*, and investigate the causes of its failure. I conclude that the Organization of American States (OAS) played an important role in deterring key segments of civil society from supporting the coup, thus keeping constitutional rule safe in Guatemala.

Guatemala: democratic history

Guatemala, Central America's most populous country, has little experience with democracy. Its land and wealth have been (and still are) concentrated in very few hands, many of those hands coming from outside the country.[17] Indeed, Guatemala was often identified as the quintessential "banana republic" (Trudeau 1993: 20). Despite many would-be impediments, democracy did begin to take root in Guatemala in the mid-1940s. Free elections for president were held in 1945, which ushered in roughly ten years of democratic rule. President Juan José Arévalo served as president until 1951, instituting military and political reform, including some limited land reform to help integrate the indigenous Indian population into political society.

The 1951 elections brought Jacobo Arbenz Guzmán to the office of president. Arbenz continued his predecessor's reform policies including land reform (Arbenz was a former military officer who supported the October 1944 revolution). As land reform began to encroach on the interests of the urban business community and the interests of the traditional officers in the military, Arbenz's support began to lag. The land reform also began to encroach on the interests of foreign investors, including the United Fruit Company, who began to rally anti-Arbenz actors in Guatemalan society. By 1954, the United States began to paint the Arbenz regime as pro-Soviet and sympathetic to the Communist cause. The CIA began to infiltrate Guatemala and gather support for an opposition movement against Arbenz, which culminated in the 1954 counterrevolution, led by Colonel Carlos Castillo Armas.[18]

From 1954 until 1982, despite intermittent elections, Guatemala was largely a military dictatorship (Black 1984). Only military candidates were permitted in elections and although a civilian president was elected in 1966, the military still maintained tremendous influence and control in Guatemalan politics (Trudeau 1993).

Like Peru, Guatemala has faced an uprising in the countryside that, while less militaristic than the *Sendero* movement, has taxed the government and its people. In Guatemala's case, the uprising centered on the country's indigenous Indian population. This armed movement began in the wake of the 1954 CIA-sponsored coup when most legal and political rights enjoyed under the Arbenz administration were suspended. From 1960 until 1996, the country has been ravaged by civil war (Jonas 1999).

---

[17] In the words of one scholar of Guatemalan politics: "Guatemala's socio-economic structure is so skewed that even the World Bank recommends more state spending." See Jonas 1994.

[18] On US actions in Guatemala, see Immerman 1982 and Schlesinger and Kinzer 1982.

In the late 1970s and early 1980s, many of the nation's Mayan peoples joined the armed rebellion, known by its Spanish acronym, URNG (Unidad Revolucionaria Nacional Guatemalteca).[19] The indigenous peoples' actions were largely a response to strong military repression in the countryside where many of the original rebels took refuge. By 1980, violence filled both the countryside and urban areas, as both the rebels and the military adopted increasingly brutal tactics.

The presence of the armed rebellion gave the military an excuse to stay heavily involved in the politics of Guatemala. Business elites strongly supported military rule in order to defeat the URNG (McCleary 1997: 130), while the military's repression of the rebellion remained brutal (Hakim 1993b). By the early to mid-1980s, however, the insurgency began to succumb to the efforts of the military and the business sector began to abandon their support of the regime (McCleary 1997).

The move to democracy began in March 1982, when General Efraín Rios Montt came to power in a coup.[20] Rios Montt's government lasted less than a year. He was replaced by General Mejia Victores, who organized democratic elections for a Constituent Assembly. After elections in 1984, the Assembly drafted a new constitution that went into effect in January 1986. Concurrently, Vinicio Cerezo Arévalo began his tenure as Guatemala's third civilian president since 1945.

A Central American autogolpe

Cerezo's administration was marred by corruption and a lack of credibility. Although his party (the DCG – Christian Democratic Party) had won a narrow majority in Congress, the party failed to enact many of its promised reforms. During Cerezo's final year, the military began to play an increasing role in the government, which discredited the DCG. Rios Montt, now the head of a political party, led in most pre-election polls in 1990, but was disqualified from running because of his participation in the 1982 coup (McCleary 1997). Into this void came a political outsider, Jorge Serrano Elias, who had never before held elected office. Serrano was elected in a runoff in January 1991.

Serrano initially continued the pace of democratic reform. He began to assert civilian supremacy over the military, even beginning the

---

[19] Technically, the URNG is an umbrella or coordinating group of movements (Trudeau 1993: 41).

[20] The coup was brought on largely by a tainted attempt at presidential elections in the spring of 1982. Hard-line military officials had to overturn electoral results to keep power, which led to dissension within the military and the coup in March (Trudeau 1993: 47).

prosecution of officers who had overseen the suppression of human rights. His relations with Congress and the Supreme Court were less cordial. Congress had consistently thwarted his efforts to enact legislation (despite his continued bribery of many members of Congress) and the Supreme Court was threatening to bring corruption charges against him.[21]

The democratic experiment in Guatemala appeared to have come to another disappointing end on May 25, 1993. Serrano suspended the country's constitution and dissolved the legislature and the Supreme Court – an action similar to Fujimori's *autogolpe*.[22] Unlike Fujimori's actions, however, the Serrano *autogolpe* was not immediately popular with the populace and the military wavered many times during the May crisis. Finally, on June 1, the military ousted Serrano. This crisis, however, did not end there.

The question of Serrano's replacement was a touchy one with the military, the business, elite, and the populace. His vice-president, Gustavo Espina, initially took office promising to serve out Serrano's term until the end of 1996 (Constable 1993). Many viewed Espina suspiciously, given his close ties to Serrano and his appearance of support for Serrano during the *autogolpe*. The military met with the Supreme Court, which had refused to disband, and agreed that Espina must also be removed from power to allow for a continuation of democracy. The Court found Espina guilty of violating the constitution and ruled him ineligible for the presidency (Villagran de León 1993: 122).

At this point, all sides began to agree on a replacement for Serrano/ Espina: a human rights ombudsman named Ramiro de León Carpio (Jonas 1994: 4–5). De León Carpio had been an outspoken critic of Serrano during his presidency and had escaped arrest at the beginning of the *autogolpe*, fleeing to a television station to rally civil society in defense of democracy (Villagran de León 1993: 121). With his appointment as president, de León Carpio agreed to serve out the remainder of Serrano's term.

Many factors, both internal and external, influenced the continuation of democracy in Guatemala. The military was essential in pushing both Serrano and Espina to leave office. Although the military did initially waver over its opposition to the *autogolpe*, at no point did Serrano believe

---

[21] "Why Did He Do It?" *The Economist*, May 29, 1993, 44. This is not to imply that neither Congress nor the Supreme Court was without flaw.

[22] I classify Guatemala as a consolidation case (similar to Paraguay) since Serrano's *autogolpe* failed so quickly. As I discuss below, few supported Serrano and there was less than two weeks' interruption in government. The Peru case is classified as a transition since Fujimori's actions lasted much longer and his coup was partially consolidated, forcing a redemocratization.

he would have the active *backing* of the military. Rather, he apparently hoped they would remain out of the picture. When apprised of his plans, observers note that military leaders "offered only half-hearted support" (Cameron 1998b: 228). According to a former military officer "there were three or four in the military hierarchy who vacillated, but not the institution as a whole."[23] When the military refused to publicly support the coup, opposition members became emboldened and took to the streets.[24]

The business community also rose up against Serrano. In fact, their movement against the *autogolpe* included trade-union leaders and leftist political organizations that they had previously eschewed.[25] Other aspects of civil society proved quite strong during the crisis. Immediately after Serrano's actions, student, labor, and Indian leaders held a meeting to plan a response (Gurnon 1993). Out of this meeting and others came the *Instancia Nacional de Consenso*, a group to coordinate civil society in exerting pressure first on Serrano, then on Espina (Villagran de León 1993). Together a wide range of groups began to cooperate to not only preserve democracy, but to strengthen it.

The deterrent effect of the OAS

While domestic actors were clearly important to the maintenance of democracy, external factors, especially the Organization of American States (OAS), were also influential in ending the crisis in a peaceful fashion. The OAS, invoking the Santiago Declaration (Resolution 1080), decried Serrano's actions and immediately sent a mission to Guatemala (Vaky 1993: 26–7). Through a combination of diplomatic pressure, economic threats, and encouragement to Guatemalan civil society, the OAS was able to assist in the short-term consolidation of democracy.

The major causal mechanism found here is the deterrent effect targeted towards segments that perceive themselves as "losing" in democratic reform. Although there is also some evidence that OAS membership had a psychological impact, the deterrent effect is the strongest. In short, a major factor in both the military and business sector opposing the *autogolpe* was each group's fear of the *international* consequences of allowing the coup to stand. Moreover, civil society received a major

---

[23] "Guatemala: Out, Out," *The Economist*, June 5, 1993, 45.

[24] It is now clear that there was a split within the Guatemalan military between hard-line officers who led the counter-revolutionary campaign of the 1970s and 1980s and the younger officers who "perceive as inevitable increased civilian control over policy" (Cameron 1998b).

[25] "Guatemala: Out, Out," *The Economist*, June 5, 1993, 45. See also Hakim 1993b.

psychological boost from the OAS when it sent the secretary-general to Guatemala to warn Serrano's supporters of international isolation early in the crisis.

As previously discussed, the army was essential to forcing Serrano and Espina from power. Given the increasingly public alliance between Serrano and the military,[26] why did the military, when push came to shove, refuse to back the president? A fear of international isolation was clearly present among a large group of junior officers, often labeled "constitutionalists" (Cameron 1998b: 229). While this group was never interested in supporting the *autogolpe* to begin with, they were able to overcome the traditional hard-liners in the military once the OAS became involved. On May 29, four days after the coup, OAS secretary-general João Baena Soares traveled to Guatemala to consult with leaders of civil society and the military. Baena emphasized to the military that OAS member states would punish the country economically if democracy did not endure. Concurrently with the Baena mission, both the US and Mexico took their first steps against Guatemala. The US cut aid to Guatemala and threatened to eliminate trade preferences, while Mexico began to mobilize the international community in support of the OAS (Millett 1994: 15–16). At this point, one of the key military leaders who had been silent concerning Serrano, General José García Samayoa, denounced the coup and called for a return to constitutional rule.[27] According to Francisco Villagran de León (1993: 122), "Baena's meeting with the military high command was probably crucial in spurring their decision to back a constitutional resolution of the crisis."

The military's concern for Guatemala's international position is not new. One of the main factors that drove the move to democratize Guatemala in the early 1980s was a concern in segments of the military that the brutal repression of the rebellion had left the country with few political allies or trade partners (Cameron 1998b: 221). It was not only the military, however, that felt the potential diplomatic and economic pressure of the OAS. Perhaps more keenly, elite business leaders feared OAS punishment. Not only have business elites traditionally sided with the military on issues of politics, but, like the military, a group of younger entrepreneurs now wields influence in the economy. Moreover, this younger class realizes the importance of Guatemala's involvement in the world economy.[28] Baena's visit to Guatemala brought news to business elites of their impending isolation which led the economic elites to pressure the army to remove Serrano and, later, Espina (Hakim 1993b).

[26] "Why Did He Do It?" *The Economist*, May 29, 1993, 44.
[27] "Guatemala: Out, Out," *The Economist*, June 5, 1993, 45.
[28] "New Broom, Slow Start," *The Economist*, June 26, 1993, 51–2.

The visit by Baena also served as a psychological boost to civil society at a key moment in the crisis. The open and public nature of the OAS mission provided encouragement to civil society's response by demonstrating that domestic opposition was not operating alone (Villagran de León 1993). Some observers have argued that the mission served to embolden civilian opposition by both providing external monitoring of the situation and coordinating the responses of the international community with domestic forces (Cameron 1998b; Hakim 1993b). The OAS mission thus served to help "in crystallizing the momentum for restoration of democratic procedures" (Vaky 1993: 27). Rather than provide legitimization to a particular administration or individual to further the process of consolidation, the OAS mission assisted in spurring support for a democratic *process*, a particularly important achievement in Guatemala.

What makes Guatemala a particularly interesting success story is the interactive nature of international and domestic actors. Civil society, the business community, and the military were key players in the return to constitutional rule, but some of these groups' strength and incentives came directly from the international community. The threat of international economic and diplomatic isolation loomed in the minds of both economic and military elites, both of which valued their international contacts. The mission of the OAS secretary-general provided a much needed psychological boost for civil society, while also providing a clear signal to economic and military elites that their fears would be realized. Divisions within the military and the unpopularity of the *autogolpe*, in turn, spurred the OAS to push harder (Cameron 1998b). In the words of one Latin American observer, "Had only one group [international or domestic] reacted, the military high command might have ridden out the storm" (Vaky 1993: 26).

Other mechanisms and arguments

There is little evidence that any of the other causal mechanisms were at work in the Guatemala case. Clearly, membership in and the joining of a regional organization did not serve to provide a credible commitment (or deterrent) to the "winners" in democratic reform (I return to this issue in the conclusion to this chapter). There is also no evidence of bribery in this case. At no point did the OAS or any other regional organization offer assistance targeted to any specific elite or mass-based group.

Finally, as in the Peru case, one could argue that unilateral US action played a more important role than the OAS, supporting the realist hypothesis concerning great power actors. While, the US did move to cut aid to Guatemala and to lift preferential trade status, the OAS as an institution was essential in this case. The counterfactual that US pressure *alone* would have been sufficient to end Serrano's power grab garners little support. While the US did possess significant economic muscle to make life difficult for Serrano, the overwhelming balance of evidence suggests that the actors within the OAS mission to Guatemala were key to ending the crisis. It is unclear whether the US could have (or would have) sent such an effective mission. US opposition was an important, but by no means defining, aspect of this crisis.

Conclusion

The long-term future of Guatemalan democracy is not guaranteed and democratic institutions are not completely consolidated. The URNG signed a peace agreement with the Arzu administration on December 29, 1996, effectively ending their rebellion against the state.[29] Nonetheless, spotty political violence continues, often assumed to be sponsored or encouraged by small pockets of radical military officers to destabilize military reform. The reform continues, however, and must continue if Guatemala is to become a truly stable democracy (McCleary 1997: 139–42). Despite these potential roadblocks, because of the outcome of the 1993 *autogolpe*, I classify Guatemala as a success in achieving short-term (or negative) democratic consolidation.

The Guatemala case points to the importance of the supply-side issue. Serrano had planed his power grab for some time, telling Congress that he wanted to "carry out a Peruvian-style self-coup" (Cameron 1998b: 219). Serrano perceived the initial international response to Fujimori's *autogolpe* in Peru as weak and calculated that he would only pay short-term costs, assuming that the OAS would only demand a long-term schedule for a return to constitutional rule (Villagran de León 1993: 119). If regional organizations refuse to enforce democratic conditionality, the conditions will become meaningless as deterrents to winners *or* losers in nascent democracies. The good news is that the OAS appeared to learn from its weak response to Fujimori in 1992, both in the context of Guatemala in 1993 and Peru in the 2000 crisis (see Chapter 5). If the deterrent effect is a key causal mechanism linking regional organizations to consolidation, members of the organization must establish the credibility of the threat. For the OAS, Guatemala helped to reestablish this credibility.

According to Viron Vaky (1993: 28), the lesson drawn from the OAS's actions in 1993 is that "international pressure works. Fear of being isolated diplomatically and appearing as pariahs was clearly a *deterrent* in

---

[29] For an in-depth discussion of the peace process see Jonas 1999 and McCleary 1997.

the Peruvian and Guatemalan cases" (emphasis added). Again, although Guatemalan democracy is far from perfect, it is in a better state thanks to the OAS. Due to a healthy civil society and strong international support, Guatemala's democratic institutions survived a strong challenge in the spring of 1993.

Conclusion: assessing the consolidation cases

Table 7.2 presents a summary of the findings across the three case studies in this chapter as well as Turkey. The strongest influence mechanism of IOs on the consolidation of democracy is found in their membership conditionality and its influence on the "losers" in democratic reform. As discussed in Chapter 2, conditionality can serve as a powerful deterrent to anti-regime forces since any benefits of the organization would end if democracy faltered. These case studies provide substantial support for this argument. In both Paraguay and Greece, the conditional benefits of MERCOSUR and the EU, respectively, provide powerful incentives for the continuance of democracy. While in Greece this seemed more of a diffuse incentive, applying to no group in particular, in Paraguay this conditionality was used to deter the military from undermining democracy. In Guatemala, the benefits of the OAS, with attendant diplomatic and economic ties that come with membership, proved a strong point of leverage in deterring the business community and the military from supporting an internal coup.

This conditionality also proved important to committing "winners" to reform as well, although less evidence was found in support of this particular causal mechanism. In both Turkey and Greece, the conditionality of membership and benefits played some role in creating a credible commitment to reform for those in power. This conditionality was most effective in signaling commitment in conjunction with the psychological benefits of membership. The major psychological benefit in these cases involved the idea of symbolic reorientation away from past authoritarian regimes, which increased the legitimacy of the young democratic regime and, perhaps more importantly, the democratic process (in Paraguay and Guatemala). Joining IOs was a high-profile signal (by the regime) that the new democratic administration was visibly breaking ranks with previous authoritarian governments. This new status is ultimately conditional, however, since membership is contingent on the continuation of democracy. Just as quickly as a regime can reorient itself through involvement in regional organizations, it could find itself isolated both regionally and internationally. This possibility creates domestic audience costs if the country were to be punished or expelled by the IO. In addition, IO membership can reinforce the public's support of democracy by signaling external support for democratic institutions, making the public more likely to support their continuation. Conditionality and audience costs thus work in tandem in helping to enhance the credibility of reform.

Bribery appeared to be a factor in only one case – Greece. One could hypothesize several reasons for the absence of this mechanism as an effective way to consolidate democracy in other cases. First, it can set a dangerous precedent that anti-system activity or leanings can have a high payoff for would-be agitators. This implies that the regime as well as the IO itself would be hesitant to open the floodgates to more demands for targeted financial assistance. Second, there is a potential difficulty in weaning the targeted group within the new democracy from the assistance. In the case of Greece, the farming sector still receives massive financial assistance under the Common Agricultural Program (CAP). Finally, I would hypothesize that bribery was especially effective in the case of Greece because there was a preexisting arrangement within the institution (the CAP) designed to help a group that could have made the consolidation of democracy difficult in Greece. If a new program had been required within the EC, it might have been more difficult to establish this system of financial support for the Greek farmers or any other disaffected group after the transition.

One additional causal mechanism was discovered in the case of Greece – institutional change. The EC requirement that institutional reform expand in Greece served as another way to consolidate Greek democracy. There is also some anecdotal evidence that similar processes occurred in both Spain and Portugal immediately preceding and during their accession to the EU (Pridham 1991c). It is possible that this is an EC/EU-specific phenomenon, or one relegated to well-established IOs. Nevertheless, it is a mechanism that should receive additional attention in future research.

Overall, these case studies help to illustrate the causal processes that explain the statistical associations between IO membership and democratic longevity. While not all the hypothesized causal mechanisms received strong support, there is evidence that each has played a role in at least one of the cases selected here. This shows that the statistical findings of Chapter 6 are not a statistical artifact – there are clear causal links between the membership in and the joining of highly democratic regional organizations and the endurance of democracy. No doubt other causal mechanisms exist (as was found in the case of Greece), but from the four studies undertaken here, it appears that many of the causal processes are captured by the mechanisms in Chapter 2.

Table 7.2 *Consolidation cases and evidence of causal mechanisms*

Case/Mechanism	Turkey (see Chapter 5)	Greece	Paraguay	Guatemala
Binding – deterrence of losers	–	Strong	Strong	Strong
Binding – commitment of winners	Moderate	Moderate	Low	–
Psychological legitimization	Moderate	Moderate	Low	Low
Bribery	–	Moderate	–	–
Institutional change*	–	Moderate	–	–

*– not included in Chapter 2 causal mechanisms.

Discussion: assessing the six case studies

The key question that arises when comparing the six cases across Chapters 5 and 7 is why do IOs occasionally have difficulty consolidating democracies in the same countries where they were able to pressure for redemocratization? The case of Turkey is telling in this regard. Why were IOs successful in pressuring the Turkish military to speed up and expand the liberalization process, yet unable to deter them from moving against democracy in the first place? One could turn to variables specific to Turkey (opposition to the secular nature of the state, fears of Islamic fundamentalism, etc.), but we find a similar outcome in Peru. Despite the OAS's clear (if unsuccessful) efforts to undo the democratic reversal in Haiti earlier that year, Fujimori undertook his actions with little regard for that regional institution. Guatemala arguably follows a similar pattern – Serrano was undeterred by potential punishment from the OAS, but quickly backed down when confronted with punishment.[30]

There are several potential answers to this puzzle, each warranting further investigation. First, it is clear in the cases of Turkey, Peru, and Guatemala that those who perpetrated the actions against the regime never considered or gave very short shrift to the influence of the international community, especially the regional organizations of which they were members. Turkish military leaders seemed unconcerned about NATO or EC reaction during the 1980 coup. Fujimori was genuinely surprised that the OAS and its members were against his *autogolpe* of 1992. Serrano felt the OAS would object diplomatically, but take no more initial

---

[30] What sets Guatemala apart, however, is that the OAS did constrain the military from joining Serrano, which was a key factor in his failure to consolidate the *autogolpe*.

action than it had in the Peru case. This underscores the importance of signaling on the part of the IO that conditions will be enforced if they are abrogated. I would argue that the supply-side of the equation failed in these three cases, and to a lesser extent Greece in 1967. In none of these cases were there clear and explicit warnings given that anti-democratic action would be met with punishment from the organization. MERCO-SUR has been very quick to warn Paraguay on multiple occasions that a suspension of democracy would spell disaster for its membership. The counterfactual is that if similar warnings had come from the OAS (in the case of Peru) and NATO and/or the EC (in the case of Turkey), would these democratic breakdowns have occurred? In Guatemala, the quick action of the OAS did forestall the army and business elites from backing Serrano, which led to the return to constitutional rule.

A second and related explanation lies in the importance of precedent in the Peru and Turkey cases. In the past coups in Turkey, NATO (and to a lesser degree the EC) had been unconcerned with domestic governance issues and seemed completely unwilling to punish Turkey out of concern for broader geo-strategic interests. As discussed in the case of Peru, the OAS's weak response to the Panama crisis of the late 1980s and its inability to set a consistent policy towards Haiti in that state's 1991 coup could have led Fujimori to infer that his actions would be accepted by the OAS. Also discussed in the Guatemala case, Serrano had planned to announce elections soon after his *autogolpe* to placate the OAS, but this turned out to be too little, too late. Again, this points to the importance of IOs in acting on the conditions set in membership agreements.

A third possibility to explain this anomaly deals with the level of internal violence and pressures on the state. One commonality across each of these cases of democratic backsliding (or near-backsliding) is that each state was in the midst of widespread civil violence (Peru and Guatemala), a high degree of external threat (Greece in 1967 in Cyprus), or both (Turkey). It is likely that under these extenuating circumstances, even the clearest signal from an IO of impending punishment or sanction will fall on deaf ears. Because of overriding concerns of civil or international war, leaders considering coups may simply not pay attention to other international factors in their decision calculus.[31]

The final possibility is that while the IOs may ultimately be successful in signaling their intent to punish movements away from democracy in member states, those who would overthrow the state may do so regardless. In other words, even if IOs can increase the costs of democratic backsliding, coup perpetrators may still believe that the benefits will outweigh

---

[31] On this argument, see Cameron 1998b.

these new costs. As discussed in the case of Turkey, many military leaders began to fear an all-out civil war unless drastic action was taken. Under these circumstances, no outside (nor internal) force may convince the military or any other group that a coup is not in its best interests. Especially if states are experiencing massive domestic unrest, I would hypothesize that this scenario is much more likely – the short-term costs of continued internal upheaval will far outweigh the costs (economic or diplomatic) that could be brought by a regional organization.

Of course, it is also possible that some unobserved set of variables, which may be specific to a state or a region, also would account for this variation in the efficacy of IOs to promote or preserve democracy. One alternative explanation receiving some support in two cases (Turkey and Greece) is the realist argument that the preferences of great powers are a better predictor of outcome than the presence of regional institutions. I return to this question in Chapter 8, but it is interesting that in both cases, the state (the US) and the organization (NATO) are identical. As I hypothesize in the next chapter, democratic great power preferences could be influenced by security threats, accounting for the lack of US pressure through NATO on Turkey or Greece.

In the end, although there are still questions concerning the nature of the causal relationship between regional organizations and the democratization process, these case studies have provided evidence concerning how these causal mechanisms function. They have also spurred the creation of new hypotheses concerning this relationship as well as questions about the conditions under which this relationship holds. Although some questions still remain, we can now be more confident about the presence and the nature of the links between regional organizations and democratization.

8   Conclusion

Since 1974, democracy has become an increasingly ubiquitous form of government. In the words of one scholar, "Democracy seems to have scored an historic victory over alternative forms of government" (Held 1993: 13). What has accounted for the rise of democracy and its prospects for continuation has become the focus of a large scholarly community. Despite the widespread interest in these issues, how international factors shape these processes has not received "sufficient attention" from these scholars (Hall 1993: 279).

The purpose of this book has been to investigate one aspect of the international influence on democratization: the effect of regional organizations. Through theorizing about causal processes, as well as testing the link between regional IOs and democracy, I attempted to bring a systematic approach to the investigation of external–internal linkages. Such an effort is essential not only for political science theory and research, but policymakers as well.

The argument

In Chapter 2, I presented several causal processes linking membership in and the joining of regional organizations to both democratic transitions and democratic endurance. The successes of regional institutions arise from their ability to create both positive and negative incentives for domestic actors. A regional organization's ability to either promote or protect democracy grows out of its capacity to influence the cost–benefit calculations as well as the perceptions of societal actors, often at the behest of these same domestic actors.

With regard to democratic transitions, regional organizations can provide a low-cost forum for neighboring democracies to pressure non-democracies to liberalize. Through public delegitimization, political isolation, suspension of benefits from the organization, even economic sanctions, regional institutions can increase the costs of remaining a non-democracy for member states. This scenario will be especially likely in cases where a member state suffers from a breakdown of democratic rule (e.g. Peru). In the face of international opposition, an autocrat may move to reliberalize or may be forced from power due to costs imposed by the international opposition. The regional institution provides a forum where surrounding states' opposition to a coup can coalesce.

Regional organizations may also encourage liberalization through a phenomenon I label the acquiescence effect. Membership in regional organizations can provide protection to the interests of key groups such as business elites and the military. Many scholars have argued that these groups often support authoritarian over democratic rule since autocrats will better protect property rights and the policies which benefit these groups (Kaufman 1986; Payne 1994). Regional organizations can provide guarantees for property rights and economic policies thus allaying the fears of business elites and/or the military. In addition, some regional organizations, especially military alliances, may socialize important elite groups to not interfere with the democratic process. Evidence of the socialization phenomenon was discussed in the context of the Spanish, Turkish, and Hungarian transitions.

Finally, membership in regional organizations can help to legitimize transitional or interim regimes to ensure a completion of the democratic transition. Often, interim regimes face problems of legitimacy and credibility since they are not elected and often contain elements from previous authoritarian regimes (Shain and Linz 1995). Membership in and accession to regional IOs can assist in the legitimization of these regimes since acceptance into these organizations can provide an essential external "seal of approval" to the regime and the transition to democracy.

With respect to democratic consolidation, regional organizations can assist nascent democracies in overcoming challenges to their survival in several ways. First, regime leaders may join IOs to make credible commitments to democratic reform. Because membership and the benefits of regional organizations are often conditional on continued democratic governance, any attempts by the new regime to consolidate its own power at the expense of the democratic process will be met with punishment from the organization. This prospect of punishment contributes to the ability of regime leaders to make a credible commitment to democratic reform. Enhancing the credibility of this measure are the costs associated with entering a new regional organization and the potential enforcement of membership conditions that are controlled by a third party. This credible commitment can be essential to the duration of democracy as elite groups (e.g. business elites) and/or the masses could undermine the new regime if they feel a commitment is not present. These audience costs are especially potent since joining a highly democratic regional organization provides a way for the new institutions to distance themselves from previous regimes and build legitimacy.

These same incentives apply to anti-regime forces as well. That is, those groups which oppose democracy out of fears that they will "lose" under the new system can be deterred from moving against a new democracy since they would also incur the costs (suspension of aid/trade, political isolation, or expulsion) imposed by the regional organization for abrogating the conditions of membership. In addition to these negative incentives, IOs may provide positive incentives as well, including bribery of key societal actors. These positive incentives can convince regime opponents that democracy can be palatable, lessening the probability that they will undermine democracy.

Because I do not expect *all* regional organizations to be associated with democratic transitions or endurance, I discuss the supply-side part of the problem in Chapter 3. Again, some organizations may be unwilling to adopt democracy-related conditions, while others may be hesitant to enforce these conditions. My contention is that the more democracies which are members of a regional organization, as a percentage of all organization members, the more likely the organization will be to enact conditions, enforce conditions, and provide a credible external seal of approval of domestic reform efforts. Only organizations with high "democratic density" will be associated with the promotion and protection of democracy. I also discussed the scope conditions of the argument, noting that the key international organizations used in the theory generation and statistical tests were regional organizations. I specifically excluded universal organizations (e.g. the UN), as well as international/regional financial institutions (e.g. the IMF; World Bank), since the theory behind their hypothesized linkages to democratization are distinct from those tested here.

Finally, I discuss an alternate realist-based hypothesis in Chapter 3. Drawing on various realist theories and some institutionalist literature, I discuss the possibility that regional institutions are not the important external actor related to the process of democratization. In this alternate hypothesis, the interests of the democratic great powers are the driving force behind democratization rather than the institutions themselves. The counterfactual drawn by this view is that great power interests would encourage or preserve democracy in the absence of the regional organization. If the large democratic state(s) in a regional IO desires democracy, this would be a better predictor than the nature of the regional organization itself. I argue that this position misses the mark theoretically. For most of the causal mechanisms to function in my argument, the key preferences in question are those of the domestic elite. Regional IOs may be tools for actors, but the theory suggests they are potent tools of domestic elites inside nascent democracies, not of the democratic great powers. Indeed, a key contribution of this work is to show domestic actors may use international institutions to achieve their domestic goals. The one causal mechanism where regional institutions (and therefore possibly great powers) choose whether or not to impose their preferences on member states is the pressure mechanism. I discuss the empirical evidence concerning this hypothesis in the next section.

The findings

To test the preceding theory, I utilized both statistical analyses and case studies. Chapter 3 presented the operationalization of the key concepts to be used in the statistical tests. The chapter also contained a description of the main data measures of regime type and IO involvement from 1950 to 1992. I also conducted a number of bivariate tests showing initial support for the idea that more homogenously democratic regional IOs were associated with transitions to and the consolidation of democracy. The full statistical tests of the argument were presented in Chapters 4 and 6. Chapter 4 presented a model of democratic transitions which controlled for other processes associated with democratic transitions (and IO involvement) including per capita income, growth rates, internal and external conflict, type of previous authoritarian regime, past experience with democracy and contagion effects, among others. The estimates of the model indicated that membership in democratic regional organizations (those organizations with more democracies as a percentage of all members, see Chapter 3) was associated with an increased probability of a transition to democracy. This result was robust across several variations of the model, including the inclusion of region-based fixed effects to control for regional phenomena excluded from the model. Joining democratic regional IOs, however, seemed to have little systematic influence on the prospects for democratic transitions.

In addition, Chapter 4 included tests focused on the various stages of democratic transitions. The model of political liberalization (Model 4.2) tested for an association between membership in democratic regional organizations and the initial loosening of authoritarian rule, which could have resulted in a partial democracy (anocracy) or a full-fledged democracy. Controlling for several other factors associated with liberalization, the statistical results indicated a strong association between membership in democratic regional organizations and political liberalization. The model of democratic completion (Model 4.3), or moving from a partial to a full democracy, however, showed far less support for this relationship.

Only occasionally was the association between IO membership and completing the transition statistically significant.

Although the large-N tests showed a broad association between IOs and democratization across space and time, it is difficult to know if the causal processes outlined in Chapter 2 are behind these statistical correlations. Chapter 5 presented three case studies of democratic transitions: Hungary, Peru, and Turkey. The Hungarian case demonstrated how IOs assist in the completion of the democratic transition. The study found support for the idea that regional organizations can have an acquiescence effect on societal elites, in this case, the military. The two strongest causal linkages in the Hungarian case are found in the psychological-legitimization benefits of membership in regional organizations and direct assistance (financial and technical) provided by these organizations (e.g. the EU, Council of Europe, the CSCE). The Peruvian case illustrated how IO membership can spur liberalization through the direct application of pressure by a regional organization against the leadership of a member state. In response to Alberto Fujimori's *autogolpe* of 1992, the OAS responded with strong condemnation, political pressure, and the threat of economic sanctions if Fujimori did not take steps to return the country to constitutional rule. Although critics have argued that the OAS did not go far enough to pressure Fujimori, its actions did alter Fujimori's plans to consolidate his own authority through a national plebiscite that would have granted him near absolute power.

Finally, the case of Turkey is another illustration of how regional institutions may pressure for redemocratization after a democratic breakdown. In the aftermath of the military takeover in 1980, several European organizations including the EC and the Council of Europe pressured the Turkish military to return the country to civilian rule. The suspension of economic assistance and institutional membership to the Council of Europe were a potent source of pressure on the government of General Evren. There is also some evidence that the psychological-legitimization factor was present in the Turkish case, but more as an additional source of pressure on the military regime. There is also some evidence that the military hastened its retreat to the barracks in Turkey because of the socialization effects of NATO membership.

Chapter 6 tested for the relationship between membership in and/or accession to democratic regional organizations and the longevity of democracy. This chapter utilized an event history model to test for this association, while controlling for factors such as per capita income, growth rates, internal and external conflict, type of governmental system (presidential or parliamentary), past experience with democracy and contagion effects, among others. The results indicated that *accession* to these organizations was associated with longer-lasting democracies. Further tests, including the introduction of fixed effects to the model, showed that joining democratic organizations had a robust association with the endurance of democracy.

Chapter 7 presented three cases to trace the influence of regional organizations in the protection of democracy: Greece, Paraguay, and Guatemala. In the Greek case, traces of all the causal mechanisms specified in Chapter 2 were present. Accession to the EC provided many benefits to Greece, all of which were conditional upon continued democratic practice. This conditionality helped create a credible commitment on the part of the Karamanlis government to continue democratic reform, while also providing a deterrent to forces that could have moved against the young democracy. In addition, the provision of assistance from the EC served to "bribe" certain domestic groups (mostly the agriculture sector) in order to gain their allegiance to the new regime.

Paraguay demonstrated the strong deterrent effect that conditions of membership may have on regime opponents. MERCOSUR membership has supported this fledgling democracy through two crises that threatened to end in military coups. In both cases, the threat of expulsion and the end of the benefits associated with MERCOSUR played a large role in convincing the military to stay out of civilian politics. Similarly in Guatemala, the OAS played a crucial role in deterring key members of civil society from supporting Jorge Serrano's self-coup. The organization not only quickly denounced the *autogolpe* but sent a high-level mission to Guatemala, including the secretary-general. Through many meetings with the mission, nearly all aspects of civil society openly denounced Serrano and his coup was short-lived. Again, the threat of diplomatic and economic isolation spurred by the OAS convinced both the military and business elites to solve the crisis peacefully and return the state to constitutional rule.

Finally, although presented in Chapter 5, the case of Turkey can be classified as a failed case of consolidation. Despite membership in several highly democratic regional organizations, Turkey has suffered three breakdowns of democracy, each at the hands of the military. This study explored why membership in such organizations as NATO, the EC/EU, and the Council of Europe has not created conditions conducive to the survival of democracy. I conclude that the lack of enforcement of conditions, largely due to Turkey's geostrategic importance, plays a large role in making this a failed case for my theory. In addition, I speculate that in some circumstances, although regional organizations may increase the costs of anti-democratic behavior, the benefits of such actions may still outweigh the costs especially given the presence of internal violence. Both of these explanations play a role in the 1980 military coup in Turkey. In both of the previous cases of military coups (1960 and 1971), European institutions had done little to punish the Turkish military. This history of turning a blind eye towards Turkey, in addition to the dire economic and political situation of Turkey, probably led the military to believe that the costs imposed for such a transgression would be low. This past behavior, in conjunction with massive internal unrest confronting the military, led to its movement to suspend civilian rule.

Overall, the evidence that major power preferences were the driving force behind transitions to or the durability of democracy was not strong. In each statistical model, I added a variable controlling for the presence of democratic major powers in the most democratic regional organization for each state. In only one case out of eight (the completion of democracy model using the Polity98 data) did any evidence emerge that great powers were correlated with democratization. An examination of the particular completion cases (all European) accounting for this result suggests that the regional IO was still an important causal mechanism at work. The evidence from the Hungarian case, for example, suggests that the legitimization effect of the regional IOs was based on the fact that Hungary was admitted to an *organization*. There is little evidence that unilateral assistance by the democratic major powers in this case would have achieved the same ends. Thus, the relationship between democratic major powers and the completion of a democratic transition appears more correlational than causal.

In the remaining seven cases, the association with membership in or the joining of a highly democratic regional IO remained a much stronger predictor of democracy than the major power variable. The case studies also showed isolated evidence that great power interests were accounting for the success or failure of regional institutions. In both the Turkish and Greek cases, the United States exerted pressure on NATO *not* to encourage returns to democracy. In the Turkish case, however, evidence emerged that other democratic great powers actually changed their behavior towards Turkey to align themselves with both the European Union and the Council of Europe. Finally, little evidence emerged in the Latin American cases suggesting that United States preferences were a better predictor of success or failure than multilateral OAS efforts. Although the interests of the US and the OAS may have been aligned in many of these cases, there is strong evidence to suggest that the OAS was essential to the outcome – US pressure alone would not have preserved or encouraged democracy in these cases. Thus, an exclusive focus on democratic major powers is not sufficient to account for the outcomes discussed here. It should be emphasized, however, that these actors are not completely unimportant in this case and any analysis of the influence of regional organizations on outcomes should not ignore these actors.

In sum, both the statistical and case-based evidence support the contention that homogenously democratic regional organizations can play a role in promoting and protecting democracy by altering the incentives of domestic actors. Some of the hypothesized causal processes received more support than others in the case research, while new avenues of causality were uncovered. I return to these in my discussion of future research on this topic.

The implications

The relationship between regional organizations and domestic political processes has important implications for both academic theory and political practice. Specifically, these findings challenge current thinking about the role and functions of international institutions in international relations theory, and they call into question the assumption in comparative politics that the major influences and determinants of democratization lie only inside the nation-state. In addition, the empirical findings and scope of conditions discussed in this work establish some important guidelines for policymakers who wish to use these organizations to foster and/or protect democracy.

International relations theory

The "institutions debate" in international relations theory has centered on issues relating to conflict and cooperation between states. For example, a common argument/assumption of neoliberal institutionalists is that international institutions are formed to solve coordination problems between states (cf. Keohane and Martin 1995; Martin 1992). While I do not address the question of the *international* influence of these institutions, I have shown that *domestic* political processes can shape state involvement in international institutions.

Choices concerning accession to international institutions can be shaped by domestic incentives, not merely a desire to coordinate policy internationally. This is especially important when thinking about incentives to *join* institutions. Most of the international institutions literature focuses on the *formation* of institutions and regimes. Today, much of the activity surrounding international institutions involves the expansion of existing structures. Institutionalist theory is largely silent as to whether the act of joining these institutions will have a similar impetus as the act of forming them. My findings indicate that decisions of whether to join an institution may be based as much (or more) on domestic political considerations as on international ones.

As called for by recent institutionalist work (cf. Martin and Simmons 1998), I have attempted to show not only *how* institutions matter, but also how variation among institutions influences their performance. First, in line with other recent institutionalist works (e.g. Goldstein 1996; Mansfield, Milner, and Rosendorff 2002), this work has shown how the direct causal linkages between the international and domestic levels of analysis function. Regional organizations may pressure domestic governments, provide incentives for certain types of behavior, or provide an anchor of legitimacy for interim governments. Rather than merely external agents for change, however, these same regional organizations function as a tool for domestic actors. By binding themselves to the rules and regulations of an organization, domestic agents limit not only their own autonomy, but other elites' autonomy as well. These constraints can be essential to encourage the transition to and the consolidation of democracy.

Variations among regional organizations set important limits to these findings. The more democratic the membership of a regional organization, the more credible are its guarantees of assistance and protection, the more interested it will be in promoting liberal reforms, the more likely it will be to set constraining conditions on the behavior of new members, and the more likely it will be to enforce those conditions if they are violated. Of course, variation along other dimensions may be important to an organization's ability or interest in democracy promotion. Other factors such as the distribution of wealth (or military power) among the members or the democraticness of the rules of the organization could correlate with the efficacy in this area, as well as suggest other causal processes linking these organizations to democracy. Still, we can be assured that along at least one dimension (level of democracy of membership), variations in institutions matter for outcome.

The findings of this study are also suggestive for several bodies of literature discussed in Chapter 1. The "two-level games" literature argues that domestic actors will use constraints arising from international institutions to further their domestic agenda, yet domestic political constraints will also be a source of leverage in international negotiations. This study proposes that in post-transitional states, these dynamics may occur quite often. Yet, in these instances, only the "outside-in" constraint is important. That is, domestic agents will use membership in or the joining of regional organizations to limit their own (or their opponents') options domestically, yet it is difficult to conclude that their domestic situation is a source of leverage internationally. Indeed, it is surprising that post-transitional states do not attempt to lever more favorable treatment from these organizations. Rather, in their quest for membership and its attendant benefits, domestic elites will rarely press for the best possible bargain. This is clearly evident in the European Union association agreements, for example, where Hungary, Poland, and the Czech Republic received very few guarantees of open markets in Western Europe, in exchange for future consideration as EU members (Pinder 1991).

The new institutionalist contention that international and domestic institutions interact in distinct and strategic ways also receives support in this study. Although many of the models underlying this new institutionalist work require complete information concerning the preferences of the actors, one finds evidence that domestic agents do use membership in regional institutions to bind their own hands, signal intentions, and make side-payments to disaffected domestic political groups. Despite the fact that information about the preferences (or even identity) of important actors in the transition stage can be scarce, this study suggests that the ideas of the new institutionalists may apply to more than the developed and consolidated Western democracies.

Interest group based explanations for involvement in regional organizations (cf. Solingen 1994; 1998) also receive some support, although this research suggests a broader range of concerns that can lead to joining regional organizations. Rather than solely economic-based agendas driving membership in these organizations, I have argued that concerns of domestic legitimacy, placating or paying off domestic interest groups, as well as binding groups, can be important factors in the drive to join regional organizations. Although economic motives are important in many cases, these other interests can be important as well.

In a similar vein, my argument concerning transitions to democracy shows how membership in these organizations can have unforeseen consequences for elites. If "internationalist" coalitions push governments to join regional organizations for simply economic benefits, they may find themselves under pressure from these organizations to liberalize domestically. Even if not an initial requirement of entry to the organization, regional institutions may evolve to include such requirements. One example is the OAS which has implemented a democratic charter many years after its founding.

Comparative politics

Although much of the research in comparative politics on democratic transitions and consolidation has eschewed international factors, this work has shown that even when controlling for important domestic factors, regional organizations play a significant role in the democratization process. In many instances, domestic factors are the dominant force in shaping democratic transitions and consolidation, but to ignore the role of actors external to the nation-state is to ignore a potent force for change.

Since membership in a regional organization is inherently a domestic political decision, my argument does not minimize the importance of domestic actors. Rather, I argue that when specifying the influences on these actors' decisions regarding democratization, international forces can be important. Regional organizations can influence the cost and benefit calculations of these domestic agents by encouraging, committing, or deterring them in a variety of ways. This influence may arise from an actor's desire to constrain themselves or opponents.

In the face of these costs imposed by regional IOs, the influence of many traditionally important domestic variables may be mitigated or changed. For example, economic crises may bring domestic pressure from regime opponents, yet their behavior will be circumscribed by anticipated costs deriving from their membership in regional IOs. Over time, membership in democratically dense organizations can help to engender long-term respect for democracy. This was one of several factors in Argentina's economic crisis in 2001–2, where a massive economic recession brought down the government of President de la Rua. In the face of economic instability, however, a smooth transition of power took place in Argentina. As noted by a former Argentine army general, "the crisis of democratic values is resolved with more democracy" (Schamis 2002: 92). MERCOSUR provided a background guarantee for the continuation of democracy in Argentina (Steves 2001).

Although some literature has developed discussing the importance of international factors in the transition or consolidation process (cf. Pridham 1994; Whitehead 1996a), much of this literature lacks systematic attempts to build theory. Much of the extant work is based on single case studies, which, while important in determining the causal mechanisms in particular instances, does little to help build broader theories which link international forces with domestic political processes. In addition, few statistical studies exist in this literature. This work fills both these theoretical and empirical voids.

To ignore the influence of actors external to the state is to ignore an important influence in domestic political processes. For example, the concept of "legitimacy" has been offered as an important factor in the success or failure of the transition and the consolidation process (cf. Mainwaring 1992). This study has shown that an important source of legitimacy for both transitional (e.g. interim) and nascent democratic regimes is acceptance by the international community. One important signal of this acceptance is membership in regional organizations. Although other domestic factors certainly influence public and elite perceptions of legitimacy, international factors are often an important constituent of this perception.

Comparative politics scholarship has identified other international factors that can influence the democratization process. Two of these (epistemic communities/spill-over and the use of force) actually coincide with causal mechanisms discussed in this study (acquiescence effect/ socialization and pressure, respectively). The importance of regional organizations in providing technical assistance to and socializing actors in fledgling democracies to help complete their transitions to democracy was noted in the case of Hungary (see Chapter 5). Although short of the physical use of force, the pressure mechanism used in the cases of Peru, Guatemala, and Paraguay also shows how direct pressure in the form of threats and sanctions can influence the democratization process. Rather than competing explanations, the extant literature offers complementary mechanisms that can work through regional IOs.

Rather than overturning or rejecting current thinking in comparative politics as to the role of external factors in the democratization process, this study has attempted to clarify how those factors function, their relative importance, and if those factors work in conjunction with other causal mechanisms discussed in comparative politics. As regional organizations continue to expand throughout the globe, the prospects for these institutions to play an increasing role in domestic politics will grow with time. As such, it is essential that those who study domestic political dynamics consider their influence on domestic politics.

Policymaking

As discussed in Chapter 1, much of the justification for the expansion of regional institutions from policymakers flows from the idea that international institutions can protect and/or promote democracy. This work has shown that simply assuming this link will always function may set the policymaking community up for great disappointments in the future. A major conclusion of this research has shown that the supply-side aspect of the IO–democracy link is an essential part of the picture. Conditions on membership are a key factor in this link. When conditions are not enforced, this threatens the democratic stability of the state in question and also sets dangerous precedents for future threats to democracy in other states. As the case of Turkey illustrates, turning a blind eye to anti-democratic behavior can lead to assumptions on the part of coup perpetrators that similar behavior in the future will lead to a similar response.

The IO–democracy link functions largely by influencing the cost–benefit calculations of domestic agents. If these agents attach a low probability to the enforcement of conditions, regional institutions will then only be able to pressure for redemocratization rather than prevent its breakdown.

The lack of enforcement may arise for a variety of reasons. Some members of the organization may refuse to cooperate with economic sanctions against another member state. In these instances, the cohesion of the organization may be valued over encouraging democracy, especially in cases where the member in question is considered a cornerstone of the organization. For example, it is clear that the US was hesitant to press Turkey on the issue of democracy because of its geostrategic importance in the Cold War. The question is, under what circumstances are conditions likely *not* to be enforced? I return to this question below.

Another important lesson drawn from this work for policymakers is the importance of conditions themselves (Carothers 1999). Because part of the importance of conditions is their "signaling value" – their ability to create credible commitments on the part of new democrats – conditions should be explicit upon accession to the organization. When conditions are not explicit, they are less likely to create credible commitments or deter anti-regime activity (e.g. NATO's lack of explicit conditionality in the case of Greece and Turkey).

What about policy implications for nascent democracies? One cynical conclusion that could be drawn from this work is that only new democracies in regions where underlying conditions are favorable will be helped by regional institutions. Do regional IOs, then, only assist on the margins? Are regional IOs useful at all in these circumstances? What is a new democratic leader to do if he or she has no equivalent of the EU to join?

In short, form your own democratic regional organization. This is exactly what three sets of newly democratic states have done over the past twenty years – in each case these states were spurred by wanting to help democratize other neighbors as well as cementing their own democratic institutions. Immediately after the transition to democracy in Argentina and Brazil, both states moved to build common regional institutions, beginning with the Argentina–Brazil Economic Integration Pact (ABEIP). As one observer of Latin American politics noted, "The ABEIP was intended by both presidents to be a means of reinforcing the consolidation of democracy domestically" (Steves 2001: 84). The ABEIP then encouraged Uruguay to join the integration process and, by the early 1990s, Paraguay was added to plans for regional integration.

The same pattern emerged in Eastern Europe, where Hungary, Poland, and Czechoslovakia (later the Czech and Slovak Republics) followed a similar strategy. Within a year of beginning their transition to democracy, these states came together to form two regional organizations: the

Visegrad Group and the Central European Free Trade Agreement (CEFTA). Both of these organizations signaled the intent of each member state to undertake and continue political and economic reforms. CEFTA's own founding documents contend that a "fundamental objective includes the consolidation of democracy and the market economy."[1] While each state desires eventual admission to the EU, as an interim solution, it is instructive that these states decided to build their own "club" of democracies.

Finally, and perhaps most importantly, *African* states appear to be adopting this strategy as well. In 1992, the Southern African Development Coordinating Conference (SADCC) was reorganized by member states into the Southern African Development Community (SADC).[2] This reorganization was meant to reflect the increasing number of democratic states of the region, especially the change in regime in South Africa, which had formerly been the target of SADCC policies. One goal of this new organization became the promotion and stabilization of democracy. South African President Nelson Mandela pressed SADC members to enact standing policies through the SADC to impose economic sanctions against states resisting moves towards democracy (Banks and Mueller 1998: 1162). Although no formal action was taken on Mandela's proposal, this set the tone for some SADC members to push the democratization agenda.

The SADC's first opportunity for action came in the fall of 1998, when Lesotho experienced massive unrest in response to controversial elections in May. After a number of violent public demonstrations and open threats of a coup against Prime Minister Mosisili, the SADC approved military intervention by South Africa and Botswana to bring calm to Lesotho and preserve the democratic regime (Neethling 1999; Southall 2003; Tsie 1998).[3]

South Africa possessed strategic as well as normative goals in the Lesotho intervention. Having a civil war in a proximate state would do nothing to help the economic or political climate in South Africa. Yet, both South Africa and Botswana chose to enact a 1994 agreement made under the auspices of the SADC that named them the guarantors of Lesotho's democracy (Tsie 1998). Such multilateral action would have

---

[1] CEFTA web page: http://www.cefta.org/cefta/historical.htm. Last accessed 10/1/03.
[2] The members of the SADC are: Angola, Botswana, Democratic Republic of the Congo, Lesotho, Malawi, Mauritius, Mozambique, Namibia, Seychelles, South Africa, Swaziland, Tanzania, Zambia, and Zimbabwe.
[3] South Africa weathered tremendous criticism for this intervention and the resulting chaos in Lesotho (see "It All Went Wrong," *The Economist*, September 26, 1998, 49), yet the intervention did lay the groundwork for future elections in Lesotho (Southall 2003).

been unthinkable fifteen years prior when South Africa, Botswana, and Lesotho were not considered democracies. Can we now say that Southern Africa will become the next regional club of democracies, anchored by the SADC? It is far too early to answer this question in the affirmative, yet if South Africa, Botswana, and Malawi continue to use the SADC as a forum to pressure neighbors to undertake and continue democratic reforms, such an outcome is certainly possible. This is extremely important for my argument, since the case of Lesotho's democratization has been labeled a "difficult" case by some Africanists (Southall 2003).

In sum, my theory predicts regional IOs to be more influential in the democratization process when those IOs are homogenously democratic. For nascent democracies in regions with few other democracies, banding together to form regional organizations with other democracies has been a successful strategy. There is reason for hope, therefore, that democratic clubs in various regions may form and be successful. The history of South America, Eastern Europe, and possibly Southern Africa bears witness to this fact.

Future research avenues

This work is by no means the definitive statement on the IO–democracy link. Many additional theoretical and empirical puzzles have arisen during the course of this analysis. This section will outline several additional directions that could add to this body of knowledge.

First, several empirical puzzles emerge from the case studies. For example, why do IOs appear to be more effective in engendering redemocratization than initial democratization? I could find little evidence that longstanding authoritarian regimes were effectively pressured to democratize by regional organizations. Rather, my cases indicate that only when a state suffers a breakdown of democracy is pressure from an IO helpful in the emergence of democracy. Again, more case studies of authoritarian regimes involved in IOs could help answer this puzzle.

Another puzzle requiring more case research is the lack of evidence of the acquiescence effect. If ideas concerning the importance of protection to societal elites (especially business interests and the military) by authoritarian regimes are correct, regional organizations should be able to serve as effective substitute commitment mechanisms for emerging democracies. Since these organizations lock in policies for important societal groups, the danger of losing these privileges under democracy is lessened. Despite arguments that this process was important in the Southern European transitions (Whitehead 1986), there is little evidence of this in other transition or consolidation cases.

One explanation for this finding could center on the idea of "reserve domains" (Linz and Stepan 1996). By creating policy guarantees which "lock in" an advantage for a certain segment of society, these arrangements create policy areas considered off-limits to the new democratic regime. Thus, even in the face of massive opposition to these policies, governments would be bound by their international commitments. If a new democratic regime fears granting such power to an elite group, it may refrain from doing so. That is, new regimes may want to place no policies "off-limits" for reasons of popular legitimacy. In these cases, they will not utilize regional organizations to protect the interests of key elite groups.[4] To test these hypotheses, however, more case studies are needed on both cases of democratic transitions and motivations to join regional organizations.

Additional causal mechanisms, such as the provision of direct assistance, also provide fertile grounds for new case research. In the case of Hungary, direct technical and monetary aid helped to complete the transition from an interim regime to an elected democratic government. Given these limited findings, it would appear that this process may be more common in the democratic completion stage, yet more case work is needed to test this hypothesis. Similarly in Greece, the EC's influence in bringing institutional reform to that country provided an additional link between regional organizations and democratic consolidation. More research on these causal processes is warranted.

Another area in which substantial research could take place is expanding the domain of inference for these findings. I included only a sample of relevant regional organizations in the statistical tests of my argument. I specifically excluded several types of organizations (both regional and international) from the scope of this study. Further work could investigate the influence of larger, global institutions such as the United Nations, as well as the international financial institutions (IFIs). As noted in Chapter 3, it is unlikely that the global, open institutions like the UN and its related agencies influence democratization in the same manner as the regional organizations included in this study since, by definition, these open organizations have no conditions on membership. IFIs and their regional counterparts (e.g. regional development banks) may also play a role in influencing democratization. This influence could be direct, through the conditions attached to assistance, although because many of the conditions in these agreements are not public knowledge, the exact causal processes probably differ. For example, the role of creating visible,

---

[4] Of course, this would not explain why authoritarian regimes would not enact these policies if the prospects of democratization were good.

credible commitments to political reform may be undermined by the secrecy of the IMF and World Bank. In addition, the link to democracy may be indirect, through economic reform. If political democracy requires neoliberal economic reform, these institutions may play a crucial role in the long-term promotion and protection of democracy. Each of these testable hypotheses should be investigated using both statistical analysis and case studies. The robustness checks of the statistical models in Chapters 4 and 6 that included non-regional organizations and IFIs suggested that there was some relationship between these institutions and democracy, but the statistical results were inconsistent. Future work should theorize about the causal linkages between these organizations and democracy, while devising appropriate statistical tests to capture those causal processes.

One factor not discussed in my theoretical argument was the domestic political dynamics concerning the decision to join a regional organization. In several of the countries under study, some segments of the domestic population voiced their opposition to membership in the regional organization. Future work could concentrate on how that opposition was dealt with in the post-transitional environment (in the cases of consolidation). In other words, how do domestic political processes concerning foreign policy play out in these settings? This work has concentrated on the broader picture of membership, its impetus, and its effects, yet this question could be equally important to understanding the domestic politics of organization membership.

Finally, besides the "democratic density" of an organization, there may be other correlates of the likelihood of enforcement of democratic conditions, some of which may actually fall close to the realist camp. The two cases which showed the clearest evidence of great-power interests driving an institution's behavior were Turkey and Greece. The democratic breakdowns in Turkey and Greece were "accepted" by the US because of Cold War military concerns. In addition, the US refused to use its leverage in NATO to pressure either state to redemocratize after the coups. As previously discussed, this behavior set dangerous precedents for future adventurers who would overthrow democratic governments. The common variable in both of these cases is geostrategic importance. This leads to a modified realist hypothesis whereby major-power preferences do not drive outcomes vis-à-vis regional institutions *unless* the major power perceives a vital security issue to be at stake. In fact, this take on institutions is perfectly consistent with the view of many realists who argue that security issues are the most difficult to confront in a multilateral setting (Jervis 1983; Mearsheimer 1995). If this hypothesis were true, it would set a significant boundary condition to the finding presented here.

Epilogue: Venezuela, the OAS, and United States foreign policy

As the preparation of this manuscript came to a close, the domestic situation in Venezuela was very much in flux. On April 11, 2002, a group of military leaders overthrew Venezuelan President Hugo Chavez and placed him under house arrest in an island off the coast of Venezuela. Ironically, barely six months earlier, the Organization of American States (OAS) had agreed to a Democratic Charter that calls for membership suspension in cases of interruption of the democratic order (Hakim 2002). What followed the coup was a series of events demonstrating that while there were still limits to OAS power in supporting democracy, that power was not dependent on the democratic great power of the region.

The April coup against Chavez was short lived. Three days after his forced exile, Chavez made a triumphant return to Caracas to reclaim the presidency. In those three days, however, the OAS and the United States displayed very different reactions to the coup. In the hours following the coup, nearly every Latin American nation decried it as a violation of the OAS Democratic Charter. The Rio Group, made up of thirteen states in the region, immediately demanded OAS action against Venezuela (Caizlez 2002). Although many Latin American leaders disliked Chavez, the coup put all civilian presidents on edge, leading to their denouncing the Venezuelan military's move (Rother 2002).

The US position was quite different. White House spokesman Ari Fleischer denied that a coup had even occurred, "the government suppressed what was a peaceful demonstration of the people [which] led very quickly to a combustible situation in which Chavez resigned" (Rother 2002). This response was not surprising given US opposition to Chavez. Since his rise to power in 1999, Chavez had continually angered the US, visiting Libya, Cuba, and Iraq, even calling the post-September 11 war in Afghanistan an exercise of "fighting terror with terror" (Coile 2002). The US had little love for Chavez and the feeling was mutual. Chavez continually directed his military to deny over-flight rights for US reconnaissance aircraft fighting the war on drugs in the region. The US clearly welcomed Chavez's ouster, establishing communication with the coup perpetrators and chastizing other OAS members for not being more concerned about Chavez's past anti-democratic behavior (DeYoung 2002).

The US position was decried in Latin America as well as by observers in America itself. Despite US preferences to the contrary, the OAS called a meeting to discuss the situation in Venezuela.[5] In that meeting, OAS

---

[5] Once Chavez returned to power, the US supported the OAS condemnation of the coup.

members condemned the coup and sent Secretary-General Cesar Gaviria to set up dialogue groups between Chavez supporters and opponents. For the past thirteen months, the OAS has continued to lead dialogues in Venezuela to prevent the outbreak of massive civil conflict or another coup.

The impact of these events on the US is clear. The US was "visibly out of step with other hemispheric leaders who condemned the military coup" (Valenzuela 2002). The action shook regional confidence in the US support for democracy (Hakim 2002). The George W. Bush administration's support of the coup perpetrators led one special assistant to Mexican President Vicente Fox to describe US policy as "multilateralism à la carte" (De Young 2002). In some ways, this case presents a perfect test for the realist hypothesis – the democratic great power expressed a preference for a new regime in Venezuela. The OAS should have had little efficacy in pressuring for a return to democracy. Yet, combined with strong domestic pressures, the OAS "helped pave the way for Hugo Chavez's stunning return to power . . . by refusing to accept the legitimacy of the coup that overthrew him and by threatening to impose sanctions" (Rother 2002). Perhaps, more importantly, after Chavez's return to power, *both* sides of the domestic unrest requested OAS assistance in setting up dialogues between the regime and opponents (Marquez 2002). This suggests that domestic elites play a key role in whether the regional IO–democracy link is strong or weak. Although the Venezuelan dialogues have progressed for over a year, as of the spring of 2004, it is still too early to judge the influence of these dialogues on the prospects for democracy in Venezuela.

The Venezuela case provides solid evidence against the predictions of the realist hypothesis concerning the influence of major powers in regional organizations. Despite US preferences to the contrary, the OAS emerged as a defender of the unpopular Chavez regime in order to stay true to its Charter for Democracy. Although the outcome is still in doubt, the initial coup overthrowing the freely elected Chavez was halted with some assistance from the OAS. Although regional institutions cannot ensure democracy all of the time, they have clearly become an important factor for societal elites in the realm of regime choice.

Conclusion

The title of this work proposes a simple question, can democracy come "from above"? That is, do regional organizations impose or create democracy where it had not existed? The conclusion of this work is that while part of the impetus for democracy may come "from above," the success and endurance of democracy depend on how domestic actors behave "from below." Regional organizations can provide powerful incentives to liberalize, complete the transition to democracy, and remain a democracy, yet domestic agents must ultimately respond to those incentives, whether positive or negative. Richard Millett (1994: 20) discusses the domestic–international nexus in these very terms:

International efforts to promote transitions to democratic rule and to prevent (or reverse) coups and other efforts to terminate constitutional rule are important, but they are by no means sufficient to ensure the consolidation of democracy . . . Prime responsibility for the success of any democratic system rests with national elected authorities.

This study has shown that in many circumstances, these domestic actors will respond to, even seek out, these incentives. In the end, regional organizations can assist in both the transition and the consolidation processes in various ways. This work has shown that there is an empirical link between membership in and accession to regional organizations and democratization. The case studies presented in the final chapters highlighted some of the causal processes surrounding this empirical link. Although this work raised many new questions for further research, there is now some theoretical and empirical basis for both scholars and policymakers to hope that regional institutions can enhance the prospects for democracy.

By influencing the costs and benefits of domestic agents who are contemplating liberalization, redemocratization, or anti-democratic coups, regional organizations can influence domestic political processes. Through the provision of pressure on authoritarians, credible commitments to societal elites and new regimes, an external seal of approval and legitimization, and direct economic benefits, these organizations can increase the likelihood of a democratic transition and of democratic consolidation. If the members of these regional organizations can remain vigilant in supplying this pressure, conditionality, approval, and resources, regional organizations may augur well for the future of democracy in member states.

References

Abente, Diego. 1989. "Constraints and Opportunities: Prospects for Democratization in Paraguay." *Journal of Interamerican Studies and World Affairs* 30 (1): 73–104.

Acevedo, Domingo E. and Claudio Grossman. 1996. "The Organization of American States and the Protection of Democracy." In *Beyond Sovereignty: Collectively Defending Democracy in the Americas*, ed. T. Farer, 132–49. Baltimore: Johns Hopkins University Press.

Agocs, Sandor. 1997. "A Dispirited Army." In *Civil-Military Relations in Post-Communist States*, ed. A. A. Bebler, 86–92. Westport: Praeger.

Aguero, Felipe. 1992. "The Military and the Limits to Democratization in South America." In *Issues in Democratic Consolidation*, ed. S. Mainwaring, G. O'Donnell, and J. S. Valenzuela, 153–98. South Bend, IN: University of Notre Dame Press.

——— 1995. "Democratic Consolidation and the Military in Southern Europe and South America." In *The Politics of Democratic Consolidation*, ed. R. Gunther, N. P. Diamandouros, and H. Puhle, 124–65. Baltimore: Johns Hopkins University Press.

Albright, Madeline. 1997. "Enlarging NATO: Why Bigger is Better." *The Economist* 342 (February).

Allison, Graham T. and R. Beschel. 1992. "Can the United States Promote Democracy?" *Political Science Quarterly* 107(1): 89–98.

Almond, Gabriel A. 1989. "The International-National Connection." *British Journal of Political Science* 19: 237–59.

Alvarez, Mike, José Antonio Cheibub, Fernando Limongi, and Adam Przeworski. 1996. "Classifying Political Regimes." *Studies in Comparative International Development* 31(Summer): 3–36.

Arat, Zehra. 1988. "Democracy and Economic Development: Modernization Theory Revisited." *Comparative Politics* 21 (1): 21–36.

Archer, Clive. 1992. *International Organizations*. London: Routledge.

Armijo, Leslie E., Thomas J. Biersteker, and Abraham F. Lowenthal. 1995. "The Problem of Simultaneous Transitions." In *Economic Reform and Democracy*, ed. L. Diamond and M. Plattner, 226–40. Baltimore: John Hopkins University Press.

Ash, Timothy Garton, Michael Mertes, and Dominique Mosi. 1991. "It's their Europe, too." *The Independent*, September 16, 17.

Asmus, Ronald D., Richard L. Kugler, and F. Stephen Larrabee. 1993. "Building a New NATO." *Foreign Affairs* 72 (4): 28–40.

Balbi, Carmen R. and David S. Palmer. 2001. "'Reinventing' Democracy in Peru." *Current History* (February): 65–72.

Banks, Arthur S. 1994. "Cross-Polity Data Codebook." Binghamton: Binghamton University. Typescript.

Various years. *Political Handbook of the World.* Binghamton: CSA Publications.

Banks, Arthur S. and Thomas C. Mueller. 1998. *Political Handbook of the World.* Binghamton: CSA Publications.

Barany, Zoltan. 1999. "Hungary: An Outpost on the Troubled Periphery." In *America's New Allies*, ed. A. A. Michta, 74–111. Seattle: University of Washington Press.

Barany, Zoltan and Peter Deak. 1999. "The Civil-Military Nexus in Postcommunist Hungary." In *The Military and Society in the Former Eastern Bloc*, ed. C. Danopoulos and D. Zirker, 31–50. Boulder, CO: Westview Press.

Barchard, David. 1985. *Turkey and the West.* London: Routledge.

Barro, Robert J. 1997. *Determinants of Economic Growth: A Cross-Country Empirical Study.* Cambridge, MA: MIT Press.

Bartlett, David. 1997. *The Political Economy of Dual Transformations: Market Reform and Democratization in Hungary.* Ann Arbor: University of Michigan Press.

Bartlett, David and Wendy Hunter. 1997. "Market Structures, Political Institutions, and Democratization: The Latin American and East European Experiences." *Review of International Political Economy* 4 (1): 87–126.

Basombrio, Carlos. 2001. "Peru: The Collapse of 'Fujimorismo.'" In *The Crisis of Democratic Governance in the Andes*, ed. C. Arnson, 11–32. Princeton, NJ: Wilson Center.

Batt, Judy. 1994. "The International Dimension of Democratisation in Czechoslovakia and Hungary." In *Building Democracy? The International Dimension of Democratization in Eastern Europe*, ed. G. Pridham, E. Herring, and G. Sanford, 168–87. New York: St. Martin's Press.

Bebler, Anton. 1997. "Postscript." In *Civil-Military Relations in Post-Communist States*, ed. A. A. Bebler, 125–35. Westport: Praeger.

Beck, Nathaniel. 1998. "Modeling Space and Time: The Event History Approach." In *Research Strategies in the Social Sciences: A Guide to New Approaches*, ed. E. Scarbrough and E. Tanenbaum, 191–213. New York: Oxford University Press.

Beck, Nathaniel and Jonathan Katz. 1995. "What to Do (and Not to Do) with Time-Series Cross-Section Data." *American Political Science Review* 89 (3): 634–47.

Beck, Nathaniel, Jonathan N. Katz, and Richard Tucker. 1998. "Beyond Ordinary Logit: Taking Time Seriously in Binary Time-Series Cross-Section Models." *American Journal of Political Science* 42 (4): 1260–88.

Bennett, D. Scott. 1999. "Parametric Models, Duration Dependence, and Time-Varying Data Revisited." *American Journal of Political Science* 43 (1): 256–70.

Bergsten, C. Fred, and Jeffrey Schott. 1997. U.S. Congress. House. Committee on Ways and Means. Subcommittee on Trade. *Preliminary Evaluation Of NAFTA.* September 11.

Black, George, with Milton Jamail and Norma Chinchilla. 1984. *Garrison Guatemala*. New York: Monthly Review Press.

Bliss, Henry, and Bruce Russett. 1998. "Democratic Trading Partners: The Liberal Connection, 1962–1989." *Journal of Politics* 60 (4): 1126–47.

Bloomfield, Richard J. 1994. "Making the Western Hemisphere Safe for Democracy? The OAS Defense-of-Democracy Regime." *Washington Quarterly* 17(Spring): 157–69.

Bollen, Kenneth. 1983. "World System Position, Dependency, and Democracy: The Cross-National Evidence." *American Sociological Review* 48 (4): 468–79.

Bollen, Kenneth and Robert Jackman. 1985. "Political Democracy and the Size Distribution of Income." *American Sociological Review* 50 (4): 438–57.

Botcheva, Liliana and Martin, Lisa L. 2001. "Institutional Effects on State Behavior: Convergence and Divergence." *International Studies Quarterly* 45 (1): 1–39.

Box-Steffensmeier, Janet M., and Bradford S. Jones. 1997. "Time Is of the Essence: Event History Models in Political Science." *American Journal of Political Science* 41 (4): 1414–61.

Boyd, Carolyn and James Boyden. 1985. "The Armed Forces and the Transition to Democracy in Spain." In *Politics and Change in Spain*, ed. T. Lancaster and G. Prevost, 94–124. Praeger: New York.

Braun, Aurel. 1999. "Introduction: The Continuing Dilemmas of Transition." In *Dilemmas of Transition: The Hungarian Experience*, ed. A. Braun and Z. Barany, 1–28. Lanham: Rowman & Littlefield Publishers, Inc.

Brown, Drusilla, Alan Deardorff, Simeon Djankov, and Robert Stern. 1997. "An Economic Assessment of the Integration of Czechoslovakia, Hungary, and Poland into the European Union." In *Europe's Economy Looks East*, ed. S. W. Black, 23–60. Cambridge: Cambridge University Press.

Bugajski, Janusz. 1992. *Nations in Turmoil: Conflict and Cooperation in Eastern Europe*. Boulder, CO: Westview Press.

Bunce, Valerie. 1997. "The Visegrad Group: Regional Cooperation and European Integration in Post-Communist Europe." In *Mitteleuropa: Between Europe and Germany*, ed. P. Katzenstein, 240–84. Providence, RI: Berghahn Books.

Burkhart, Ross and Michael Lewis-Beck. 1994. "Comparative Democracy: The Economic Development Thesis." *American Political Science Review* 88 (4): 903–10.

Burnell, Peter. 2000. *Democracy Assistance: International Cooperation for Democratization*. London: Frank Cass.

Burton, Michael, Richard Gunther, and John Higley. 1992. "Elites and Democratic Consolidation in Latin America and Southern Europe: An Overview." In *Elites and Democratic Consolidation in Latin America and Southern Europe*, ed. J. Higley and R. Gunther. New York: Cambridge University Press.

Busch, Marc L. and Helen V. Milner. 1994. "The Future of the International Trading System: International Firms, Regionalism, and Domestic Politics." In *Political Economy and the Changing Global Order*, ed. R. Stubbs and G. Underhill, 259–76. New York: St. Martin's Press.

Caizlez, Andres. 2002. "Americas: OAS Strengthened by Response to Venezuelan Coup." *Inter Press Service*, April 17. [Lexis/Nexis]

Cameron, Maxwell A. 1994. *Democracy and Authoritarianism in Peru: Political Coalitions and Social Change*. New York: St. Martin's Press.

——. 1997. "Political and Economic Origins of Regime Change in Peru." In *The Peruvian Labyrinth: Polity, Society, and Economy*, ed. M. Cameron and P. Mauceri, 37–71. University Park, PA: Penn State University Press.

——. 1998a. "Self-Coups: Peru, Guatemala, and Russia." *Journal of Democracy* 9 (1): 125–39.

——. 1998b. "Latin American *autogolpes*: Dangerous Undertows in the Third Wave of Democratization." *Third World Quarterly* 19 (2): 219–39.

Cameron, Maxwell A. and Philip Mauceri. 1997. "Threads in the Peruvian Labyrinth." In *The Peruvian Labyrinth: Polity, Society, and Economy*, ed. M. Cameron and P. Mauceri, 223–45. University Park, PA: Penn State University Press.

Candar, Cengiz. 1999. "Redefining Turkey's Political Center." *Journal of Democracy* 10 (4): 129–41.

Carothers, Thomas. 1999. *Aiding Democracy Abroad: The Learning Curve*. Washington, DC: Carnegie Endowment for International Peace.

Carr, E. H. 1946. *The Twenty Years' Crisis, 1919–1939: An Introduction to the Study of International Relations*. London: Macmillan and Co.

Chand, Vikram K. 1997."Democratization from the Outside In: NGO and International Efforts to Promote Open Elections." *Third World Quarterly* 18(3): 543–61.

Christopher, Warren. 1995. "America's Leadership, America's Opportunity." *Foreign Policy* (95): 6–27.

CIA Factbook On-line. 1999. http://www.odci.gov/.

Clemens, Elisabeth S. 1998. "To Move Mountains: Collective Action and the Possibility of Institutional Change." In *From Contention to Democracy*, ed. M. Giugni, D. McAdam, and C. Tilly. Lanham, MD: Rowman & Littlefield Publishers, Inc.

Clogg, Richard. 1979a. "The Greek Political Context." In *Greece and the European Community*, ed. L. Tsoukalis, 108–27. Westmead, UK: Saxon House.

——. 1979b. *A Short History of Modern Greece*. Cambridge: Cambridge University Press.

Coad, Malcom. 1992. "Fujimori U-Turns to Avert Tougher OAS Sanctions." *The Guardian*, May 21, 10.

Coile, Zachary. 2002. "Tepid U.S. Response to Chavez's Return." *San Francisco Chronicle*, April 15, A9.

Constable, Pamela. 1993. "OAS Neighbors Remain Wary as Guatemala Crisis Lingers." *Boston Globe*, June 4. Lexis-Nexis.

Cooper, Andrew F. and Thomas Legler. 2001. "A Model for the Future?" *Journal of Democracy* 12 (4): 123–36.

Costa, Eduardo F. 1993. "Peru's Presidential Coup." *Journal of Democracy* 4 (1): 28–40.

Coufoudakis, Van. 1977. "The European Economic Community and the 'Freezing' of the Greek Association, 1967–1974." *Journal of Common Market Studies* 16 (2): 114–31.

Couloumbis, Theodore A. 1983. *The United States, Greece, and Turkey: The Troubled Triangle*. New York: Praeger.

Cowhey, Peter F. 1993. "Domestic Institutions and the Credibility of International Commitments: Japan and the United States." *International Organization* 47: 299–326.

Crescenzi, Mark J. C. 1999. "Violence and Uncertainty in Transitions." *Journal of Conflict Resolution* 43 (2): 192–212.

Dagi, Ihsan D. 1996. "Democratic Transition in Turkey, 1980–1983: The Impact of European Diplomacy." *Middle Eastern Studies* 32 (2): 124–41.

Dahl, Robert. 1971. *Polyarchy*. New Haven: Yale University Press.

1989. *Democracy and Its Critics*. New Haven: Yale University Press.

Dassel, Kurt. 1998. "Civilians, Soldiers, and Strife: Domestic Sources of International Aggression." *International Security* 23(Summer): 107–40.

Dassel, Kurt and Eric Reinhardt. 1998. "Domestic Strife and the Initiation of Violence at Home and Abroad." *American Journal of Political Science* 43 (1): 56–85.

Degregori, Carlos I. 1997. "After the Fall of Abimael Guzman: The Limits of Sendero Luminoso." In *The Peruvian Labyrinth: Polity, Society, and Economy*, ed. M. Cameron and P. Mauceri, 179–91. University Park, PA: Penn State University Pres.

DeYoung, Karen. 2002. "U.S. Seen as Weak Patron of Latin Democracy." *Washington Post*, April 16, A15.

Di Palma, Giuseppe. 1990. "Parliaments, Consolidation, Institutionalization: A Minimalist View." In *Parliament and Democratic Consolidation in Southern Europe*, ed. U. Liebert and M. Cotta, 31–49. London: Pinter Publishers.

Diamandouros, P. N. 1986. "Regime Change and the Prospects for Democracy in Greece: 1974–1983." In *Transitions from Authoritarian Rule: Comparative Perspectives*, ed. G. O'Donnell, P. C. Schmitter, and L. Whitehead, 138–64. Baltimore: Johns Hopkins University Press.

Diamond, Larry J. 1992. "Economic Development and Democracy Reconsidered." In *Reexamining Democracy: Essays in Honor of Seymour Martin Lipset*, ed. G. Marks and L. Diamond, 93–139. Newbury Park, CA: Sage Publications.

1995. "Promoting Democracy in Africa: U.S. and International Policies in Transition." In *Africa in World Politics: Post-Cold War Challenges*, ed. J. Harbeson and D. Rothchild, 250–77. Boulder, CO: Westview Press.

1999. *Developing Democracy*. Baltimore: Johns Hopkins University Press.

Diamond, Larry, Juan J. Linz, and Seymour Martin Lipset, eds. 1989. *Democracy in Developing Countries* (4 vols.). Boulder, CO: Lynne Rienner.

Diermeier, Daniel, Joel Ericson, Timothy Frye, Steven Lewis. 1997. "Credible Commitment and Property Rights: The Role of Strategic Interaction Between Political and Economic Actors." In *The Political Economy of Property Rights: Institutional Change and Credibility in the Reform of Centrally Planned Economies*, ed. D. Weimer, 20–42. Cambridge: Cambridge University Press.

Dodd, C. H. 1990. *The Crisis of Turkish Democracy*, 2nd edn. Huntingdon: Eothen Press.

Dominguez, Jorge I. 1998. "The Americas: Found, and then Lost Again." *Foreign Policy* 112 (Fall): 125–37.

Downes, Richard. 1994. "In Defense of Democracy in the Western Hemisphere." *North-South: Magazine of the Americas* 4 (3): 20–5.

Downs, George W., David M. Rocke, and Peter N. Barsoom. 1996. "Is the Good News About Compliance Good News About Cooperation?" *International Organization* 50 (3): 379–406.

Doxey, John. 1997. "Turkey's Generals Draw a Line in the Sand." *Business Week*, May 12, 63.

Drake, Paul W. 1998. "The International Causes of Democratization, 1974–1990." In *The Origins of Liberty: Political and Economic Liberalization in the Modern World*, ed. Paul W. Drake and Mathew D. McCubbins, 70–91. Princeton: Princeton University Press.

Drezner, Daniel, ed. 2003. *Locating the Proper Authorities: The Interaction of Domestic and International Institutions*. Ann Arbor: University of Michigan Press.

Durand, Francisco. 1997. "The Growth and Limitations of the Peruvian Right." In *The Peruvian Labyrinth: Polity, Society, and Economy*, ed. M. Cameron and P. Mauceri. University Park, PA: Penn State University Press.

EC Bulletin. 1981. *EC Bulletin* 14 (5): 53.

Eckstein, Harry and Ted Robert Gurr. 1975. *Patterns of Authority: A Structural Basis for Political Inquiry*. New York: Wiley-Interscience.

Evans, Peter. 1993. "Building an Integrative Approach to International and Domestic Politics: Reflections and Projections." In *Double-Edged Diplomacy*, ed. P. Evans, H. Jacobson, and R. Putnam, 397–430. Berkeley: University of California Press.

Evans, Peter, Harold Jacobson, and Robert Putnam, eds. 1993. *Double-Edged Diplomacy*. Berkeley: University of California Press.

Faiola, Anthony. 1998. "Paraguay Faces Ghost of Its Political Past." *Washington Post*, April 10, A16.

Farber, Henry S. and Joanne Gowa. 1995. "Polities and Peace." *International Security* 20 (2): 123–46.

Farer, Tom J. 1989. "A Multilateral Arrangement to Secure Democracy." In *Democracy in the Americas*, ed. R. Pastor, 115–32. New York: Holmes and Meier.

Fearon, James D. 1994. "Domestic Political Audiences and the Escalation of Interstate Disputes." *American Political Science Review* 88 (September): 577–92.

Featherstone, Kevin. 1994. "Political Parties." In *Greece and EC Membership Evaluated*, ed. P. Kazakos and P. C. Ioakimidis, 154–65. New York: St. Martin's Press.

Feinberg, Richard. 1996. "The Coup that Wasn't." *Washington Post*, April 30, A13.

Feld, Werner J. and Robert S. Jordan, with Leon Hurwitz. 1994. *International Organizations: A Comparative Approach*, 3rd edn. Westport, CT: Praeger.

Felkay, Andrew. 1997. *Out of Russian Orbit: Hungary Gravitates to the West*. Westport, CT: Greenwood Press.

Feng, Y. and P. J. Zak. 1999. "The Determinants of Democratic Transitions." *Journal of Conflict Resolution* 43 (2): 162–77.

Fernández, Raquel and Jonathan Portes. 1998. "Returns to Regionalism: An Evaluation of Nontraditional Gains from Regional Trade Agreements." *The World Bank Economic Review* 12 (2): 197–220.

Finer, Samuel E. 1962. *The Man on Horseback*. London: Pall Mall.

Finnemore, Martha. 1996a. *National Interests in International Society*. Ithaca: Cornell University Press.

1996b. "Norms, Culture, and World Politics: Insights from Sociology's Institutionalism." *International Organization* 50 (Spring): 325–47.

Fitzmaurice, John. 1998. *Politics and Government in the Visegrad Countries*. New York: St. Martin's Press.

Foster, Gregory. 1996. "Confronting the Crisis in Civil-Military Relations." *Washington Quarterly* 20 (4): 15–33.

Freeman, Alan. 1997. "Hungary Sees NATO as Insurance: Seeks to Avoid Russian Sphere of Influence." *Cleveland Plain Dealer*, February 16, A7. Lexis-Nexis.

Frieden, Jeffry A. and Ronald Rogowski. 1996. "The Impact of the International Economy on National Policies: An Analytical Overview." In *Internationalization and Domestic Politics*, ed. R. O. Keohane and H. V. Milner, 25–47. Cambridge: Cambridge University Press.

Friedrich, Robert J. 1983. "In Defense of Multiplicative Terms in Multiple Regression Equations". *American Journal of Political Science* 26 (4): 797– 833.

Frye, Timothy. 1997. "Russian Privatization and the Limits of Credible Commitment." In *The Political Economy of Property Rights: Institutional Change and Credibility in the Reform of Centrally Planned Economies*, ed. D. Weimer, 84–108. Cambridge: Cambridge University Press.

Galvin, Kevin. 1992. "Military Shuts Media, Detains Critics as Constitution is Suspended." *Associated Press Wire*, April 7. Lexis-Nexis.

Garfinkle, Adam. 1991. "The Nadir of Greek Democracy." In *Friendly Tyrants*, ed. D. Pipes and A. Garfinkle, 63–87. New York: St. Martin's Press.

Gartzke, Erik. 1998. "Kant We All Just Get Along? Opportunity, Willingness, and the Origins of the Democratic Peace." *American Journal of Political Science* 42: 1–28.

2000. "Preferences and the Democratic Peace." *International Studies Quarterly* 44 (2): 191–212.

Gasiorowski, Mark J. 1993. "The Political Regime Change Dataset." Louisiana State University. Typescript.

1995. "Economic Crisis and Political Regime Change: An Event History Analysis." *American Political Science Review* 89 (4): 882–97.

1996. "An Overview of the Political Regime Change Dataset." *Comparative Political Studies* 29 (August): 469–83.

Gasiorowski, Mark J. and Timothy J. Power. 1998. "The Structural Determinants of Democratic Consolidation: Evidence from the Third World." *Comparative Political Studies* 31 (6): 740–71.

Gastil, Raymond D. 1990. "The Comparative Survey of Freedom: Experiences and Suggestions." *Studies in Comparative International Development* 25 (1): 25–50.

Gaubatz, Kurt T. 1996. "Democratic States and Commitment in International Relations." *International Organization* 50 (Winter): 109–39.

Geddes, Barbara. 1999. "What Do We Know About Democratization after Twenty Years?" *Annual Review of Political Science* 2: 115–44.

Gedeon, Peter. 1997. "Hungary: German and European Influences on the Post-Socialist Transition." In *Mitteleuropa: Between Europe and Germany*, ed. P. Katzenstein, 101–48. Providence, RI: Berghahn Books.

George, Alexander and Timothy McKeown. 1985. "Case Studies and Theories of Organizational Decision Making." *Advances in Information Processing in Organizations* 2: 21–58.

Gerschenkron, Alexander. 1962. *Economic Backwardness in Historical Perspective*. Cambridge: Belknap Press.

Gleditsch, Kristian. 2002. "Expanded Trade and GDP Data." *Journal of Conflict Resolution* 46: 712–24.

Goldman, Minton F. 1997. *Revolution and Change in Central and Eastern Europe*. Armonk, NY: M. E. Sharpe.

Goldstein, Judith. 1996. "International Law and Domestic Institutions: Reconciling North American 'Unfair' Trade Laws." *International Organization* 50 (4): 541–64.

    1998. "International Institutions and Domestic Politics: GATT, WTO, and the Liberalization of International Trade." In *The WTO as an International Organization*, ed. A. O. Krueger, 133–60. Chicago: University of Chicago Press.

Gonick, Lev S. and Robert M. Rosh. 1988. "The Structural Constraints of the World-Economy on National Political Development." *Comparative Political Studies* 21 (2): 171–99.

Gonzalez, Gustavo. 1991. "Americas: Proposal for Automatic OAS Anti-Coup Sanctions." *Inter Press Service*, June 4. [Lexis/Nexis]

Gourevitch, Peter A. 1978. "The Second Image Reversed: The International Sources of Domestic Politics." *International Organization* 32 (4): 881–912.

Gower, Jackie. 1993. "EC Relations with Central and Eastern Europe." In *The European Community and the Challenge of the Future*, 2nd edn, ed. J. Lodge, 283–99. New York: St. Martin's Press.

Grabendorff, Wolf. 1993. "The Price of Integration: Reducing or Redefining State Sovereignty?" In *The Challenge of Integration: Europe and the Americas* ed. P. Smith, 333–60. New Brunswick: Transaction.

    1996. "International Support for Democracy in Contemporary Latin America: The Role of the Party Internationals." In *The International Aspects of Democratization: Europe and the Americas*, ed. L. Whitehead, 201–26. Oxford: Oxford University Press.

Grieco, Joseph. 1988. "Anarchy and the Limits of Cooperation: A Realist Critique of the Newest Liberal Institutionalism." *International Organization* 42: 485–507.

    1996. "State Interests and Institutional Rule Trajectories: A Neorealist Interpretation of the Maastricht Treaty and European Economic and Monetary Union." *Security Studies* 5 (Spring): 261–306.

Grugel, Jean, ed. 1999. *Democracy Without Borders: Transnationalization and Conditionality in New Democracies*. London: Routledge.

Gunther, Richard, Hans-Jurgen Puhle, P. Nikiforos Diamandouros. 1995. "Introduction." In *The Politics of Democratic Consolidation*, ed. R. Gunther, N. Diamandouros, and H. Puhle, 1–30. Baltimore: Johns Hopkins University Press.

Gurnon, Emily. 1993. "Adios, Jorge." *The Nation*, June 28, 892–3.

Gurr, Ted R. 1990. *Polity II: Political Structures and Regime Change, 1800–1986*. Study no. 9263, Ann Arbor: ICPSR [distributor].

    1993. *Minorities at Risk*. Washington: United States Institute of Peace.

Gurr, Ted R., Keith Jaggers, and Will Moore. 1990. "The Transformation of the Western State: The Growth of Democracy, Autocracy, and State Power Since 1800." *Studies in Comparative International Development* 25 (1): 73–108.

Gyarmati, Istvan. 1999. "Hungary's Security and the Enlargement." In *The Challenge of NATO Enlargement*, ed. A. Bebler, 110–15. Westport, CT: Praeger.

Haas, Ernst B. 1964. *Beyond the Nation-State: Functionalism and International Organization*. Stanford: Stanford University Press.

Haggard, Stephen and Robert Kaufman. 1992. "Economic Adjustment and the Prospects for Democracy." In *The Politics of Economic Adjustment*, ed. S. Haggard and R. Kaufman, 319–50. Princeton: Princeton University Press.

    1995a. "The Challenges of Consolidation." In *Economic Reform and Democracy*, ed. L. Diamond and M. Plattner, 1–12. Baltimore: Johns Hopkins University Press.

    1995b. *The Political Economy of Democratic Transitions*. Princeton: Princeton University Press.

Hakim, Peter. 1992. "Democracy in Peru: Fanning a Faint Ember." *Los Angeles Times*, December 6, M2.

    1993a. "The OAS: Putting Principles into Practice." *Journal of Democracy* 4 (3): 39–49.

    1993b. "Behind Guatemala's 'Miracle'". *Christian Science Monitor*, June 23. Lexis-Nexis.

    1996. "Good News from Paraguay: A Coup d'Etat Falls Flat." *Christian Science Monitor*, May 30. Lexis-Nexis.

    2000. "Peru is No Democracy." *Christian Science Monitor*, February 24, 11.

    2002. "Democracy and U.S. Credibility." *New York Times*, April 21. [Lexis/Nexis]

    2003. "Dispirited Politics." *Journal of Democracy* 14 (2): 108–22.

Hall, John A. 1993. "Consolidations of Democracy." In *Prospects for Democracy: North, South, East, West*, ed. D. Held, 271–90. Stanford, CA: Stanford University Press.

Halperin, Morton and Kristen Lomasney. 1998. "Guaranteeing Democracy: A Review of the Record." *Journal of Democracy* 9 (2): 134–47.

Hayes, Monte. 1992. "Peru's President Has Earned His Nickname 'The Emperor.'" *Associated Press Wire*, April 9. Lexis-Nexis.

Held, David. 1993 "Democracy: From City-States to a Cosmopolitan Order?" In *Prospects for Democracy: North, South, East, West*, ed. D. Held, 13–52. Stanford, CA: Stanford University Press.

Hellman, Joel. 1998. "Winners Take All: The Politics of Partial Reform in Post Communist Transitions." *World Politics* 50 (2): 203–34.

Henze, Paul B. 1991. "Why Turkey is Not a Friendly Tyrant." In *Friendly Tyrants*, ed. D. Pipes and A. Garfinkle, 91–108. New York: St. Martin's Press.

Heper, Metin. 1987. "The State, the Military, and Democracy in Turkey." *Jerusalem Journal of International Relations* 9 (3): 52–64.

    1992. "Consolidating Turkish Democracy." *Journal of Democracy* 3 (2): 105–17.

Herring, Eric. 1994. "International Security and Democratisation in Eastern Europe." In *Building Democracy? The International Dimension of Democratization in Eastern Europe*, ed. G. Pridham, E. Herring, and G. Sanford, 87–118. New York: St. Martin's Press.

Hill, Kevin and John Hughes. 1999. "Is the Internet an Instrument of Global Democratization?" *Democratization* 6 (2): 99–127.

Huntington, Samuel. 1968. *Political Order in Changing Societies*. New Haven: Yale University Press.

    1981. *American Politics: The Promise of Disharmony*. Cambridge, MA: Harvard University Press.

    1991. *The Third Wave*. Norman, OK: Oklahoma University Press.

Hurrell, Andrew. 1994. "Regionalism in the Americas." In *Latin America in a New World*, ed. A. F. Lowenthal and G. F. Treverton, 167–90. Boulder, CO: Westview Press.

    1996. "The International Dimensions of Democratization in Latin America: The Case of Brazil." In *The International Aspects of Democratization: Europe and the Americas*, ed. L. Whitehead, 146–74. Oxford: Oxford University Press.

Hyde-Price, Adrian G. V. 1994. "Democratization in Eastern Europe: The External Dimension." In *Democratization in Eastern Europe: Domestic and International Perspectives*, ed. G. Pridham and T. Vanhanen, 220–54. London: Routledge.

    1996. *The International Politics of East Central Europe*. Manchester: Manchester University Press.

Ikenberry, G. John. 2001. *After Victory: Institutions, Strategic Restraint, and the Rebuilding of Order after Major Wars*. Princeton: Princeton University Press.

Immerman, Richard H. 1982. *The CIA in Guatemala: The Foreign Policy of Intervention*. Austin: University of Texas Press.

Inotai, Andras and Jurgen Notzold. 1995. "Hungary". In *Central and Eastern Europe on the Way into the European Union*, ed. W. Weidenfeld, 89–110. Gutersloh: Bertelsmann Foundation Publishers.

Inter Press Service. 1991. "France: Junta in Haiti Will Transfer Power to Civilians." October 2. Lexis/Nexis.

Ioakimidis, P. C. 1994. "The EC and the Greek Political System: An Overview." In *Greece and EC Membership Evaluated*, ed. P. Kazakos and P. C. Ioakimidis, 139–53. New York: St. Martin's Press.

Jacobson, Harold K., William Reisinger, and Todd Mathers. 1986. "National Entanglements in International Governmental Organizations." *American Political Science Review* 80 (1): 141–59.

Jaggers, Keith and Ted Robert Gurr. 1995. "Tracking Democracy's Third Wave with the Polity III Data." *Journal of Peace Research* 32 (November): 469–82.
1996. *Polity III: Regime Change and Political Authority, 1800–1994.* Study no. 6695. Ann Arbor: ICPSR [distributor].
Jervis, Robert 1983. "Security Regimes." In Stephen D. Krasner, ed., *International Regimes*, 173–94. Ithaca: Cornell University Press.
Jonas, Susanne. 1994. "Text and Subtext of the Guatemalan Political Drama." *LASA Forum* 24 (4): 3–9.
1999. *The Mined Road to Peace in Guatemala.* Miami: North-South Center.
Jones, Daniel, Stuart Bremer, and J. D. Singer. 1996. "Militarized Interstate Disputes, 1816–1992: Rationale, Coding Rules, and Empirical Patterns." *Conflict Management and Peace Science* 15 (2): 163–213.
Kadera, Kelly, Mark Crescenzi, and Megan Shannon. 2003. "Democratic Survival, Peace, and War in the International System." *American Journal of Political Science* 47 (2): 234–47.
Kahler, Miles. 1992. "External Influence, Conditionality, and the Politics of Adjustment." In *The Politics of Economic Adjustment: International Constraints, Distributive Politics, and the State*, ed. S. Haggard and R. Kaufman, 89–136. Princeton: Princeton University Press.
1997. "Liberalization as a Foreign Policy Determinant and Goal." In *Liberalization and Foreign Policy*, ed. M. Kahler, 287–313. New York: Columbia University Press.
Kamrava, Mehrah and Frank Mora. 1998. "Civil Society and Democratization in Comparative Perspective: Latin America and the Middle East." *Third World Quarterly* 19 (5): 593–615.
Karaosmanoglu, Ali L. 1991. "The International Context of Democratic Transition in Turkey." In *Encouraging Democracy: The International Context of Regime Transition in Southern Europe*, ed. G, Pridham, 159–74. New York: St. Martin's Press.
1993. "Officers: Westernization and Democracy." In *Turkey and the West: Changing Political and Cultural Identities*, ed. M. Heper, A. Oncu, and H. Kramer, 19–38. London: I. B. Tauris and Co.
1994. "The Limits of International Influence for Democratization." In *Politics in the Third Turkish Republic*, ed. M. Heper and A. Evin, 117–33. Boulder, CO: Westview Press.
Karp, Larry and Thierry Paul. 1998. "Labor Adjustment and Gradual Reform: When is Commitment Important?" *Journal of International Economics* 46 (2): 333–62.
Katseli, L. T. 1990. "Economic Integration in the enlarged Community: Structural Adjustment of the Greek Economy." In *Unity with Diversity in the European Community*, ed. C. Bliss and J. B. Macedo. Cambridge: Cambridge University Press.
Katzenstein, Peter and Christopher Hemmer. 2002. "Why is There No NATO in Asia? Collective Identity, Regionalism, and the Origins of Multilateralism." *International Organization* 56 (3): 575–608.
Kaufman, Robert. 1986. "Liberalization and Democratization in South America: Perspectives from the 1970s." In *Transitions from Authoritarian*

Rule: Comparative Perspectives, ed. G. O'Donnell, P. C. Schmitter, and L. Whitehead, 85–107. Baltimore: Johns Hopkins University Press.

Kay, Bruce H. 1996. "'Fujipopulism' and the Liberal State in Peru, 1990–1995." *Journal of Interamerican Studies and World Affairs* 38 (4): 55–98.

Keefer, Philip and Stephen Knack. 1995. "Institutions and Economic Performance: Cross-Country Tests Using Alternative Institutional Measures." *Economics and Politics* 7 (3), 207–27.

1997. "Why Don't Poor Countries Catch Up? A Cross-National Test of Institutional Explanation." *Economic-Inquiry* 35 (3), 590–602.

Keiswetter, Allen L. 1997. "The Partnership for Peace and Civil-Military Relations in a Democracy." In *Civil-Military Relations in Post-Communist States*, ed. A. A. Bebler, 3–7. Westport, CT: Praeger.

Keohane, Robert O. 1984. *After Hegemony: Cooperation and Discord in the World Political Economy*. Princeton: Princeton University Press.

1993. "Institutional Theory and the Realist Challenge After the Cold War." In *Neorealism and Neoliberalism: The Contemporary Debate*, ed. D. Baldwin, 269–300. New York: Columbia University Press.

Keohane, Robert O. and Lisa L. Martin. 1995. "The Promise of Institutionalist Theory." *International Security* 20 (1): 39–51.

Keohane, Robert O. and Joseph Nye. 2001. *Power and Interdependence*, 3rd edn. New York: Longman Press.

King, Gary, and Robert O. Keohane, and Sydney Verba. 1994. *Designing Social Inquiry*. Princeton: Princeton University Press.

Kis, Janos. 1989. *Politics in Hungary: For a Democratic Alternative*. Highland Lakes, NJ: Atlantic Research and Publications.

Klebes, Heinrich. 1999. *The Quest for Democratic Security: The Role of the Council of Europe and U.S. Foreign Policy*. Washington, DC: United States Institute of Peace.

Knight, Jack. 1992. *Institutions and Social Conflict*. Cambridge: Cambridge University Press.

Kolozsi, Bela. 1995. "Hungary's Return to Traditional European Foreign Policy Patterns." In *Monitoring Association and Beyond: The European Union and the Visegrad States*, ed. B. Lippert and H. Schneider, 97–109. Bonn: Europa Union Verlag.

Koop, Michael. 1997. "Joining the Club: Options for Integrating Central and Eastern European Countries into the European Union." In *Europe's Economy Looks East*, ed. S. W. Black, 315–41. Cambridge: Cambridge University Press.

Korosenyi, Andras. 1992. "The Decay of Communist Rule in Hungary." In *Post-Communist Transition: Emerging Pluralism in Hungary*, ed. A. Bozoki, A. Korosenyi, and G. Schopflin, 1–12. New York: St. Martin's Press.

Kovrig, Bennett. 1999. "European Integration." In *Dilemmas of Transition: The Hungarian Experience*, ed. A. Braun and Z. Barany, 253–72. Lanham: Rowman & Littlefield Publishers, Inc.

Kozhemiakin, Alexander V. 1998. *Expanding the Zone of Peace? Democratization and International Security*. New York: St. Martin's Press.

Kritz, Neil J. 1993. "The CSCE in the New Era." *Journal of Democracy* 4 (3): 17–28.

Kun, Joseph C. 1993. *Hungarian Foreign Policy: The Experience of a New Democracy.* Westport, CT: Praeger.

Kuniholm, Bruce R. 1985. "Turkey and NATO." In *NATO and the Mediterranean,* ed. L. Kaplan, R. Clawson, and R. Luraghi, 215–37. Wilmington: Scholarly Resources, Inc.

Kurth, James. 1979. "The Political Consequences of the Product Cycle: Industrial History and Political Outcomes." *International Organization* 33 (1): 1–34.

LaFranchi, Howard. 1999. "Democracy: 'A Little Help from its Friends.'" *Christian Science Monitor* 91 (99): 6.

Lake, Anthony. 1993. "From Containment to Enlargement". *Department of State Dispatch* 4 (39): 3.

Lambert, Peter. 1997. "Assessing the Transition." In *The Transition to Democracy in Paraguay,* ed. P. Lambert and A. Nickson, 200–13. London: Macmillan.

Lane, Frederic C. 1979. *Profits from Power: Readings in Protection Rent and Violence Controlling Enterprises.* Albany: SUNY Press.

Leeds, Brett Ashley. 1999. "Domestic Political Institutions, Credible Commitments, and International Cooperation." *American Journal of Political Science* 43 (4): 979–1002.

Linz, Juan J. 1978. *The Breakdown of Democratic Regimes: Crisis, Breakdown, and Reequilibration.* Baltimore: Johns Hopkins University Press.

1990. "The Perils of Presidentialism." *Journal of Democracy* 1: 51–69.

Linz, Juan J., and Alfred Stepan. 1996. *Problems of Democratic Transition and Consolidation.* Baltimore: Johns Hopkins University Press.

Linz, Juan J., Alfred Stepan, and Richard Gunther. 1995. "Democratic Transition and Consolidation in Southern Europe, with Reflections on Latin America and Eastern Europe." In *The Politics of Democratic Consolidation,* ed. R. Gunther, N. Diamandouros, and J. Puhle, 77–123. Baltimore: Johns Hopkins University Press.

Lipset, Seymour M. 1959. "Some Social Requisites for Democracy: Economic Development and Political Legitimacy." *American Political Science Review* 53 (1): 69–105.

Lomax, Bill. 1991. "Hungary – From Kadarism to Democracy: The Successful Failure of Reform Communism." In *The Impact of Gorbachev,* ed. D. W. Spring, 154–74. London: Pinter Publishers.

Londregan, John B., and Keith T. Poole. 1990. "Poverty, the Coup Trap, and the Seizure of Executive Power." *World Politics* 42 (January): 151–83.

1996. "Does High Income Promote Democracy?" *World Politics* 49 (1): 1–30.

Mackenzie, Kenneth. 1984. *Turkey in Transition: The West's Neglected Ally.* London: Institution for European Defense and Strategic Studies.

Macridis, Roy. 1979. "Greek Foreign Policy: Reality, Illusions, Options." In *Greece and the European Community,* ed. L. Tsoukalis, 135–48. Farnborough, UK: Saxon House.

Madison, Christopher. 1992. "U.S.–Latin Tango." *The National Journal* 24 (24): 1408–9.

Mainwaring, Scott. 1992. "Transitions to Democracy and Democratic Consolidation: Theoretical and Comparative Issues." In *Issues in Democratic Consolidation*, ed. S. Mainwaring, G. O'Donnell, and A. Valenzuela, 294–342. South Bend, IN: University of Notre Dame Press.

Mainwaring, Scott, Guillermo O'Donnell, and Arturo Valenzuela. 1992. "Introduction." In *Issues in Democratic Consolidation*, ed. S. Mainwaring, G. O'Donnell, and A. Valenzuela, 1–16. South Bend, IN: University of Notre Dame Press.

Mair, Stefan. 2000."Germany's Stiftungen and Democracy Assistance: Comparative Advantages, New Challenges." In *Democracy Assistance: International Cooperation for Democratization*, ed. P. Burnell, 128–49. London: Frank Cass.

Malloy, James M. 1987. "The Politics of Transition in Latin America." In *Authoritarians and Democrats: Regime Transition in Latin America*, ed. J. Malloy and M. Seligson, 235–58. Pittsburgh: University of Pittsburgh Press.

Mango, Andrew J. A. 1997. "Testing Time in Turkey." *The Washington Quarterly* 20 (1): 3–20.

Mansfield, Edward D. 1998. "The Proliferation of Preferential Trading Arrangements." *Journal of Conflict Resolution* 42 (5): 523–43.

Mansfield, Edward D. and Jon C. Pevehouse. 2000. "Trade Blocs, Trade Flows, and International Conflict." *International Organization* 54 (4): 775–808.

Mansfield, Edward D. and Jack Snyder. 1995. "Democratization and the Danger of War." *International Security* 20 (1): 5–38.

2002. "Democratic Transitions, Institutional Strength, and War." *International Organization* 56 (2): 297–337.

Mansfield, Edward D., Helen V. Milner, and B. Peter Rosendorff. 2000. "Free to Trade: Democracies, Autocracies, and International Trade." *American Political Science Review* 94 (2): 305–321.

2002. "Why Democracies Cooperate More: Electoral Control and International Trade Agreements." *International Organization* 56 (3): 477–513.

Manuel, Paul C. 1996. *The Challenges of Democratic Consolidation in Portugal*. Westport, CT: Praeger.

Marks, Gary. 1992. "Rational Sources of Chaos in Democratic Transition." In *Reexamining Democracy: Essays in Honor of Seymour Martin Lipset*, ed. G. Marks and L. Diamond, 47–69. Newbury Park, CA: Sage Publications.

Marquez, Humberto. 2002. "Venezuela: OAS Chief Convinces Government and Opposition to Talk." *Inter Press Service*, November 1. [Lexis/Nexis]

Marshall, Monty. 1999. *Polity 98 Dataset*. http://www.bsos.umd.edu/cidcm/polity.

Martin, Lisa L. 1992. *Coercive Cooperation: Explaining Multilateral Economic Sanctions*. Princeton: Princeton University Press.

2000.*Democratic Commitments*. Princeton: Princeton University Press.

Martin Lisa L. and Beth A. Simmons. 1998. "Theories and Empirical Studies of International Institutions." *International Organization* 52 (4): 729–57.

Masi, Fernando. 1997. "Foreign Policy." In *The Transition to Democracy in Paraguay*, ed. P. Lambert and A. Nickson, 174–82. London: Macmillan.

Mauceri, Philip. 1997. "Return of the Caudillo: Autocratic Democracy in Peru." *Third World Quarterly* 18 (5): 899–911.

1998. "State Reform, Coalitions, and the Neoliberal Autogolpe in Peru." *Latin American Research Review* 30 (1): 7–37.

Mayhew, Alan. 1998. *Recreating Europe: The European Union's Policy Towards Central and Eastern Europe.* Cambridge: Cambridge University Press.

McCleary, Rachel. 1997. "Guatemala's Postwar Prospects." *Journal of Democracy* 8 (2): 129–43.

1999. *Dictating Democracy: Guatemala and the End of Violent Revolution.* Gainesville: University Press of Florida.

McClintock, Cynthia. 1989. "The Prospects for Democratic Consolidation in a 'Least Likely' Case." *Comparative Politics* 21 (2): 127–48.

1993. "Peru's Fujimori: A Caudillo Derails Democracy." *Current History* 92 (572): 112–19.

2001. "Room for Improvement". *Journal of Democracy* 12 (4): 137–40.

McCormick, James. 1980. "Intergovernmental Organizations and Cooperation Among Nations". *International Studies Quarterly* 24 (1): 75–98.

Mearsheimer, John J. 1995. "The False Promise of International Institutions." *International Security* 19 (3): 5–49.

Messerlin, Patrick A. 1992. "The Association Agreements Between the EC and Central Europe: Trade Liberalization vs. Constitutional Failure?" In *Trade, Payments, and Adjustment in Central and Eastern Europe,* ed. J. Flemming and J. M. C. Rollo, 111–43. London: Royal Institute for International Affairs.

Millett, Richard L. 1994. "Beyond Sovereignty: International Efforts to Support Latin American Democracy." *Journal of Interamerican Studies and World Affairs* 36 (3): 1–23.

Milner, Helen V. 1997. *Interests, Institutions, and Information: Domestic Politics and International Relations.* Princeton: Princeton University Press.

1998. "Regional Economic Co-operation, Global Markets, and Domestic Politics." In *Regionalism and Global Economic Integration,* ed. W. Coleman and G. R. D. Underhill, 19–41. London: Routledge.

Mitchell, Brian R. 1995. *International Historical Statistics: Africa, Asia and Oceania 1750–1988.* New York: Stockton.

1998. *International Historical Statistics: The Americas 1750–1993.* London: Macmillan Reference.

Mitchell, Sarah M. 2002. "A Kantian System? Democracy and Third-party Conflict Resolution." *American Journal of Political Science* 46 (4): 749–59.

Mitrany, David. 1966. *A Working Peace System.* Chicago: Quadrangle Press.

Monshipouri, Mahmood. 1995. *Democratization, Liberalization, and Human Rights in the Third World.* Boulder, CO: Lynne Rienner Press.

Moore, Barrington. 1966. *Social Origins of Dictatorship and Democracy.* Boston: Beacon Press.

Mora, Frank O. 1998. "From Dictatorship to Democracy: the U.S. and Regime Change in Paraguay, 1954–1994." *Bulletin of Latin American Research* 17 (1): 59–79.

Morgenthau, Hans J. 1967. *Politics Among Nations: The Struggle for Power and Peace.* 4th edn. New York: Alfred A. Knopf.

Morrow, James D., Randolph M. Siverson, and Tressa E. Tabares. 1998. "The Political Determinants of International Trade: The Major Powers, 1907–1990." *American Political Science Review* 92 (3): 649–61.

Muftuler-Bac, Meltem. 1998. "The Never-Ending Story: Turkey and the European Union." *Middle Eastern Studies* 34 (4): 240–58.

Muñoz, Heraldo. 1993. "The OAS and Democratic Governance." *Journal of Democracy* 4 (3): 29–38.

1998. "The Right to Democracy in the Americas." *Journal of Interamerican Studies and World Affairs* 40 (1): 1–18.

Neethling, Theo. 1999. "Military Intervention in Lesotho : Perspectives on Operation Boleas and Beyond." *Online Journal of Peace and Conflict Resolution* 2 (2). http://www.trininstitute.org/ojpcr

Nelson, Daniel N. 1999. "Regional Security and Ethnic Minorities." In *Dilemmas of Transition: The Hungarian Experience*, ed. A. Braun and Z. Barany, 301–22. Lanham, MD: Rowman & Littlefield Publishers, Inc.

Nierop, Tom. 1994. *Systems and Regions in Global Politics*. New York: John Wiley & Sons.

North, Douglass C. and Barry W. Weingast. 1989. "The Evolution of Institutions Governing Public Choice in 17th Century England." *Journal of Economic History* 49 (4): 803–32.

Nye, Joseph S., Jr. 1987. *Peace in Parts: Integration and Conflict in Regional Organization*. Reprint. Latham, MD: University Press of America.

1996. "Epilogue: The Liberal Tradition." In *Civil-Military Relations and Democracy*, ed. L. Diamond and M. Plattner, 151–56. Baltimore: Johns Hopkins University Press.

O'Donnell, Guillermo A. 1973. *Modernization and Bureaucratic-authoritarianism: Studies in South American Politics*. Berkeley: University of California Institute for International Studies.

1979. *Modernization and Bureaucratic-Authoritarianism: Studies in South America Politics*. Berkeley: Institute of International Studies.

1996. "Illusions about Consolidation." *Journal of Democracy* 7 (2): 34–51.

O'Donnell, Guillermo and Philippe C. Schmitter. 1986. *Transitions from Authoritarian Rule: Tentative Conclusions About Uncertain Democracies*. Baltimore: Johns Hopkins University Press.

OECD. 1990. *Main Economic Indicators*. Paris: OECD.

O'Loughlin J., M. D. Ward, C. L. Lofdahl, J. S. Cohen, D. S. Brown, D. Reilly, K. S. Gleditsch, and M. Shin. 1998. "The Diffusion of Democracy, 1946–1994." *Annals of the Association of American Geographers* 88 (4): 545–74.

Oneal, John R. and Bruce Russett. 1996. "The Classical Liberals Were Right: Democracy, Interdependence and Conflict, 1950–1985." *International Studies Quarterly* 41 (2): 267–93.

Onis, Ziya. 2001. "Political Islam at the Crossroads: From Hegemony to Coexistence." *Contemporary Politics* 7 (December): 281–98.

Onis, Ziya and E. Fuat Keyman. 2003. "A New Path Emerges." *Journal of Democracy* 14 (2): 95–107.

Owen, John M. 2002. "The Foreign Imposition of Domestic Institutions." *International Organization* 56 (2): 375–409.

Ozbudun, Ergun. 1995. "Turkey: Crises, Interruptions, and Reequilibrations." In *Politics in Developing Countries*, ed. L. Diamond, J. Linz, and S. M. Lipset, 219–61. Boulder, CO: Lynne Rienner.

Ozel, Soli. 2003. "After the Tsunami." *Journal of Democracy* 14 (2): 80–94.

Palmer, David Scott. 1996. "'Fujipopulism' and Peru's Progress." *Current History* 95 (February): 70–5.

2000. "Democracy and Its Discontents in Fujimori's Peru." *Current History* 99 (February): 60–5.

Palmer, John. 1995. "Eastern Four in First Steps to Join EU." *The Guardian* 2 February, 9.

Papacosma, S. Victor. 1985. "Greece and NATO." In *NATO and the Mediterranean*, ed. L. Kaplan, R. Clawson, and R. Luraghi, 189–214. Wilmington: Scholarly Resources, Inc.

Pastor, Robert, ed. 1989. *Democracy in the Americas*. New York: Holmes and Meier.

1999. "The Third Dimension of Accountability: The International Community in National Elections." In *The Self-Restraining State: Power and Accountability in New Democracies*, A. Schedler, L. Diamond and M. F. Plattner, eds., 123–41. Boulder, CO: Lynne Rienner.

Payne, Leigh. 1994. *Brazilian Industrialists and Democratic Change*. Baltimore: Johns Hopkins University Press.

Pena, Felix. 1995. "New Approaches to Economic Integration in the Southern Cone." *The Washington Quarterly* 18 (3): 113–22.

Perry, William and Michael May. 1996. "Wasmosy's Fragile Democracy is Upset." *Jane's Intelligence Review* 3 (7): 14–15.

Pevehouse, Jon C., Timothy Nordstrom, and Kevin Warnke. 2004. "Intergovernmental Organizations, 1815–2000: A New Correlates of War Data Set." *Conflict Management and Peace Studies*, forthcoming.

Pinder, John. 1991. *The European Community and Eastern Europe*. London: Pinter Publishers.

1994. "The European Community and Democracy in Central and Eastern Europe." In *Building Democracy? The International Dimension of Democratization in Eastern Europe*, ed. G. Pridham, E. Herring, and G. Sanford, 32–59. New York: St. Martin's Press.

Pion-Berlin, David. 1991. "Between Confrontation and Accommodation: Military and Government Policy in Democratic Argentina." *Journal of Latin American Studies* 23 (October): 543–71.

Polachek, Solomon W. 1997. "Why Democracies Cooperate More and Fight Less: The Relationship between International Trade and Cooperation." *Review of International Economics* 5 (3): 295–309.

Powell, Charles. 1996. "International Aspects of Democratization: The Case of Spain." In *The International Dimensions of Democratization* ed. L. Whitehead, 285–314. Oxford: Oxford University Press.

Power, Timothy J., and Mark J. Gasiorowski. 1997. "Institutional Design and Democratic Consolidation in the Third World." *Comparative Political Studies* 30 (April): 123–55.

Powers, Nancy R. 1992. *The Transition to Democracy in Paraguay: Problems and Prospects*. Kellogg Working Paper no. 171. Notre Dame, IN: Kellogg Center.

Pridham, Geoffrey. 1991a. "International Influences and Democratic Transition: Problems of Theory and Practice in Linkage Politics." In *Encouraging Democracy: The International Context of Regime Transition in Southern Europe*, ed. G. Pridham, 1–30. New York: St. Martin's Press.

1991b. *Encouraging Democracy: The International Context of Regime Transition in Southern Europe*. New York: St. Martin's Press.

1991c. "The Politics of the European Community, Transnational Networks and Democratic Transition in Southern Europe." In *Encouraging Democracy: The International Context of Regime Transition in Southern Europe*, ed. G. Pridham, 212–45. New York: St. Martin's Press.

1994. "The International Dimension of Democratization: Theory, Practice, and Inter-regional Comparisons." In *Building Democracy? The International Dimension of Democratization in Eastern Europe*, ed. G. Pridham, E. Herring, and G. Sanford, 7–31. New York: St. Martin's Press.

1995. "The International Context of Democratic Consolidation: Southern Europe in Comparative Perspective." In *The Politics of Democratic Consolidation: Southern Europe in Comparative Perspective*, ed. R. Gunther, P. Diamandouros, and H. J. Puhle, 166–203. Baltimore: Johns Hopkins University Press.

1999. "The European Union, Democratic Conditionality and Transnational Party Linkages: The Case of Eastern Europe." In *Democracy Without Borders*, ed. Jean Grugel, 59–73. London: Routledge.

Pridham, Geoffrey, E. Herring, and G. Sanford, eds. 1994. *Building Democracy? The International Dimension of Democratization in Eastern Europe*. New York: St. Martin's Press.

Przeworski, Adam. 1986. "Some Problems in the Study of the Transition to Democracy." In *Transitions from Authoritarian Rule: Comparative Perspectives*, ed. G. O'Donnell, P. Schmitter, and L. Whitehead, 47–63. Baltimore: Johns Hopkins University Press.

1991. *Democracy and the Market*. Cambridge: Cambridge University Press.

Przeworski, Adam, and Fernando Limongi. 1997. "Modernization: Theories and Facts." *World Politics* 49 (January): 155–83.

Przeworski, Adam, Michael Alvarez, José Antonio Cheibub, and Fernando Limongi. 1996. "What Makes Democracies Endure?" *Journal of Democracy* 7 (1): 39–55.

Putnam, Robert. 1988. "Diplomacy and Domestic Politics: The Logic of Two-Level Games." *International Organization* 42 (3): 427–60.

Reinhardt, Eric. 2003. "Tying Hands without a Rope: Rational Domestic Response to International Institutional Constraints." In *Locating the Proper Authorities*, ed. D. Drezner, 77–104. Ann Arbor: University of Michigan Press.

Reiter, Dan. 2001a. "Does Peace Nurture Democracy?" *Journal of Politics* 63 (3): 935–949.

2001b. "Why NATO Enlargement Does Not Spread Democracy." *International Security* 25 (4): 41–68.

Richards, Diana, T. Clifton Morgan, Rick Wilson, Valarie Schwebach, and Garry Young. 1993. "Good Times, Bad Times, and the Diversionary Use of Force." *Journal of Conflict Resolution* 37 (3): 504–36.

Roberts, Kenneth and Mark Peceny. 1997. "Human Rights and United States Policy Toward Peru." In *The Peruvian Labyrinth: Polity, Society, and Economy*, ed. M. Cameron and P. Mauceri, 192–222. University Park, PA: Penn State University Press.

Rodrik, Dani. 1989. "Credibility of Trade Reform – A Policy Maker's Guide." *The World Economy* (March): 1–16.

Root, Hilton. 1994. *The Fountain of Privilege: Political Foundations of Markets in Old Regime France and England*. Berkeley: University of California Press.

Rosenau, James, ed. 1969. *Linkage Politics: Essays on the Convergence of National and International Systems*. New York: Free Press.

Rother, Larry. 2002. "Uprising in Venezuela: Latin America." *New York Times*, April 15, A8.

Ruhl, Mark J. 1996. "Unlikely Candidates for Democracy: The Role of Structural Context in Democratic Consolidation." *Studies in Comparative International Development* 31 (1): 3–23.

Russett, Bruce. 1967. *International Regions and the International System*. Chicago: Rand McNally.

　　　1993. *Grasping the Democratic Peace*. Princeton: Princeton University Press.

　　　1998. "A Neo-Kantian Perspective: Democracy, Interdependence, and International Organizations in Building Security Communities." In *Security Communities*, ed. E. Adler and M. Barnett, 368–94. Cambridge: Cambridge University Press.

Russett, Bruce and John R. Oneal. 2001. *Triangulating Peace*. New York: W.W. Norton.

Russett, Bruce, John Oneal, and David R. Davis. 1998. "The Third Leg of the Kantian Tripod: International Organizations and Militarized Disputes, 1950–1985." *International Organization* 52 (Summer): 441–67.

Rustow, Dankwart A. 1993. "A Democratic Turkey Faces New Challenges." *Global Affairs* 8 (2): 58–70.

Santiso, Carlos. 2000. "Towards Democratic Governance: The Contribution of Multilateral Development Banks in Latin America." In *Democracy Assistance: International Cooperation for Democratization*, ed. P. Burnell, 150–87. London: Frank Cass.

Sartori, Giovanni. 1976. *Parties and Party Systems*. Cambridge: Cambridge University Press.

Saxonhouse, Gary R. 1993. "Trading Blocs and East Asia." In *New Dimensions in Regional Integration*, ed. J. de Melo and A. Panagariya, 388–414. New York: Cambridge University Press.

Schamis, Hector. 2002. "Argentina: Crisis and Democratic Consolidtion." *Journal of Democracy* 13 (2): 81–94.

Schedler, Andreas. 1998. "What is Democratic Consolidation?" *Journal of Democracy* 9 (2): 91–107.

Schiff, Maurice, and L. Alan Winters. 1998. "Regional Integration as Diplomacy." *The World Bank Economic Review* 12 (2): 271–95.

Schlesinger, Stephen and Stephen Kinzer. 1982. *Bitter Fruit: The Untold Story of the American Coup in Guatemala*. Garden City, NY: Doubleday.

Schmitter, Phillipe. 1986. "An Introduction to Southern European Transitions from Authoritarian Rule: Italy, Greece, Portugal, Spain, and Turkey." In

Transitions from Authoritarian Rule: Southern Europe, ed. G. O'Donnell, P. Schmitter, and L. Whitehead, 3–10. Baltimore: Johns Hopkins University Press.

1996. "The Influence of the International Context upon the Choice of National Institutions and Policies in Neo-Democracies." In *The International Aspects of Democratization: Europe and the Americas*, ed. L. Whitehead, 26–54. Oxford: Oxford University Press.

Schmitter, Phillipe C., and Terry L. Karl. 1991. "What Democracy Is . . . and Is Not." *Journal of Democracy* 2 (3): 75–88.

Schultz, Kenneth A. 1998. "Domestic Opposition and Signaling in International Crises." *American Political Science Review* 92 (4): 829–844.

1999. "Do Democratic Institutions Constrain or Inform? Contrasting Two Institutional Perspectives on Democracy and War." *International Organization* 53 (2): 233–66.

Schweller, Randall L. and David Priess. 1997. "A Tale of Two Realisms: Expanding the Institutions Debate." *Mershon International Studies Review* 41 (1): 1–32.

Shain, Yossi and Juan Linz. 1995. *Between States: Interim Governments and Democratic Transition*. New York: Cambridge University Press.

Shanks, Cheryl, Harold K. Jacobson, and Jeffrey H. Kaplan. 1996. "Inertia and Change in the Constellation of International Governmental Organizations." *International Organization* 50 (Autumn): 593–627.

Sheahan, John. 1986. "Economic Policies and the Prospects for Successful Transition from Authoritarian Rule in Latin America." In *Transitions from Authoritarian Rule: Comparative Perspectives*, ed. G. O'Donnell, P. C. Schmitter, and L. Whitehead, 154–64. Baltimore: Johns Hopkins University Press.

Shin, Doh Chull. 1994. "On the Third Wave of Democratization". *World Politics* 47 (1): 135–71.

Shugart, Matthew S. and John M. Carey. 1992. *Presidents and Assemblies: Constitutional Design and Electoral Dynamics*. Cambridge: Cambridge University Press.

Sidjanski, Dusan. 1991. "Transition to Democracy and European Integration: The Role of Interest Groups in Southern Europe." In *Encouraging Democracy: The International Context of Regime Transition in Southern Europe*, ed. G. Pridham, 195–211. New York: St. Martin's Press.

Sikkink, Kathryn. 1996. "The Effectiveness of US Human Rights Policy, 1973–1980." In *The International Aspects of Democratization: Europe and the Americas*, ed. L. Whitehead, 93–124. Oxford: Oxford University Press.

Simmons, Beth A. 1998. "Compliance with International Agreements." *Annual Review of Political Science* 1: 75–93.

2000. "International Law and State Behavior: Commitment and Compliance in International Monetary Affairs." *American Political Science Review* 94 (4): 819–36.

Simon, Michael W. and Erik Gartzke. 1996. "Political System Similarity and the Choice of Allies: Do Democracies Flock Together, or Do Opposites Attract?" *Journal of Conflict Resolution* 40 (4): 617–35.

Siotis, Jean. 1983. "Characteristics and Motives for Entry." In *The Enlargement of the European Community: Case Studies of Greece, Portugal, and Spain*, ed. J. L. Sampedro and J. A. Payno, 57–69. London: Macmillan Press.

Siverson, Randolph M. and Juliann Emmons. 1991. "Birds of a Feather: Democratic Political Systems and Alliance Choices in the Twentieth Century." *Journal of Conflict Resolution* 35 (2), 285–306.

Small, Melvin and J. David Singer. 1994. *Correlates of War Project: International and Civil War Data, 1816–1992*. Study no. 9905. Ann Arbor, MI: Inter-University Consortium for Political and Social Research.

Smith, Alastair. 1998. "International Crises and Domestic Politics." *American Political Science Review* 92 (3): 623–39.

Smith, Tony. 1994. "In Defense of Intervention." *Foreign Affairs* 73 (6): 34–46.

Snyder, Jack. 1990. "Averting Anarchy in the New Europe." *International Security* (14) 4: 5–41.

2000. *From Voting to Violence*. New York: W.W. Norton.

Snyder, Jack and Karen Ballentine. 1996. "Nationalism and the Marketplace of Ideas." *International Security* 21 (2): 5–40.

Solingen, Etel. 1994. "The Political Economy of Nuclear Restraint." *International Security* 19 (2): 126–69.

1998. *Regional Order at Century's Dawn*. Princeton: Princeton University Press.

Southall, Roger. 2003. "An Unlikely Success: South Africa and Lesotho's Election of 2002." *Journal of Modern African Studies* 41 (2): 269–96.

Spain, J. W. and N. Ludington. 1983. "Dateline Turkey: The Case for Patience." *Foreign Policy* 50: 150–68.

Steinbach, Udo. 1994. "The European Community, the United States, the Middle East, and Turkey." In *Politics in the Third Turkish Republic*, ed. M. Heper and A. Evin, 103–16. Boulder, CO: Westview Press.

Steves, Franklin. 2001. "Regional Integration and Democratic Consolidation in the Southern Cone of Latin America." *Democratization* 8 (3): 75–100.

Story, Jonathan and Benny Pollack. 1991. "Spain's Transition: Domestic and External Linkages." In *Encouraging Democracy: The International Context of Regime Transition in Southern Europe*, ed. G. Pridham, 125–58. New York: St. Martin's Press.

Strang, David and Patricia M. Y. Chang. 1993. "The International Labor Organization and the Welfare State: Institutional Effects on National Welfare Spending, 1960–1980." *International Organization* 47 (2): 235–62.

Summers, Robert, Alan Heston, Daniel A. Nuxoll and Bettina Aten. 1995. *The Penn World Table (Mark 5.6a)*. Cambridge, MA: National Bureau of Economic Research.

Sunar, Ilkay and Sabri Sayari. 1986. "Democracy in Turkey: Problems and Prospects." In *Transitions from Authoritarian Rule: Southern Europe*, ed. G. O'Donnell, P. Schmitter, and L. Whitehead, 165–86. Baltimore: Johns Hopkins University Press.

Tachau, Frank. 1984. *Turkey: The Politics of Authority, Democracy, and Development*. New York: Praeger.

Tharp, Paul A. 1971. *Regional International Organizations: Structures and Functions*. New York: St. Martin's Press.

Thomas, Daniel. 2001. *The Helsinki Effect: International Norms, Human Rights, and the Demise of Communism.* Princeton: Princeton University Press.

Thomas, George M., John W. Meyer, Francisco O. Ramirez, and John Boli. 1987. *Institutional Structure: Constituting State, Society and the Individual.* Newbury Park: Sage Publications.

Thompson, William R. 1996. "Democracy and Peace: Putting the Cart Before the Horse?" *International Organization* 50 (1): 141–74.

Tirman, John. 1998. "Improving Turkey's 'Bad Neighborhood'." *World Policy Journal* 15 (Spring): 60–7.

Tovias, Alfred. 1984. "The International Context of Democratic Transition." In *The New Mediterranean Democracies: Regime Transition in Spain, Greece and Portugal,* ed. G. Pridham, 158–71. London: Frank Cass.

Treverton, Gregory. 1986. *Spain: Domestic Politics and Security Policy.* London: IISS.

Trudeau, Robert H. 1993. *Guatemalan Politics: The Popular Struggle for Democracy.* Boulder, CO: Lynne Reinner.

Tsie, Balefi. 1998. "Regional Security in Southern Africa: Whither the SADC Organ on Politics, Defence and Security?" *Global Dialogue* 3 (3): http://www.igd.org.za/pub/g-dialogue/africa/sadc.html.

Tsingos, Basilios. 1996. "Underwriting Democracy: The European Community and Greece." In *The International Aspects of Democratization: Europe and the Americas,* ed. L. Whitehead, 315–55. Oxford: Oxford University Press.

Tsoukalis, Loukas. 1981. *The European Community and its Mediterranean Enlargement.* London: George Allen & Unwin.

Tuohy, William. 1991. "'Good Shepherd' Gathers East European States to the Fold." *Los Angeles Times,* March, 19, 2.

Union of International Associations. 1996. *Yearbook of International Organizations CD-ROM1996.* New York: K. G. Saur.

Vaky, Viron P. 1993. "The Organization of American States and Multilateralism in the Americas." In *The Future of the Organization of American States,* ed. V. Vaky and H. Munoz, 1–66. New York: Twentieth Century Fund Press.

Valenzuela, Arturo. 1997. "Paraguay: The Coup that Didn't Happen." *Journal of Democracy* 8 (1): 43–55.

1999. *The Collective Defense of Democracy: Lessons from the Paraguayan Crisis of 1996.* Washington: Carnegie Commission on Preventing Deadly Conflict.

2002. "Bush's Betrayal of Democracy." *Washington Post,* April 16, A19.

Valenzuela, J. Samuel. 1992. "Democratic Consolidation in Post-Transitional Settings: Notion, Process, and Facilitating Conditions." In *Issues in Democratic Consolidation,* ed. S. Mainwaring, G. O'Donnell, and A. Valenzuela, 57–104. South Bend, IN: University of Notre Dame Press.

Valki, Laszlo. 1998. "Hungary and the Future of European Security." In *European Security and NATO Enlargement: A View From Central Europe,* ed. S. J. Blank, 91–118. Carlisle, PA: Strategic Studies Institute.

van Babrant, Jozef M. 1994. *The Transformation of Eastern Europe: Joining the European Integration Movement.* Commack, NY: Nova Science Publishers, Inc.

van Klaveren, Alberto. 1993. "Why Integration Now? Options for Latin America." In *The Challenges of Integration: Europe and the Americas,* ed. Peter H. Smith, 115–45. New Brunswick: Transaction Publishers.

Verney, Susannah. 1994. "Central State-Local Government Relations." In *Greece and EC Membership Evaluated*, ed. P. Kazakos and P. C. Ioakimidis, 166–80. London: Pinter.

Verney, Susannah and Theodore Couloumbis. 1991. "State-International System Interaction and the Greek Transition to Democracy in the mid-1970s." In *Encouraging Democracy: The International Context of Regime Transition in Southern Europe*, ed. G. Pridham, 103–24. New York: St. Martin's Press.

Verney, S. and T. Tsakaloyannis. 1986. "Linkage Politics: the Role of the European Community in Greek Politics in 1973." *Byzantine and Modern Greek Studies* 10: 179–95.

Vetschera, Heinz. 1997. "Security Policy and Democratic Control." In *Civil-Military Relations in Post-Communist States*, ed. A. A. Bebler, 15–21. Westport, CT: Praeger.

Villagran de León, Francisco. 1993. "Thwarting the Guatemalan Coup." *Journal of Democracy* 4 (3): 117–24.

Wallace, William. 1994. *Regional Integration: The Western European Experience*. Washington, DC: Brookings Institution.

Waltz, Kenneth. 1959. *Man, the State and War: A Theoretical Analysis*. New York: Columbia University Press.

Weart, Spencer R. 1998. *Never at War: Why Democracies Will Never Fight One Another*. New Haven: Yale University Press.

Whalley, John. 1998. "Why Do Countries Seek Regional Trade Arrangements?" In *The Regionalization of the World Economy*, ed. J. A. Frankel, 63–83. Chicago: University of Chicago Press.

White, David. 1986. "The Taboos Start to Lift." *The Financial Times*, December 1, S1.

White, Nigel D. 2000. "The United Nations and Democracy Assistance: Developing Practice within a Constitutional Framework." In *Democracy Assistance: International Cooperation for Democratization*, ed. P. Burnell, 67–89. London: Frank Cass.

Whitehead, Laurence. 1986. "International Aspects of Democratization." In *Transitions from Authoritarian Rule: Comparative Perspectives*, ed. G. O'Donnell, P. C. Schmitter, and L. Whitehead, 3–46. Baltimore: Johns Hopkins University Press.

1989. "The Consolidation of Fragile Democracies: A Discussion with Illustrations." In *Democracy in the Americas*, ed. R. Pastor, 79–95. New York: Holmes and Meier.

1991. "Democracy by Convergence and Southern Europe: A Comparative Politics Perspective." In *Encouraging Democracy: The International Context of Regime Transition in Southern Europe*, ed. G. Pridham, 45–61. New York: St. Martin's Press.

1993. "Requisites for Admission." In *The Challenge of Integration: Europe and the Americas*, ed. P. H. Smith, 149–82. New Brunswick, NJ: Transaction Publishers.

1994. "East-Central Europe in Comparative Perspective." In *Building Democracy? The International Dimension of Democratization in Eastern Europe*, ed. G. Pridham, E. Herring, and G. Sanford, 32–59. New York: St. Martin's Press.

1996a. *The International Aspects of Democratization: Europe and the Americas.* Oxford: Oxford University Press.

1996b. "Democratic Regions, Ostracism, and Pariahs." In *The International Aspects of Democratization: Europe and the Americas,* ed. L. Whitehead, 395–412. Oxford: Oxford University Press.

1996c. "Three International Dimensions of Democratization." In *The International Aspects of Democratization: Europe and the Americas,* ed. L. Whitehead, 3–25. Oxford: Oxford University Press.

1996d. "Concerning International Support for Democracy in the South." In *Democratization in the South: The Jagged Wave,* ed. R. Luckham and G. White, 243–73. Manchester: Manchester University Press.

Wiarda, Howard J. 1995. "The Future of Political Reform in the Southern Cone: Can Democracy be Sustained?" *The Washington Quarterly* 18 (3): 89–112.

1997. *Cracks in the Consensus: Debating the Democracy Agenda in US Foreign Policy.* Westport, CT: Praeger.

Wilkenfeld, Jonathan, ed. 1973. *Conflict Behavior and Linkage Politics.* New York: David MacKay.

Wilkenfeld, Jonathan and Dinna Zinnes. 1973. "A Linkage Model of Domestic Conflict Behavior." In Wilkenfeld, ed. *Conflict Behavior and Linkage Politics,* 325–56. New York: David MacKay.

World Bank. 1998. *The World Development Indicators.* CD-ROM.

Wright, Robert. 1998. "A New Security Blanket." *Financial Times,* December 7, 3.

Writer, Rashna. 1996. "Paraguay's April Near-Coup Shows the Fragility of Transitioning from Authoritarian Government." *Defense and Foreign Affairs' Strategic Policy* (April). Lexis-Nexis.

Yamaguchi, Kazuo. 1991. *Event History Analysis.* Newbury Park: Sage Publications.

Yannopoulos, George N. 1975. *Greece and the European Economic Communities: The First Decade of a Troubled Association.* Beverly Hills: Sage Publications.

Yarbrough, Beth V., and Robert M. Yarbrough. 1992. *Cooperation and Governance in International Trade: The Strategic Organizational Approach.* Princeton, NJ: Princeton University Press.

Yesilada, Birol A. 1999. "The Worsening EU–Turkey Relations." *SAIS Review* 19 (Winter-Spring): 144–61.

Yilmaz, Hakan. 2002. "External-Internal Linkages in Democratization: Developing an Open Model of Democratic Change." *Democratization* 9 (2): 67–84.

Yost, David. 1998. *NATO Transformed: The Alliance's New Roles in International Security.* Washington, DC: United States Institute of Peace.

Youngers, Coletta. 1994. *After the Autogolpe: Human Rights in Peru and the U.S. Response.* Washington: Washington Office on Latin America.

Zakaria, Fareed. 1997. "The Rise of Illiberal Democracy." *Foreign Affairs* 76 (6): 22–43.

Index